A HISTORY
OF THE WORLD IN
500
RAILWAY
JOURNEYS

Inspiring | Educating | Creating | Entertaining

First published in Great Britain 2017 by
Aurum Press, an imprint of The Quarto Group,
The Old Brewery, 6 Blundell Street,
London, N7 9BH, United Kingdom.

All correspondence concerning this book's content should be addressed to the Editorial Department at the address below.

This book was conceived, designed, and produced by
The Bright Press, an imprint of The Quarto Group.
The Old Brewery, 6 Blundell Street,
London N7 9BH, United Kingdom.
T (0)20 7700 6700 www.QuartoKnows.com
HWRW

A catalogue record for this book is available from the British Library.

ISBN 978 1 78131 678 8

2021 2020 2019

10 9 8 7 6 5 4 3 2

Printed and bound in China by
C&C Offset Printing Co., Ltd.

Editorial Director: Emma Bastow
Senior Editor: Caroline Elliker
Editor: Sonya Patel Ellis
Designers: Tony Seddon, Tania Gomes
Illustrator: Lynn Hatzius
Picture Researcher: Emma Brown
Publisher: Mark Searle

For Rod and Marcus, old friends

Christian Wolmar is an award-winning writer and broadcaster specialising in transport. He is the author of a series of books on rail history, including, most recently, *Railways and the Raj: The Story of Indian Railways.*

A HISTORY
OF THE WORLD IN
500
RAILWAY
JOURNEYS

SARAH BAXTER

Foreword by
Christian Wolmar

Aurum
Press

A steam train runs across the majestic Glenfinnan Viaduct, on the West Highland Line in Inverness-shire, Scotland (pp. 217–219).

CONTENTS

FOREWORD

Railways – a 19th century invention – not only survived the 20th century but are now thriving in the 21st. There was no guarantee that would happen. After the Second World War, as motor car ownership soared and jets made air travel safe and relatively inexpensive, what role was left for the railways? There was no end of predictions that they would disappear, as trams and trolleybuses did in so many places. Lots of lines were closed, steam engines disappeared and lorries carried most of the freight. Now, however, that process has been reversed and the railways are enjoying a fantastic renaissance as high speed lines spread around the world, suburban services are jammed full of commuters and new passenger routes spring up, often on routes once abandoned.

Just as the cinema has survived the arrival of television, and traditional books the invention of digital versions, so railways seem set for a long and healthy future despite the popularity of the motor car. And one of the key reasons is that people love the railway journey. Travelling by train is an enjoyable experience in itself. It is not all about simply getting there. Sure, air travel might have its attractions but once you have been up in the sky a few times, the sight of clouds and distant land pales. Likewise, car travel is not often the fantasy portrayed in advertisements where new models speed along empty, 'bucket-list' countryside – dull trips along motorways or slow crawls through traffic-jammed towns are much likelier scenarios. That's why there will probably never be a book called *A History of the World in 500 Car Trips*.

Rail journeys, on the other hand, allow you to look out of the window or sit quietly reading a book, knowing you will not be disturbed. Railways often fit more seamlessly with the environment; trains travel at a more palatable pace. Even a business trip or a routine journey can turn into a source of unexpected pleasure, with spectacular views or

insights into people's backyards. It's no surprise then that railway travel has inspired so much great literature, photography and film.

Train travel retains a romanticism that is lost from much of modern life. Getting there on a train is still part of the fun. And as so many of the examples in this book show, there are great train journeys to be taken almost anywhere in the world. The experiences can be so completely different. My personal favourite trips include numerous journeys in India, where it's not necessarily the scenery that is most notable but simply the adventure of the journey amid the chaos and colour of one of the most fascinating countries in the world, and its diverse people. By contrast, check out another of my favourites: the Glacier Express (pp. 36–38). As the author Sarah Baxter notes, it is the slowest as well as the most scenic express train in the world. Or take the longest journey, the Trans-Siberian Railway (pp. 255) – 6.5 days to traverse half a continent . . .

Enjoy the book and make sure you go on some of these wonderful trips.

Christian Wolmar

LEFT: The steam train is a defining image of historic railway travel but also a symbol of a bygone era.

INTRODUCTION

Trains are a little bit like time machines. There's just something about them that seems able to whisk us back to a bygone age when travel was new, exciting and overspilling with possibilities and romance. Granted, this sensation is less apparent on a crowded 8 a.m. commuter service to London Waterloo than it is aboard the wood-pannelled carriages of the Venice Simplon-Orient-Express, but it *is* there somewhere. Trains retain an allure that buses, planes and automobiles can't match.

When you're on a train, it's easy to cast your mind back to when this new form of transportation began transforming the world. From the early 19th century, railways began forging routes into remote areas and connecting once-distant communities, making the planet a smaller, more explorable place. Previously, human overland travel had been restricted by the speed of your feet or your horse. Suddenly, faraway cities, countries, even continents were within realistic reach.

However, trains don't just transport us back nearly 200 years. Even though the history of the railways is largely limited to the past two centuries, they are capable of carrying us much, much further into the past – because you can see so much from a train window. Indeed, one of the many beauties of train travel is the fact that it enables every passenger to relax and admire the view. Planes are fast but remove us from the landscape. Cars are versatile, but oblige us to concentrate on driving. Buses have to fight for space amid the cars. Walking and cycling are excellent but require more fitness and time than many have or can afford. Trains, meanwhile, offer an effortless, up-close unfurling. With no

RIGHT: Ecuador's Tren Crucero (pp. 210–213), which launched in 2013, is a great example of railway revival.

need to engage your body or brain in the business of locomotion, you are free to sit back and enjoy the movie steadily streaming by outside.

To that end, *A History of the World in 500 Railways* is your guide to these time-travelling motion pictures. Arranged chronologically, in six chapters, this book tells the story of the planet through a collection of train journeys, by turns astonishing, groundbreaking, luxurious, little-known, high-speed, super slow, steam pulled, epic, endangered and sadly defunct. Each has something to say about life on Earth: how our canyons were formed, our mountains raised, our civilisations founded, our religions born, our wars started, our culture spread. For instance, some of the trains included here travel right past ancient petroglyphs or through glacier-gouged gorges; others trundle along tracks laid to secure empires, transport armies or open up wild frontiers.

Of course, the story begins aeons before the first track was ever laid. Chapter 1 looks at prehistory, well pre-dating written records, let alone railways. And yet there are some spectacular train journeys that can deliver us to, through, over and around our geological beginnings and evidence of the earliest mankind. The subsequent chapters rumble from the dawn of time into the centuries Anno Domini (AD), via pharaohs, Romans, First Nations tribes, Berbers, Buddhists and biblical lands. There's even the world's first 'railway', courtesy of the ancient Greeks.

Then, tucked into the later pages, there are railways that follow old trade routes, medieval pilgrimages, military campaigns, human migrations and trailblazing explorers. By Chapter 5, we hit the advent of railways themselves, and hop aboard some of the pioneering lines that set trends, mastered 'impossible' terrain and pushed the boundaries of human engineering. From here, we see how railways shaped nations, boosted economies, contributed to wars and assisted genocides, and also how they brought leisure travel to the masses. We end in the modern era, as trains are getting ever faster – yet nostalgia for the slower, steam-powered era of rail travel has never been greater.

This, of course, is not a comprehensive guide. There are many railways that I've had to leave out. Likewise, there are areas of the world that barely feature, simply because they don't have any or many railways. But I have tried to give a good spread of lines – from long-distance icons to short-but-key routes – that have both historical interest and

The history of the world via railway travel includes streetcars and funiculars as well as trains. San Francisco's streetcar system is the world's last, manually operated network, used by commuters and tourists alike.

rail-fan fascination. Some of these rides pass great sites; others cross dizzying viaducts. Some are covered in detail; others are described in tantalising snippets that will make you want to find out more. The 500 individual journeys are accompanied by inspirational maps and take-me-there photography, designed to be enjoyed by both armchair train travellers and those who are likely to head off to buy a ticket immediately.

My own hottest tickets? I think I'd start by forging my way across Canada on the appropriately named Canadian (pp. 46–50) – a near 3,000-mile (4,800km) geography and geology lesson, with plenty of 'how the West was won' spirit thrown in. Perhaps then I'd dash off to trace the Nile by rail (pp. 76–78), to admire riverbank scenes that have changed little since the time of the ancient Egyptians. Then I might board a train through Peru's Sacred Valley (pp. 152–156), to marvel at how the Inca managed to build Machu Picchu amid the Andes mountains. Or perhaps I'd plot an action-filled Viking route through Denmark (pp. 164–166), to follow the world's most notorious seafarers by rail.

Where next? I'd follow Spanish conquistadores through Mexico's Copper Canyon on a ridge-teetering railway that defies belief (pp. 226–229) and follow sugar traders around St Kitts (pp. 248–250) on one of the Caribbean's few operational lines. I'd plunge across the Continental Divide and into the American West aboard the California Zephyr (pp. 300–303), to understand how this line united a nation. And I'd take the Little Train of the Upper Somme (pp. 334–335) to try to picture how the Great War tore a world apart. I might end aboard the Zurich–Milan train (pp. 357–359), to whizz through the new Gotthard Base Tunnel, one of the most audacious rail projects of the 21st century.

Well, for now, at least. Because railways are, quite literally, moving all the time. New lines open, old routes close, forgotten routes get reborn, diesel replaces steam, magnets replace wheels, steam comes back again. The world is connected and reconnected as politics and populations dictate. And always, the train provides a window to the present and the past.

Sarah Baxter

CHAPTER ONE
PREHISTORY

Take trains via timeless canyons, mighty mountains and the earliest marks of mankind for a better understanding of the planet outside the window.

1
DESERT EXPRESS

Central Namibia

Take your time crossing an ancient desert that separates
Namibia's capital city from the Atlantic Ocean.

Need to know
- *Point in time: 55–80 million years ago (age of Namib Desert)*
- *Length: 220 miles (380km)*
- *Minimum time: 19 hours*
- *Key stops: Windhoek, Okahandja, Swakopmund*
- *Countries crossed: Namibia*

There are moments, looking out the window of the Desert Express, when you have no idea not just where you are but also *when* you are. So much of Namibia, one of the most sparsely populated countries in the world, seems utterly timeless. It feels empty, endless, unfathomably old.

Perhaps that's no surprise. A large swathe of Namibia is covered by the world's most ancient desert. Arid conditions have been the norm in the Namib (a Nama word meaning 'vast place') for at least 55 million years. These days, the region's annual average rainfall is no more than a few centimetres. It's a spectacularly thirsty spot.

The Desert Express tackles part of this venerable wilderness. From the capital, Windhoek, on Namibia's central plateau, the railway runs north through the highlands. At Okahandja, the 'Garden Town of Namibia', it then turns hard west. It cuts across the Namib's gravel plains and apricot sands. And it finishes amid the Germanic architecture of the city of Swakopmund, by the crashing Atlantic Ocean.

The Namibian rail network dates from the days of the German Empire, when Namibia was part of German South West Africa. Started in 1897, the narrow gauge Swakopmund–Windhoek Staatsbahn was the first line to be built, connecting Windhoek with the empire's main harbour. Before then, goods were moved by ox-cart. But an outbreak of the rinderpest virus that killed more than 5 million cattle across southern Africa forced the need for an alternative mode of transport. The line was completed in 1902.

Windhoek's elegant Railway Station, built by the Germans in 1912, still dominates Bahnhof Street. Not only does it continue to perform its intended function, it also houses the TransNamib Railway Museum. On display is a range of historic railway equipment, maps and documents – even crockery from old dining cars. Outside, on a plinth, sits one half of a 1900 Zwillinge twin-tank steam locomotive, which chugged some 371,000 miles (597,000km) across the desert before being retired in 1939.

At the beginning of the 20th century, the 220-mile (380km) rail journey between Windhoek, in central Namibia, and Swakopmund, on the South Atlantic coast, took 3 days. Things have speeded up a little since then, although today's Desert Express still takes its time, dawdling cross-country in around 19 hours. This is because it's a tourist train: it stops en route for a game-viewing excursion, and pulls in at a secure, off-track siding after dark, so that the sleeping cars don't bump around in the night.

BELOW: The Desert Express trundles across the ancient sands of the Namib.

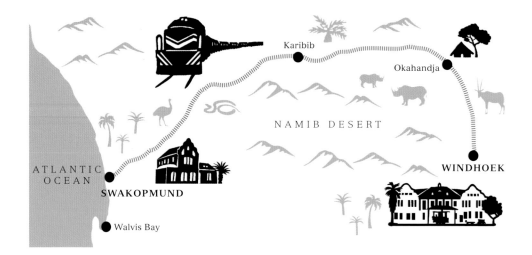

Karibib

Okahandja

NAMIB DESERT

ATLANTIC
OCEAN

WINDHOEK

SWAKOPMUND

Walvis Bay

You could save time and money by making the same journey aboard a regular Starline train, which link the two cities in just over 10 hours. However, as Starline's scheduled service leaves Windhoek every weekday at 7.15 p.m., the whole journey is run in the dark.

Conversely, when the Desert Express runs (which can be unpredictable), it leaves the capital at around 12 noon. This ensures that the countryside unfolds in daylight, through the oversized windows of comfortable lounge and bistro cars. It also enables a safari side trip on which rhino, oryx antelope and ostrich might be seen.

En route, the train passes Okahandja, founded in 1800 by the Herero and Nama people. Jostling for regional control, the two tribes fought each other here in 1850. Later, both were decimated by the Germans during the 1904–07 genocide. This was sparked by a Herero uprising in 1903 – the Herero were angered by the news that their territory was to be severed by a new railway.

The timing of the Desert Express ensures perfect placement for the unfailingly spectacular sunset over the vast, red-pink-golden Namib. The stars here are also out of this world. The next morning, there's time to admire the sunrise and walk up a soft, sandy dune before the train follows the desert and rolls to Swakopmund to meet the Atlantic's waves.

MORE DESERT JOURNEYS

2. Red Lizard Train
Tunisia

Ride for 9 miles (14.5km) between the towns of Metlaoui and Redeyef, through the otherworldly rock formations of Seldja Gorge (unsurprisingly, *Star Wars* was filmed nearby).

3. Jaipur–Jaisalmer
Rajasthan, India

Take the train across the shifting dunes of the ancient Thar Desert between two of Rajasthan's most regal cities, a journey of 380 miles (612km).

RIGHT: Not even trains can access the wildest reaches of Namibia's Atlantic coast.

4
PILBARA RAILWAYS

Western Australia

The Pilbara Craton, a crust of granite-greenstone in northwestern Australia, contains rocks that are 3.5 billion years old. And, on top, sit iron-ore-rich sedimentary rocks. Mining began in the Pilbara in the 1960s and tracks were built to transport ore from the pits around the region to the coast. The railway lines are 186–250 miles (300–400km) long but more noteworthy is the length of the vehicles that ply them. They are the world's largest scheduled trains, comprising up to 330 cars. The record belongs to the 'Mt Goldsworthy' freight train, which in 2001 hauled 99,732 tons in 682 cars, coupled up to measure a massive 4.5 miles (7.3km) long.

NORTHERN EXPLORER

North Island, New Zealand

Ride the old main trunk railway from Auckland to Wellington, via volatile volcanoes and train-testing terrain.

Need to know

- *Point in time: 15 million years ago (period of tectonic activity)*
- *Length: 423 miles (681km)*
- *Minimum time: 11 hours*
- *Key stops: Auckland, Hamilton, Otorohanga, National Park, Ohakune, Palmerston North, Wellington*
- *Countries crossed: New Zealand*

LIKE THAT? TRY THIS

- - - - - - - - - - - - - - - - - - -

6. Taieri Gorge Railway
South Island, New Zealand

The 96-mile (154km) line from the city of Dunedin to the town of Middlemarch uses innumerable tunnels, bridges and viaducts to tackle Taieri Gorge, hewn over aeons by the Taieri River.

RIGHT: The Northern Explorer passes hills, volcanoes, farmland and forest.

New Zealand is a rambunctious place. Straddling the edges of two tectonic plates, the earth here is often to be found fizzing and steaming, eructing and erupting, or simply rippling in exuberant fashion. Around 15 million years ago there was a particularly boisterous period of tectonic and volcanic activity, which laid the foundations of the landscape that's visible today.

The Northern Explorer train is a good way to get an overview of the North Island's terrific topography. It runs along the North Island Main Trunk railway line, built between 1885 and 1908 to provide a link between Auckland, now New Zealand's biggest city, with its capital Wellington. Given the lay of the land, it was a huge engineering challenge.

The line was completed south from Auckland to Te Awamutu by 1880 and north from Wellington to Longburn by 1886. But bridging the gap in the middle was the trickier bit. There was the small matter of crossing the central volcanic plateau, a ravine-sliced region dominated by the volcanoes of Tongariro National Park. Nine viaducts had to be constructed as well as the single track Raurimu Spiral (near National Park), a system of two tunnels and three horseshoe curves that enables the train to climb 139m (456ft) in less than 3.7 miles (6km). There were also territorial issues to resolve. Sections of the proposed route ran through Maori land, and building stalled while negotiations were made with the local tribes.

The railway is no longer a vital economic link. It's a leisurely sightseeing jaunt, taking passengers past Hobbiton-like green hills, undulating farmland, dense forest, tiny towns, lava flows, active volcanoes and rocky shores. The train also descends the sweeping Turangarere Horseshoe and crosses the 79m-high (260ft) Makatote Viaduct, just below active stratovolcano Mount Ruapehu. The panoramic carriages, with large side and roof windows, ensure you don't miss a thing.

South Island, New Zealand

It's easy to appreciate the spectacular geography of New Zealand's South Island on a railway that cuts right across it. The 139-mile (224km) TranzAlpine links the east-coast city of Christchurch with the town of Greymouth on the west, navigating the Southern Alps in-between. First, it skims the Canterbury Plains, which were formed from glacial moraines over the past 3 million years. Then the line climbs with the channels of the Waimakariri River before topping out at Arthur's Pass township (740m / 2,428ft); this sits below Arthur's Pass itself, a 920m (2,959ft) high niche long used by Maori to travel between east and west. The railway burrows under the pass via the Otira Tunnel and descends via beech forest and old mining towns to reach the sea.

8
QINGHAI–TIBET RAILWAY

Western China

Gasp at the landscapes – and the altitude – of the Tibetan
Plateau while aboard the world's highest railway.

Need to know

- *Point in time: 50 million years ago (Tibetan Plateau formation began)*
- *Length: 1,215 miles (1,956km)*
- *Minimum time: 22 hours*
- *Key stops: Xining, Golmud, Tanggula, Lhasa*
- *Countries crossed: China*

HIGH AND MIGHTY
- - - - - - - - - - - - - - - - - - - -

9. Petit train d'Artouste
Pyrénées-Atlantiques, France

Climb into the glacial mountains and valleys of the Pyrenees, close to the Spanish border, on the 6.2-mile-long (10km) narrow gauge tourist railway, opened in 1920.

Breathtaking. That's the best word for the Qinghai–Tibet Railway. Not only does this engineering marvel inch through magnificent mountain scenery, it also reaches astonishing, air-starved heights. The zenith of the line is the 5,072m (16,640ft) Tanggula Pass, the highest point on any railway, anywhere in the world.

For much of its 1,215 miles (1,956km), the Qinghai–Tibet Railway crosses the vast, lofty Tibetan Plateau, the 'Roof of the World'. Despite its sometimes bleak appearance, it's a vital giver of life: the tens of thousands of glaciers here melt into rivers such as the Indus and Yangtze, and provide water for more than half the population of Asia.

It's taken a while to create those peaks and icecaps. The Tibetan Plateau and fringing Himalayan range began forming 50 million years ago, when the Indian and Eurasian tectonic plates first began to collide. The subsequent pile-up and compression of these two mighty landmasses has given us the world's tallest mountains. It's also resulted in the highest plateau, where the Earth's crust is twice as thick as the norm; where the climate dictates extreme weather patterns, flicking from summer sandstorms to winter blizzards; and where conditions for constructing a railway are challenging, to say the least.

Consequently, the line took some time to complete. Xining, in Qinghai province, could be reached by railway in 1959. The stretch from Xining to Golmud was built by 1984. But it took until 2006 to extend the railway south to Lhasa. This section involved tackling obstacles such as the Kunlun and Tanggula Mountains, and the areas of permafrost between.

Permafrost (a subsurface soil layer that's almost permanently frozen) is weak, and very susceptible to temperature fluctuations. To combat this, engineers constructed elevated tracks on deep concrete pillars as well as a stabilising network of underground pipes that are pumped with liquid nitrogen to keep the permafrost frozen.

Whether this will be enough to withstand any future climate change remains to be seen. For now, though, the Qinghai–Tibet line has mastered Mother Nature.

From Xining, the train heads west, skirting the northern shores of immense Qinghai Lake, the country's largest saltwater lake and a popular spot for migratory birds and Tibetan pilgrims. More lakes surround the industrial town of Golmud, beyond which the line has to tackle the 4,772m (15,656ft) Kunlun Pass, shoving through the mountains to access the hill-edged expanse of the plateau.

Once here, it dashes through Fenghuoshan Tunnel, which at 4,905m (16,093ft) is the world's highest railway tunnel. It crosses the Tuotuo River, the source of the Yangtze. And it traverses the Hoh Xil grasslands, roamed by more than 200 animal species, from wild yak to Tibetan antelope. Aside from the odd horseman or string of Buddhist prayer flags, signs of human life are few and far between.

MORE MOUNTAINS

- - - - - - - - - - - - - - - - -

10. Arlberg Line
Austria

The gorgeous but troublesome 85-mile (137km) Innsbruck–Bludenz mountain railway, through the 6.5-mile (10km) Arlberg Tunnel, opened in 1884.

BELOW: The Qinghai–Tibet railway, running across the Tibetan Plateau, was opened in 2006.

At Tanggula station (5,068m / 16,627ft), passengers will be grateful for another piece of train innovation: to combat the effects of altitude sickness, carriages are pumped with additional oxygen and each seat has its own oxygen supply. Even so, all passengers must sign a health declaration form before travel.

From Tanggula the long descent towards Lhasa begins. After the Amdo grasslands and the glacier-licked Nyenchen Tanglha Mountains, the view becomes gradually greener. Villages crop up with distinctly Tibetan-style houses. After around 22 hours and 675 bridges, the train pulls into Lhasa's enormous terminus. The city has been the epicentre of the Tibetan Buddhist world for over 1,000 years. It is modernising, in part due to the influx of Han Chinese brought by the train. But, with its prostrating monks, narrow back-alleys and all-dominating Potala Palace, Lhasa still feels removed from the rest of the world.

LIKE THAT? TRY THIS

----

11. Montenvers Railway
Haute-Savoie, France

Ride this 3.2-mile (5.1km) rack and pinion railway, built in 1909, from the ski resort of Chamonix to Montenvers for access to the Mer de Glace, France's biggest glacier.

RIGHT: The Potala Palace in Lhasa used to be the chief residence of the Dalai Lama.

12
POSTOJNA CAVE TRAIN

Southwest Slovenia

This train provides a historic trundle through a magnificent maze of karst. Slovenia's subterranean labyrinth at Postojna – known today as the Postojna Cave Park – was formed 4 million years ago by the eroding action of the Pivka River. Around 15 miles (24km) of passages have been explored so far, with 3.2 miles (5.1km) accessible by visitors – most of it by train. The first railway to zip tourists through Postojna's caverns opened in 1872; those carriages were pushed by hand. Today electric trains loop through the tunnels via the vast, acoustically exquisite 'Concert Hall' (performances do actually take place here) and past shiny-white stalagmites and stalactites, which grow at a rate of 1cm (0.4in) every 100 years.

13
FLUGLEST

Southwest Iceland

There are no trains in Iceland. But if the proposed Fluglest ('Flight Train') does go ahead, it will not only provide a window onto the subarctic island's vigorous geology, it will be powered by it, too. Iceland, one of the planet's most tectonically active places, generates 100 percent of its electricity from renewable sources such as rivers, glaciers and geothermal shenanigans. The Fluglest would run off that electricity, linking the airport at Keflavík with Iceland's capital Reykjavík (31 miles/50km) in 15 minutes, via the lava fields and hot springs of the Reykjanes peninsula. If plans are approved, the line could open by 2019.

FERROCARRIL CENTRAL ANDINO

Central Highlands, Peru

Enter the lair of the llamas aboard this audacious
railway line through the towering Andes range.

Need to know
- *Point in time: 25
  million years ago
  (uplift of the Andes)*
- *Length: 332 miles
  (535km)*
- *Minimum time:
  14 hours*
- *Key stops: Lima, San
  Bartolomé, Matucana,
  Galera, La Oroya,
  Concepción, Huancayo*
- *Countries crossed:
  Peru*

Peruvians must have been miffed when China's Qinghai–
Tibet Railway (pp. 20–22) opened in 2006. Because
previously – indeed, since 1893 – Peru had been home to the
world's highest railway. More than a century before Chinese
engineers mastered the Tibetan Plateau, the Ferrocarril
Central Andino had tackled the Andes, the enormous
South-American range that's been 25 million years in the
raising. According to the American entrepreneur Henry
Meiggs, who helped drive the enterprise, his men would
'place rails there, where the llamas walk'.

    The first stretch of the line, from the Pacific port of Callao
to Peru's capital Lima, opened in 1851. By 1873 it had made
it to 4,818m (15,806ft) Ticlio Pass (which is now bypassed by

a slightly lower tunnel) and 4,782m (15,689ft) Galera.
By 1908, the line ran all the way to the highland city of
Huancayo. En route lay fifty-eight bridges, six switchbacks
and sixty-nine tunnels hacked out of Andean rock.

There's no regular passenger service on the line these
days. It stopped after Peru's militant communist group,
Shining Path, bombed the line in 1992. But since 2003 there
has been an infrequent tourist service (complete with
supplementary oxygen to help combat altitude sickness).

The train leaves from Lima's Beaux Arts–style
Desamparados Station, and runs through the lush Rimac
Valley, beside wildflower fields, via villages and along hills
cut with steep Inca terraces. As it ascends to the altiplano
– the high tableland of central South America – the
landscape becomes more desolate, the air thinner, the
engineering feats more impressive, not least the 175m
(574ft) long ravine-spanning Verrugas Bridge.

After Galera, now the world's second-highest railway
station, located just east of the world's second-highest tunnel,
the train passes snow peaks, glacial lakes and herds of llamas.
After some industrial ugliness, the verdant Mantaro Valley
beckons, then the town of Jauja, established by Spanish
conquistador Francisco Pizarro in the 16th century. After
14 hours, the train arrives at the thronging altiplano
metropolis of Huancayo, the end of a breath-stealing ride.

**MORE ANDES
ADVENTURES**
- - - - - - - - - - - - - - - - - -

15. Tren Macho
Peru
Continue through Peru's
Central Highlands from
the city of Huancayo,
taking the slow 80-mile
(128km) Tren Macho
through llama-grazed
valleys to the hot-spring
town of Huancavelica.

FAR LEFT: The railway
reached Ticlio Pass, in Peru's
Cordillera Central, in 1873.

LEFT: Cutting through the
lofty Andes, the Ferrocarril
Central Andino is the world's
second-highest railway.

16
TRAIN TO THE CLOUDS

Northern Argentina

Keep your fingers crossed for the future of this high-altitude,
highly dramatic route across the Andes.

Need to know
- *Point in time: 25 million years ago (uplift of the Andes)*
- *Length: 270 miles (434km)*
- *Minimum time: 15 hours return*
- *Key stops: Salta, Campo Quijano, Alfarcito, San Antonio de los Cobres, La Polvorilla Viaduct*
- *Countries crossed: Argentina*

ALTERNATIVE HIGH LINE
- - - - - - - - - - - - - - - -

17. Zugspitze Railway
Bavaria, Germany

Master Germany's highest peak via Europe's third-highest railway. Trains run from the mountain resort of Garmisch-Partenkirchen to Lake Eibsee, through the Zugspitze and Rosi tunnels to Zugspitzplatt, just below the Zugspitze's 2,962m (9,718ft) summit.

Building and maintaining a train line from northern Argentina to northern Chile, across the Andes, was always going to be a challenge. Topping 6,000m (19,685ft), the Andes are the highest mountain range outside Asia. They were born from a geological uplift that began some 25 million years ago, and which has resulted in a landscape of breathtakingly high plateaus topped with even higher peaks.

So, not an easy place to build a railway. But the desire to service the region's mines was strong, and a narrow gauge line opened in 1948, linking Salta in Argentina with Antofagasta on Chile's Pacific coast. En route it crossed La Polvorilla Viaduct, a 64m (210ft) high trestle bridge at 4,220m (13,850ft) above sea level, making it the fifth-highest train track in the world.

These days the full line is used mainly for freight, but the 270-mile (434km) portion from Salta to La Polvorilla in Argentina also runs as a tourist experience: the Tren a las Nubes, or Train to the Clouds. A 15-hour out-and-back tour, it offers an astonishing breadth of scenery, from the lush Lerma Valley to the multicoloured gorges of the Quebrada del Toro and the endless *puna* (high-altitude grasslands). On the way it negotiates twenty-nine bridges, twenty-one tunnels, thirteen viaducts, two spirals and two zigzags.

Or, it did. At the time of writing parts of the railway had been damaged by flooding, and the experience somewhat compromised. Instead of boarding the train at Salta, tourists travel along the line by bus, looking at – rather than riding – its various twists and turns all the way to the mining village of San Antonio de los Cobres. Here, passengers can finally hop on a train for an hour-long ride to La Polvorilla, which has so far withstood the Andes' inclement climes. Hopefully the whole line will eventually be restored.

18
TREN PATAGÓNICO

Río Negro, Argentina

There's no better way to traverse Patagonia, surely one of the planet's most enticing wildernesses, then aboard the Tren Patagónico. Start in the Argentinian city of Viedma, just inland from the Atlantic Ocean. Consume excellent Argentine steak and wine in the dining car. Drift off in your own sleeper as the train zips across Río Negro province. And wake up on the northern edge of Patagonia, after a journey of 510 miles (820km). The train terminates at the chocolate-box Swiss-style town of San Carlos de Bariloche, on the shores of Lake Nahuel Huapi, and provides access to a transitional wonderland where Andean forest merges into Patagonian steppe.

BELOW: The Train to the Clouds negotiates La Polvorilla Viaduct.

THE GHAN

Australia

Slice through the rich-red Australian outback, following a modern-day songline on a historic, cross-country ride.

Need to know

- *Point in time: 50,000 years ago (humans first arrived in Australia)*
- *Length: 1,851 miles (2,979km)*
- *Minimum time: 54 hours*
- *Key stops: Darwin, Katherine, Alice Springs, Adelaide*
- *Countries crossed: Australia*

LIKE THAT? TRY THIS
- - - - - - - - - - - - - - - - - - -

20. Gippsland Line
Victoria, Australia

The 172-mile (277km) Melbourne–Bairnsdale railway enters the heartland of the Gunaikurnai people. At Bairnsdale's Krowathunkooloong Keeping Place, learn how to make baskets and spears.

RIGHT: The great Ghan curves out of Alice Springs on its journey between Darwin and Adelaide.

Australia is enormous. Top to bottom, from north-coast Darwin to south-coast Adelaide, is a distance of almost 1,900 miles (3,000km). Now there's a nice, comfortable train that links the two in a near-straight line. However, people have been travelling huge distances across the Red Centre for millennia, long before the advent of air-conditioning and bar cars.

The first modern humans probably arrived on Australia's north coast around 50,000 years ago. From here, they fanned out across the country and, at some point, developed their own mythologies regarding its creation. According to many Dreamtime stories, at the beginning of the world ancestral beings roamed the land and created the hills, lakes, rocks and caves; the pathways between these features became known as songlines, tracks that are still followed by Australia's indigenous peoples today.

The Ghan is a sort of songline for rail fans. This thrilling route trundles through the heart of Australia, linking the tropical Top End's crocs and rock art to the crashing Southern Ocean. En route lie many outback icons that those ancestor spirits allegedly created. However, instead of the indigenous peoples' chants and didgeridoos providing the music, on this journey it is the clack and rumble of wheels on tracks.

The first white man to successfully traverse Australia south–north through the Red Centre was Scottish-born John McDouall Stuart in 1862. He was mapping a route for an overland telegraph, and when it came to constructing a railway several decades later, Stuart's route was used. The original steam-hauled 'Afghan Express' between Adelaide and Alice Springs was launched in 1929. It was nicknamed for the pioneering Afghan cameleers who, in the late 19th century, opened up the outback.

However, the original track proved unfit for purpose. It was laid in areas prone to flash flooding, fire and termite infestation. Long delays were common. In the 1980s new standard gauge, termite-proof lines were laid slightly further west. And, in 2004, the railway was finally extended to Darwin. A full traverse by train became possible at last.

Various comfort levels are available. Budget travellers can opt for Red class, with its recliner seats and shared

**MORE
AUSTRALIAN
ADVENTURES**
- -

**21. Transwa
Australind**
Western Australia

Travel through the Noongar people's ancestral lands on the 104-mile (167km) Perth–Bunbury route. The train stops in Pinjarra, site of the 1834 massacre of Noongar by British soldiers.

22. The Inlander
Queensland, Australia

This 607-mile (977km) ride from Pacific-side Townsville cuts across the timeless outback to Mount Isa, a mining boomtown and homeland of the Kalkadoon people.

bathrooms. Gold class offers twin cabins. Platinum is most luxurious, with more space, double beds and fancy food.

The former frontier outpost of Darwin was badly damaged by Japanese air raids during the Second World War; now it's a thriving, multicultural city. From here, the train plunges south into tropical lushness, heading for Nitmiluk (Katherine) Gorge, where the train stops to allow time for a river cruise or kayak paddle. Then it rumbles on, through the infinity-and-beyondness of the bush, a seemingly endless sweep of raw earth, orange rock and bouncing kangaroos. As the sun sinks low, the pink-purple dusk is soon replaced by an astronomical dazzle of stars.

Alice Springs awaits after an outback sunrise. Again, the train pulls in for a while, giving time for a quick excursion, perhaps to Alice's original Telegraph Station or to see spiny lizards in Alice Springs Desert Park. It's worth breaking your journey here to spend a few days in Uluru-Kata Tjuta National Park, the superstar of sacred Australian sites. Uluru (formerly Ayers Rock) is no longer available to climb, but the Anangu people who own the site lead walks around the sacred peak, filled with Dreaming tales.

Those riding the train in one go will need to be back on board by lunchtime as the Ghan continues south, pausing for spectacular stargazing in the middle-of-nowhere town of Manguri before another night on the move. By morning, the train is cutting through the Flinders Ranges, and the landscape's rich reds segue into verdant greens. As genteel Adelaide approaches, a glass of South Australian Barossa Valley wine is just the thing to toast the ride.

LIKE THAT? TRY THIS

----

23. Hotham Valley Tourist Railway
Western Australia

Ride a steam train along an old 9-mile (14km) logging line from the town of Dwellingup (meaning 'place nearby water') through unspoiled jarrah forest.

24
PICHI RICHI RAILWAY

South Australia

It took a long time for early rail engineers to master the ancient, inhospitable Australian outback. The 24-mile (39km) section from the natural harbour city of Port Augusta over the Pichi Richi Pass to the township of Quorn in the Flinders Ranges opened in 1879, part of the long-distance Ghan service that would eventually link Adelaide to Alice Springs (1929) and Darwin (2004). However, the Pichi Richi stretch was closed to regular traffic in 1957 when the Ghan was converted to standard gauge and diverted west. Now it lives on as a heritage line. Every now and then vintage steam and diesel locomotives haul 100-year-old timber carriages through blue-bush plains and ochre-hued outcrops towards the ancient, sun-scorched Flinders Ranges.

25
SOUTH EAST LIGHT RAIL

New South Wales, Australia

When Transport for NSW planned a new light rail link for the state capital of Sydney, they never planned for what happened next. Work on the 7.5-mile (12km) line, due to connect the city's Circular Quay harbour to the southeastern suburbs, began in October 2015. But while excavating the stabling yard in the suburb of Randwick, an enormous cache of more than 22,500 indigenous artefacts was uncovered. The profusion of spearheads and knife blades prompted experts to suggest that it could be a massacre site; its date is unknown, although indigenous peoples have inhabited the country for at least 50,000 years. The removal of the artefacts from the site, without full archaeological investigation, was not without controversy, but railway construction has continued. The line is due to open in 2019.

EMPIRE LINE

New York, United States

Leave an island, follow a river and bypass a load
of lakes to reach a mighty waterfall by rail.

Need to know

- *Point in time: 10,000
  years ago (Wisconsin
  glaciation formed
  Niagara Falls)*
- *Length: 460 miles
  (740km)*
- *Minimum time:
  7 hours 20 minutes*
- *Key stops: New York,
  Albany, Syracuse,
  Rochester, Buffalo,
  Niagara Falls*
- *Countries crossed:
  United States*

The Empire Line is a scenic journey across the 'Empire State', New York. It's also a wonderfully wet ride, in terms of what you get to gaze at en route. Starting from New York City's Penn Station, in the shadow of the Empire State Building, it first needs to find its way off the island of Manhattan. For this, it crosses the Harlem River into the Bronx via the Spuyten Duyvil Bridge (built in 1900), a low steel truss that can swing open to allow boats through; it is opened around 1,000 times a year.

Once across, the Empire Line heads north, following the old Hudson River Railroad (opened fully in 1851) along the eastern shore of the Hudson River. It passes the steep cliffs of the New Jersey Palisades, the Beaux Arts–style station at Yonkers and the grand Bear Mountain Bridge as it continues alongside the water to reach state capital Albany.

Here, the train turns hard left into rail history. The Mohawk and Hudson Railroad, which was founded in 1826 and connected the Hudson River at Albany to the Mohawk River at Schenectady, was the first line in the state. It was also the first in the country designed to carry a locomotive engine.

After Schenectady, the train continues west, rumbling through the Finger Lakes region. Here, there are eleven deep lagoons gouged by glaciers – or, according to the early Native American inhabitants, made by the fingerprints of the Great Spirit.

The Empire Line's most dramatic watery treat is at its terminus. The immense Niagara Falls was formed as ice retreated at the end of the Wisconsin glaciation, and water from the freshly created Great Lakes sliced through the Niagara Escarpment. Though relatively short, the combined falls are extremely wide, monstrously powerful and incredibly popular – in part because, from 1845, tourists could get to them by train.

27. Madgaon–Belgaum
Goa and Karnataka, India

This 78-mile (126km) rail journey rumbles right across the middle of 310m (1,017ft) high Dudhsagar Falls, one of India's highest cascades.

28. Giessbachbahn
Bernese Oberland, Switzerland

Switzerland's first tourist funicular, opened in 1879, climbs 363m (1,191ft) from the shores of Lake Brienz to the Grandhotel Giessbach, for views of Giessbach Falls.

LEFT: The Bear Mountain suspension bridge stretches over the Hudson River.

DENALI STAR

Alaska, United States

Crawl through the glorious, glacier-sculpted
landscapes of the 'Last Frontier' state.

Need to know
- *Point in time: 2.5 million years ago (northern hemisphere's first continental glaciation)*
- *Length: 356 miles (573km)*
- *Minimum time: 12 hours*
- *Key stops: Anchorage, Wasilla, Talkeetna, Denali, Fairbanks*
- *Countries crossed: United States*

ALTERNATIVE ALASKA

30. Glacier Discovery
Alaska, United States

Board the Alaska Railroad line from Anchorage to Grandview (68 miles / 110km) to glimpse some of Alaska's ancient and awesome tongues of ice.

As myriad tongues of ice creep slowly through the Alaskan wilds, so too does the Alaska Railroad. With a top speed of 59 miles per hour (95kph) but a tendency to go at half that pace, travelling by train is the glacial way to tour the 'Last Frontier' state. Alaska's 100,000-plus glaciers cover almost 5 percent of its area. However, from 2.5 million to 9,000 years ago, glaciers cloaked much larger areas and helped shape this spectacular place.

Alaska Railroad's flagship train, the iconic Denali Star, offers a great window onto all this ancient natural architecture. It runs daily, from mid-May to mid-September, between Anchorage, on Cook Inlet, and Fairbanks, in the subarctic interior, revealing a riot of wildflowers or autumn colours, depending on the season. En route lie pristine rivers, mighty mountains, historic towns and a lot of untamed hinterland. Even Anchorage is pretty wild: there are sixty glaciers within 50 miles (80km) of Alaska's most populous city.

The railway leaves Anchorage and wends through birch forest and river valleys where moose and bear roam. It traverses the state's agricultural heartland around the city of Wasilla and, just before the historic village of Talkeetna, offers its first glimpses of 5,500m (18,045ft) Denali / Mount McKinley, North America's highest peak. Between here and Denali National Park, the railway part follows the snaking Susitna River. This section is one of the United States' last flag-stop lines – here, backcountry adventurers can jump off or wave down the train at any point.

After crossing Hurricane Gulch via the line's longest, tallest bridge, the railroad reaches 720m (2,363ft) Broad Pass, its highest point. It then winds through the snow-capped peaks of the journey's star attraction, Denali National Park – many passengers disembark at Denali Depot to look for grizzlies and caribou or hike into the park's 6 million acres (2.5 million hectares) of pristine wilderness.

FAIRBANKS

Nenana

Mears Memorial Bridge

Healy Canyon

ALASKA

DENALI NATIONAL PARK

Denali Depot

DENALI (Mount McKinley)

Broad Pass

Hurricane Gulch

Susitna River

Talkeetna

Matanuska River

Wasilla

COOK INLET

ANCHORAGE

ABOVE LEFT: The Denali Star train runs from May to September.

LEFT: The train passes eons of Alaskan geology, including peaks, lakes and glaciers.

Those staying aboard inch through Healy Canyon and progress through an increasingly desolate landscape. At the little town of Nenana (a former railroad construction camp) the line crosses 210m (700ft) long Mears Memorial Bridge. This was the final link in the Alaska Railroad, completing the main line in 1923. Then it's a short run through boreal forest to finish in the former gold-rush city of Fairbanks.

GLACIER EXPRESS

Southern Switzerland

Hop aboard a master stroke of Swiss engineering to witness
the magnificent mountain-building of Mother Nature.

Need to know
- *Point in time: 2.58 million years ago (Quaternary glaciation began)*
- *Length: 180 miles (290km)*
- *Minimum time: 8 hours*
- *Key stops: Zermatt, Brig, Andermatt, Disentis, Chur, St Moritz*
- *Countries crossed: Switzerland*

LIKE THAT? TRY THIS
- - - - - - - - - - - - - - - - - - -

32. Wilderswil–Schynige Platte Railway
Bernese Oberland, Switzerland

As well as majestic scenery, this 4.5-mile (7.25km) cog railway, opened in 1893, leads to the Schynige Platte Botanical Alpine Garden, a glorious collection of mountain flowers and plants.

Welcome aboard the self-proclaimed slowest – though arguably most scenic – express train in the world. The Glacier Express ambles from the mountain resort of Zermatt to glitzy St Moritz in a leisurely 8 hours. It proceeds cautiously, having to master many obstacles en route – and to give passengers time to soak up the views.

Switzerland is not short of great train journeys. The combination of Alpine landscapes with precision engineering (not to mention faultless timekeeping) is a marriage made in rail heaven. Even so, the Glacier Express deserves special mention. Over its 180-mile (290km) length, this narrow gauge line negotiates 291 bridges and ninety-one tunnels, passing some of the world's most magnificent mountains as it goes.

Architect of all this Alpine gloriousness was the Quaternary glaciation, a series of ice ages fluxing between glacial expansion and warmer interglacial intervals (one of which we're in now) over the past 2.5 million years. Colossal glaciers have oozed through the Swiss valleys towards the plains, gouging ravines and cirques, scattering boulders, building hills and forming lakes in their wake.

Sadly, you won't see many actual glaciers from a regular Glacier Express window. The tongues of ice are higher up the mountains, and retreating ever further these days. You won't even glimpse the ice river for which the service is named: the Rhône Glacier. When the line first opened, in 1930, it crossed the 2,429m (7,969ft) Furka Pass via the Rhône Glacier, source of the River Rhône. However, due to heavy snowfall the pass became unnavigable in winter. So the 9.6-mile (15.4km) Furka Base Tunnel was constructed, bypassing the climb, allowing the first year-round Glacier Express service to run from 1982. In summer, visitors can still traverse the original Glacier Express route as the steam locos of the Furka Cogwheel Railway ply the 11.1-mile-long (17.8km) section between the villages of Oberwald and Realp.

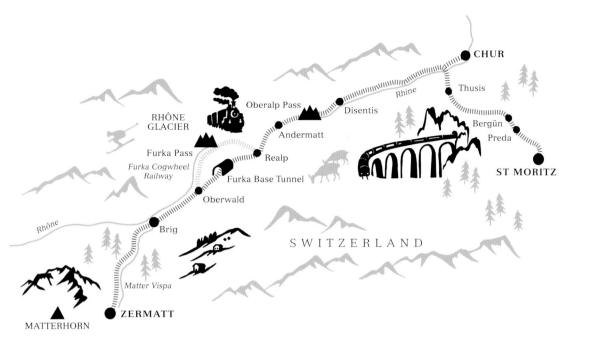

Still, the tunnel diversion doesn't much diminish the splendour of the current Glacier Express journey. Zermatt makes a fine starting point. This car-free, chocolate-box town, dominated by the pointy 4,477m (14,688ft) Matterhorn, is accessible only by train. From here, the Glacier Express meanders east along the Matter Vispa River, squeezed between towering rock walls and Switzerland's highest summits. The 1,000m (3,280ft) of descent to the town of Brig is managed with the aid of a toothed rack-and-cogwheel system.

From Brig, the train picks up the Rhône Valley, crossing the river and passing more mountains, fir trees and a scatter

BELOW: The Glacier Express leaves from Zermatt, in the shadow of the Matterhorn.

of villages for its climb back up to Oberwald. Then the train catches its breath through the Furka Base Tunnel, before the hard graft begins again after the village of Andermatt. From here, it's a hearty haul up to the 2,034m (6,673ft) Oberalp Pass, source of the River Rhine and the railway's highest point, before a drop down the Rhine Valley – the 'Swiss Grand Canyon' – to the railway's lowest point at the city of Chur.

From Chur, the train backtracks a little before veering south to pick up the Albula Line (linking the 697m / 2,287ft high village of Thusis with the 1,774m / 5,820ft high resort of St Moritz), a railway master stroke that climbs over 1,000m (3,300ft) in around 38 miles (62km). On leaving Thusis, the train has to bore through nine tunnels in just 3.7 miles (6km). Then there are the viaducts, not least the 65m (213ft) high Landwasser Viaduct, where the train teeters along a cliff edge before crossing this curvaceous, six-arched span, plunging straight into a tunnel on the other side.

Most testing for those early engineers, however, was the ascent of the valley between Bergün and Preda – some 400 vertical metres (1,300 vertical feet) in just 3.2 miles (5km). Two curved tunnels, three spiral tunnels and several bridges do the trick, winding the track like a corkscrew. Finally, the Glacier Express pulls into the upscale resort of St Moritz, a suitably glamorous finale to a spectacular Alpine ride.

33
JUNGFRAUBAHN

Bernese Oberland, Switzerland

It's hard to know which is more astonishing: the majesty of the Jungfrau itself – at 4,158m (13,642ft), one of Europe's most impressive mountains. Or the fact that for over 100 years this geological Alpine behemoth, formed some 23 to 34 million years ago, has been accessible by train. The 5.5-mile-long (9km) Jungfraubahn opened in 1912, running from the 2,061m (6,762ft) mountain pass of Kleine Scheidegg up to Jungfraujoch (3,454m / 11,332ft), Europe's highest train station. For most of the way this cogwheel railway climbs through a tunnel bored through the neighbouring Eiger and Mönch mountains, but it emerges into high Alpine splendour, with views of the Aletsch Glacier (highest in the Alps), soaring peaks and untrodden snow all around.

34
TRANSALPINA

Slovenia

Investigate the Alpine geology of Slovenia on an old Austro–Hungarian railway. Completed in 1906, the Transalpina line allowed trains to run from the sea at the Italian port of Trieste to the Austrian capital Vienna and beyond. These days you can ride the 82-mile (129km) section between the modernist Slovenian town of Nova Gorica (on the Italian border) and Jesenice (on the Austrian border) – a scenic treat. The line climbs along the green-blue Soča River, passes clusters of highland villages, skirts crystal-clear Lake Bohinj and stops off at postcard-perfect Lake Bled, with its medieval castle and church-topped island. Regular regional trains operate the route year round, but in summer steam-hauled services add extra style.

Entering the Arctic Circle can feel like regressing to the last ice age. Above 66°N, the landscapes are pristine and spectacular, and human settlement sparse – although Sami people have lived here for at least 6,000 years. The 105-mile (169km) railway link from the town of Kiruna (in Sweden's far north) to the Norwegian port of Narvik was built in 1902 to transport iron ore from Sweden's mines to the sea. It's also a scenic slice of the ancient Arctic. The train leaves Kiruna's mine-scarred mountains and heads northwest, skirting glacier-fed Lake Torne and Abisko National Park in Swedish Lapland (a great spot to see the Northern Lights), crossing the border at the ski resort of Riksgränsen and running high along valleys and fjords. Finally it descends to Narvik, where the harbour's striking industrial machinery is offset by the islands, fjords and mountains crowding in on all sides.

The remnants of a 458-million-year-old volcanic caldera, 1,085m (3,560ft) Mount Snowdon is the highest peak in Wales. It's also one of the busiest, thanks to the fact that, since 1896, a rack and pinion railway has been carrying people to the top. The railway runs 4.75 miles (7.6km) from the village of Llanberis, up Yr Wyddfa (Snowdon's Welsh name), offering unfettered views over Snowdonia National Park's rivers, waterfalls, glacially gouged cwms (corries) and knife-edge ridges. At the summit, as well as a visitor centre there is (allegedly) the tomb of Rhitta Gawr, a giant who was slain by King Arthur because he demanded the king's beard.

RIGHT: Remote Finse is the highest station on the Bergen–Oslo Railway.

OSLO–BERGEN RAILWAY

Southern Norway

Cross one of Europe's most hostile environments
on one of its most brilliant railways.

Need to know
- *Point in time: 1.5 billion years ago (oldest rocks on Hardangervidda plateau)*
- *Length: 308 miles (496km)*
- *Minimum time: 6.5 hours*
- *Key stops: Oslo, Hønefoss, Finse, Myrdal, Voss, Bergen*
- *Countries crossed: Norway*

The Oslo–Bergen Railway might just be the toughest battle between man and Mother Nature ever to have been fought in the name of train travel. This link between Norway's capital and its second city, on the west coast, has to cross the remote Hardangervidda, the largest eroded plain in Europe.

Hardangervidda is a stark, treeless moorland, riddled with lakes and streams. Its oldest rocks are over 1.5 billion years old, and fossils show that 550 million years ago it was below the sea. As a result of a collision between tectonic plates 419 million years ago, Hardangervidda rose by 3,000m (9,800ft); many millennia of erosion have gnawed away to create today's plateau, which now averages 1,100m (3,600ft) above sea level.

Being high, isolated, cold and old makes Hardangervidda a tough place to build a railway. Multiple routes were surveyed, but still engineers were faced with the necessity of boring tunnels through unyielding gneiss (metamorphic

rock) in sub-zero temperatures in the middle of nowhere. The line was built in sections, with construction of the Bergen–Voss stage begun in 1876 (originally narrow gauge). The first full Oslo–Bergen standard gauge through service didn't run until 1909.

The journey starts at Oslo Central, a new terminus built on the site of the 1880s Oslo Ø station (the old building is now a shopping mall). First, the train runs through the lengthy Oslo Tunnel – Norway's busiest section of railway – then returns to the surface in time for views across the island-dotted fjord. Veering north, the railway tickles Tyrifjorden (Lake Tyri) to arrive at the town of Hønefoss, where the 216m (709ft) Begna Railway Bridge spans the Ådal River above Hønefoss falls. The bridge was built in 1898, when it was decided the Bergen Line would officially start here.

After Hønefoss, rural scenes give way to ever-wilder countryside as the line continues west. A tunnel shoots the train onto a rock ledge above Lake Krøderen, followed by a section alongside the Hallingdal River and up into the Hallingdal Valley, long used as a thoroughfare for traders travelling west. The views become increasingly mountainous as the train nears Geilo, one of Norway's main ski resorts – a level of development enabled by the Oslo–Bergen Railway.

Bidding farewell to the treeline, the train continues to climb, passing often-frozen Lake Ustevatn. Indeed, it can be inhospitably chilly up here for much of the year. Snow sheds

BRILLIANT BRANCH LINE
- - - - - - - - - - - - - - - - - - - -

38. Flåm Railway
Norway

Slice through mountains and fjords on one of the world's steepest regular train lines: almost 80 percent of the 12-mile (20km) Flåmsbana has a gradient of 5.5 percent.

protect the railway in places, but it's still a chore to keep it open through winter. In the 1990s the line between Haugastøl and Hallingskeid, the highest section, was upgraded, and new tunnels were built. Despite unpredictable weather, the old station at Haugastøl is a popular stop-off: cyclists disembark to ride the Rallarvegen, the access road used by the navvies who built the railway.

The highest station is 1,222m (4,009ft) Finse. Perched near the Hardangerjøkulen ice cap, and frequently cloaked by snow, it feels like the Antarctic – which is why Scott and team trained here before their ill-fated 1912 South Pole expedition.

Soon after, the line's zenith is reached at Taugevann (1,301m / 4,270ft), from where the train starts its descent, offering vertiginous views down into the Flåm Valley and Sognefjord, the longest, deepest fjord in Norway. Many passengers hop off at the mountain station of Myrdal to ride the steep and scenic branch line down to picturesque Flåm.

Otherwise, it's onwards via the River Raundal to the fjord-side town of Voss. The 66-mile (107km) line from Voss to Bergen was the first section to open, in 1883. It skimmed the river and travelled via headlands, birch trees and boathouses before veering around the last obstructive mountains. However, in 1964 the Ulriken Tunnel blasted a quicker way through, so the final run in is more direct. The train emerges at Bergen's National Romantic–style station, having truly mastered some of Europe's most hostile terrain.

BELOW: The wilderness of Hardangervidda National Park is ideally accessed by train.

MUKUBA EXPRESS / KILIMANJARO

Tanzania and Zambia

Celebrate railway engineering and human evolution
on a ride across the wilds of East Africa.

Need to know

- *Point in time: 1.9 million years ago (Homo habilis inhabited East Africa)*
- *Length: 1,155 miles (1,860km)*
- *Minimum time: 46 hours*
- *Key stops: Dar es Salaam, Mbeya, Tunduma, Nakondé, Kapiri Mposhi*
- *Countries crossed: Tanzania, Zambia*

LIKE THAT? TRY THIS

- - - - - - - - - - - - - - - - - - -

40. Dar es Salaam–Mwanza
Tanzania

Currently out of service, this 764-mile (1,229km) railway should link the city of Dar es Salaam with the Cradle of Humanity: *Homo habilis* fossils were found near the Lake Victoria port of Mwanza.

ABOVE RIGHT: Giraffe and other wildlife might be seen from the train window.

RIGHT: Refreshments come by way of goods sellers at stations along the way.

If the East African Rift Valley system is the 'Cradle of Humanity', it's also, by creative extension, the birthplace of the railway. It was here, around 1.9 million years ago, that *Homo habilis* evolved. Sometimes considered the first human, *H. habilis* had a brain 50 percent larger than earlier australopithecines – a factor that distinguished it from the apes, and that would, millennia later, enable its descendants (us) to build great things: trains for example.

A tenuous connection, perhaps, but riding either the faster Mukuba Express or Kilimanjaro ordinary train between the Indian Ocean-side metropolis of Dar es Salaam across

southwest Tanzania and into Zambia feels like a trip back to prehistory. These cross-border passenger trains pass terrain that feels little changed in 2 million years.

The railway also shows how essential those big human brains have become. The line, which was built by the Chinese and opened in 1975, was a colossal engineering challenge. It involved moving 330,000 tons of steel rail and building ninety-three stations, 320 bridges and twenty-two tunnels. Obstacles that had to be overcome included intense heat, torrential rain, wide swamps, plunging ravines, big climbs and wild animals.

From Dar es Salaam the railway heads through arid bushland, eventually entering the 20,850-square-mile (54,000 sq. km) Selous Game Reserve, the biggest wildlife sanctuary in Africa. Giraffes, elephants, baboons, zebras and more might be seen from the window – and they seem unfazed by the trains rumbling by. After this, the landscape grows gradually more mountainous and the railway is punctuated with tunnels and bridges – notably the 50m (164ft) high span across the Mpanga River.

Entering the Southern Highlands and rolling via tea and coffee plantations, the tracks reach their zenith at the 1,789m (5,871ft) high town of Uyole. After border-crossing red tape at Tunduma-Nakonde, the line continues south through Zambia with a flatter, quicker ride that crosses the Chambeshi River and runs along the foothills of the Muchinga Mountains to finish in Kapiri Mposhi. The town itself is no great shakes but it's a handy gateway to the rest of Zambia, with capital Lusaka a short, bumpy bus ride south.

EARLY HUMAN ENCOUNTERS

41. Diré Dawa–Djibouti
Ethiopia and Djibouti

Hominid fossils from Ethiopia's Afar region date back 3.2 million years. The new 470-mile (756km) electrified line between Diré Dawa in Ethiopia and the Red Sea port of Djibouti crosses this ancient land.

42. Zambezi Train
Zambia

The 529-mile (851km) Kitwe–Livingstone line passes Kabwe, where in 1921 archaeologists discovered an 125,000–300,000-year-old *Homo rhodesiensis* skull. The line finishes at Victoria Falls.

43. Amtrak Cascades
Canada and United States

On its 446-mile (718km) journey, Amtrak's Cascades service visits Portland and Seattle. It also skims the coast and mountains that supported early peoples who travelled across the Bering Sea land bridge around 20,000 years ago.

44. Rutland Railway
Vermont, United States

While digging the Rutland Railway between Burlington and Charlotte, workmen discovered the skeleton of an 11,500-year-old beluga whale. 'Charlotte' the whale now resides at Perkins Geology Museum in Burlington.

It was tough to build a trans-Canada railway (next page), partly because of the Canadian Shield, a vast exposed chunk of the Earth's crust that is home to the world's oldest known rocks.

THE CANADIAN

Canada

Cross the Canadian Shield and the Rocky Mountains
on a pioneer-feel transcontinental ride.

Need to know
- *Point in time: 4 billion years ago (age of Canada's oldest rocks)*
- *Length: 2,775 miles (4,466km)*
- *Minimum time: 5 days*
- *Key stops: Toronto, Winnipeg, Saskatoon, Edmonton, Jasper, Vancouver*
- *Countries crossed: Canada*

The Canadian, VIA Rail's cross-country service, is billed as 'Your Window to Canada', which is no marketeer's exaggeration. This transcontinental train ride covers a goodly part of the planet's second-biggest country, showcasing the scale and scope of environments it encompasses. And they are truly ancient environments.

The Canadian Shield, a vast exposed chunk of the Earth's crust, is home to the world's oldest known rocks. The Acasta Gneiss of Canada's Northwest Territories and Québec's Nuvvuagittuq Greenstone Belt are both around 4 billion years old.

When railway builders reached the country's wild west in the late 19th century to construct the Canadian Pacific Railway (CPR), the tracks had to be blasted through this geological suit of armour – a heroic undertaking. Indeed, in the 1952 poem 'Towards the Last Spike' (a narrative of the building of the CPR by Canadian poet E.J. Pratt), the Canadian Shield is likened to a dragon and the railway the knight that defeats it. Of course, even after this particular enemy had been vanquished, the railway still had the Canadian Rockies to contend with. It's a miracle that a trans-Canada train ever made it, but the political will to unite the country was strong. In 1885 the line was completed; in 1886 the CPR's first east-west journey was made.

The original train route across Canada ploughed a westerly course through the country's major provinces, cities and towns. From Montréal and Toronto it ran to Winnipeg, Regina, Moose Jaw, Calgary and Banff, over the Rockies at Kicking Horse Pass, then through British Columbia (BC) via Kamloops to Vancouver. Today's Canadian service takes a line further to the north, pioneered by the Canadian National Railway (CNR). This veers off after Winnipeg, running via Edmonton and over the Yellowhead Pass in the Canadian Rockies, before hitting Kamloops. Now, only the Rocky Mountaineer tourist train still uses the 1885 CPR line.

ABOVE: The Rockies range presents a monumental obstacle to railway routes across Canada.

Even so, The Canadian is an epic journey, taking 4 nights to cross the country. The train's 1950s-look stainless steel carriages leave Toronto's Beaux Arts–style station at 10 p.m., three times a week (twice weekly in winter). Almost immediately the train passes the monument to the 17,000 Chinese workers who helped build the CPR in the late 19th century; more than 4,000 died doing so. Soon, though, the bright lights of the metropolis fade and the route plunges onto the Canadian Shield and passes a seemingly endless expanse of boreal forest, bare rock, lakes and rivers. Moose and even bears might be spotted as you trundle through.

Eventually, the sea of spruce gives way to the flat plains of the province of Manitoba and, a day and a half after leaving Toronto, Winnipeg's skyscrapers appear. There's time for a little leg-stretch in this old trading post town – the train arrives at 8 a.m. but is off again at 11.45 a.m., bounding across the prairies into the province of Saskatchewan, then into Alberta.

At around 6.30 a.m. on day four, the Canadian pulls into Edmonton, stopping briefly to catch its breath for the Rockies. As the train approaches Jasper – the commercial centre of Jasper National Park – the snowy heights of the Miette Range start to loom. From here on, the perspex-roofed Vistadome cars of the Canadian come into their own as the train inches forward amid towering mountains, sparkling lakes and snowy peaks on all sides.

The railway crosses into BC at Yellowhead Pass. When a rail route across the Continental Divide was first mooted, engineer Sir Sandford Fleming recommended using this relatively easy thoroughfare. However, the more direct route over Kicking Horse Pass was preferred, despite the greater technical difficulty – it required building the steepest stretch of main line in North America.

Once in BC, the Canadian route drops towards Kamloops before negotiating the narrow, Wild West-feel Fraser River Canyon via a set of bridges and tunnels. Here the CPR and CNR tracks occupy opposite banks; at Siska, truss bridges span the gorge of the Fraser River and the two railways switch sides. After this hostile frontier, the train enters the friendlier Fraser Valley, lined with fields and grazing cows. Finally, at around 9.40 a.m. on day five, the train pulls into Vancouver's 1919-vintage neoclassical Pacific Central Station, having completed its transcontinental adventure.

LIKE THAT?
TRY THIS
- - - - - - - - - - - - - - - - - -

46. Rocky Mountaineer: Rainforest to Gold Rush
British Columbia, Canada

Mix pioneer history and geological marvels – Fraser Canyon, Cariboo Plateau, the Rocky Mountains – on a luxurious 3-day train trip from the city of Vancouver to the town of Jasper in Alberta via Quesnel in British Columbia.

RIGHT: Crossing Java by train offers views to volcanoes across rice terraces.

SUMATRA–JAVA–BALI

Indonesia

Experience an ancient Asian super-region by taking trains –
and a few ferries – through the Indonesian archipelago.

Need to know
- *Point in time: 110,000–12,000 years ago (last Ice Age)*
- *Length: Around 1,055 miles (1,700km)*
- *Minimum time: 40 hours*
- *Key stops: Palembang, Bandar Lampung, Bakauheni, Merak, Jakarta, Surabaya, Banyuwangi, Gilimanuk*
- *Countries crossed: Indonesia*

It's not logistically possible to take a train all the way
from Sumatra across Java to Bali. These days the three
Indonesian islands are separated by the Bali and Sunda
Straits. But this wasn't always so. During the last Ice Age,
until around 12,000 years ago, these islands were joined,
forming the edge of the Asian biogeographical region of
Sundaland. This region was separated from the region to
the east, which became Australasia – resulting in a distinct
natural history different from that of its neighbour. The
phenomenon was recognised in 1859 by British naturalist
Alfred Russel Wallace, who drew a hypothetical faunal
boundary between the two ecozones.

To make your own Sundaland connection now is to
embark on a multi-transportation adventure, using what
remains of Indonesia's original railways (constructed
during Dutch colonial days), plus a few ferry rides
between the islands.

Start in the ancient Sumatran city of Palembang, former capital of the Buddhist Srivijaya empire that ruled the region from AD 650 to 1377. From here, the railway makes a slow traverse of southern Sumatra, via the megalithic-monument-speckled Pasemah Highlands. After about 11 hours it reaches the hillside coastal city of Bandar Lampung, jumping-off point for the port of Bakauheni, the major ferry terminal for boats to Java.

A 2-hour sail across the Sunda Strait delivers you to the west Javan seaport of Merak, where you can take trains right across to the island's east. Various routes are possible – Java has a relatively comprehensive rail network. The northernmost option will take around 24 hours and runs via seething capital Jakarta, the colonial port of Semarang (home to the grand Lawang Sewu building, HQ of the Dutch East Indies Railway Company between 1907 and 1942) and unprepossessing Surabaya, once the largest city in the Dutch East Indies.

It also runs via a resplendence of green, from stream-tickled valleys to hillsides cut with vibrant rice terraces. Volcanoes simmer in the distance. The penultimate stop is the rail terminus at Banyuwangi at the easternmost end of Java. From there you can take a 30-minute ferry ride to the port of Gilimanuk on Bali – Sundaland's easternmost extent. Here, surf beaches, rice paddies, tranquil temples and general laidback loveliness await.

BERING STRAIT RAILROAD

Russia and United States

It's been about 11,000 years since a land bridge existed across the Bering Strait, briefly facilitating land travel from Russia to Alaska. The notional Bering Strait Railroad would re-establish this link. The idea of a railway across the 51-mile (82km) channel, via a tunnel or bridge, was first mooted in the 1890s. Recent estimates suggest building a so-called 'Intercontinental Peace Bridge' would cost over US$100 billion. This hasn't deterred the Chinese, however. In 2014, reports suggested that China was contemplating an 8,080-mile (13,000km) China–Russia–Canada–America bullet train, travelling through a Bering Sea tunnel, that would scoot passengers between Beijing and the contiguous United States in 2 days.

ABOVE: Ijen volcano looms near the port of Banyuwangi, eastern Java.

LEFT: Hop off the train to soak up colourful Indonesian art and culture.

GRAND CANYON RAILWAY

Arizona, United States

Ride restored vintage railcars along a historic line to reach the world's most gorgeous gorge.

Need to know
- *Point in time: 17 million years ago (Grand Canyon first formed)*
- *Length: 65 miles (105km)*
- *Minimum time: 2 hours 15 minutes*
- *Key stops: Williams, South Rim*
- *Countries crossed: United States*

ROCK-HEWN RAILWAYS
- - - - - - - - - - - - - - - - - - -

53. Kurobe Gorge Railway
Honshu, Japan

Some twenty-one bridges and forty-one tunnels help this 12-mile (20km) line negotiate the Japanese Alps, best seen when autumn foliage is in full flame.

54. Al Hoota Cave Train
Oman

A short electric train ride delivers visitors through the mountains and right into the mouth of this 2-million-year-old cave in the Western Hajar range.

The first steam locos of the Grand Canyon Railway (GCR) chugged north from Williams to the canyon's South Rim in 1901. In doing so, the railway opened up one of the United States' most jaw-dropping sites, allowing ordinary, everyday folks the means to glimpse the view that, said Teddy Roosevelt, 'every American should see'. Previously, the vast, mile-deep rip in the blood-red rock was remote, accessible only to hardy pioneers. After 1901, anyone with a US$3.95 ticket could make the short journey to gaze into the beautiful bowels of northern Arizona.

Of course, by 1901 the Grand Canyon had already been an awfully long time in the making. This magnificent gash through the Colorado Plateau measuring 277 miles (446km) long and up to 18 miles (29km) wide was created over millions of years. The very oldest rock at its bottom, the canyon's underbelly of Vishnu Schist, dates back 1.75 billion years. Atop that, stacked like a geological layer cake, are multicoloured strata of Tapeats Sandstone, Muav Limestone, Bright Angel Shale, the deep-red rocks of the Supai Group and glittering, quartzite-rich Coconino Sandstone. Even the youngest layer, the Kaibab Limestone cap, is 270 million years old, well predating the dinosaurs. The Colorado River, aqueous architect of it all, started carving the canyon around 17 million years ago. It's done a top-class job.

The train doesn't delve down into the canyon itself. You'll need a good pair of boots or a trusty mule to do that. No, the railway sticks to the heights of the plateau. It starts at the Williams Depot, 30 miles (48km) west of Flagstaff and 2,130m (7,000ft) above sea level. The poured-concrete depot, dating from 1908, is now on the National Register of Historic Places. It was once abuzz with travellers heading cross-country between Los Angeles and Chicago, who would stop off here for a snooze or a bite to eat at the Fray Marcos Hotel. These days, the new Grand Canyon Railway Hotel, next door to the depot, offers a bygone-feel stay.

The railway operates six different classes of service, utilising a collection of historic passenger cars. Luxury Parlor is the most plush, with its fancy lounges and open-air rear platforms for invigorating wind-in-your-hair views. The oldest carriages in use are restored 1920s Harriman-style vintage Pullmans that until 1984 plied a San Jose–San Francisco commuter line.

A fleet of historic diesel locomotives power most of the services. However, the GCR also has two steam engines, which date from 1906 and 1923, converted to run on recycled vegetable oil. About once a month, one of them is employed to chug across the plateau, adding extra nostalgia to the ride.

LEFT: A 1923 Baldwin steam locomotive arrives at Grand Canyon Village.

LIKE THAT?
TRY THIS
- - - - - - - - - - - - - - - - - - - -

**55. Royal Gorge
Railroad**
Colorado, United States
Follow 24 miles (39km)
of the old Denver and
Rio Grande Western
Railroad, from Cañon
City through the Royal
Gorge, known as the
'Grand Canyon of the
Arkansas River'.

RIGHT: The Kylling Bridge is
one of thirty-two spans along
the Rauma Railway.

BELOW: The stations and
rolling stock of the Grand
Canyon Railway give the
journey a bygone feel.

The class of carriage doesn't alter the splendour of the
scenery, however. Pulling away from Williams, the train
cuts through forests of ponderosa pine, Douglas fir, aspen
and spruce, travelling at around 30–40 miles per hour
(48–64 kph). Then it gradually drops to expansive prairie,
speckled with sagebrush and mountain ash, before climbing
to the canyon rim. The area is rich in wildlife, from
pronghorn antelope and elk to bald eagles, mule deer, even
mountain lion. It's also laced with human history. Native
American Navajo, Havasupai and Hopi peoples all have
deep connections to the region, while there's plenty of
pioneer-era heritage, too. Indeed, it's possible your carriage
will be 'held up' by an array of (fake) gun-totin' Wild West
characters at the station, while singing cowboys may
serenade you en route.

Finally, the train halts at the Grand Canyon Depot – the
South Rim terminus – another National Historic Landmark.
It was completed in 1910 and is the only operational log-built
depot in the country. The El Tovar Hotel, constructed in 1905,
from pine and stone to serve arriving passengers, is nearby
– and still open for business. Beyond that, the earth simply
falls away to the Grand Canyon's chasm snaking through the
ancient rock.

56
RAUMA RAILWAY

Western Norway

For an in-your-face geology lesson, you could do worse than ride the Rauma Railway. This 71-mile (114km) line, running from the town of Åndalsnes on the shores of Romesdalsfjorden to the strategically placed village of Dombås, inches along the ancient gneiss Troll Wall. This is the tallest vertical rock face in Europe, measuring 1,100m (3,600ft) from base to top. The Rauma Railway officially opened in 1924, transporting post and people between communities en route. It encounters thirty-two bridges (including gorgeous, gorge-crossing Kylling Bridge) and six tunnels (including the Stavem horseshoe tunnel). It takes an hour and 40 minutes, although there's talk of replacing it with a high-speed line.

57
ALGOMA CENTRAL RAILWAY

Ontario, Canada

Around 1.2 billion years ago, faulting ruptured the Canadian Shield's ancient rock. Since then, ice ages have sculpted this crack into the wide, wonderful Agawa Canyon. Begun in 1899, the Algoma Central Railway was originally an industrial link, running for 296 miles (476km) between the Ontarian city of Sault Ste Marie, on the Canada-United States border, and the lumber town of Hearst. Now it delivers nature lovers to the boreal forest in between, which is only accessible by foot or rail. Most dramatic is the train's descent from the canyon wall to the canyon floor, a drop of around 150m (500ft).

CUMBRES AND TOLTEC SCENIC RAILROAD

New Mexico and Colorado, United States

You can learn a lot about really old rock on this narrow gauge 64-mile (103km) heritage line between the village of Chama, New Mexico, and the town of Antonito, Colorado. The railroad was originally constructed in 1880–81 as a silver-mining line. Now its original steam locomotives haul passenger cars across the steep 3,053m (10,015ft) high Cumbres Pass and through the Toltec Gorge, offering a dynamic geology lesson through one of the United States' most varied regions. From the train window, look out on the Rio Grande Rift, the San Juan volcanic field, the Precambrian core of the Tusas Mountains and metamorphic rock as old as the bottom of the Grand Canyon.

CHENGDU–KUNMING RAILWAY

Southwest China

The train link between the bustling cities of Chengdu (Sichuan province) and Kunming (Yunnan) is nicknamed China's 'geological museum' route. Over its 681 miles (1,096km) it passes through a gamut of diverse natural environments. These posed a real challenge for railway builders in the 1970s, but provide an extremely scenic ride for today's travellers. The train has to negotiate high mountains (up to almost 2,000m / 6,560ft), as well as precipitous cliffs, canyons and a network of wide rivers. There are also a few geological oddities such as Yunnan's Stone Forest, comprising curious towers of karst believed to be 270 million years old.

RIGHT: The Kuranda Scenic Railway cuts through some of the planet's oldest, most important forests.

KURANDA SCENIC RAILWAY

Queensland, Australia

Trundle through some of the last tracts of Gondwana Rainforest, a portal into Earth's past plants.

Need to know

- *Point in time: 570–510 million years ago (split of Gondwana supercontinent)*
- *Length: 23 miles (37km)*
- *Minimum time: 1 hour 45 minutes*
- *Key stops: Cairns, Freshwater, Kuranda*
- *Countries crossed: Australia*

The UNESCO World Heritage–listed Gondwana Rainforests of Australia comprise one of the most important natural history records on the planet. The species that exist here are the same types that existed in the same place over 570 million years ago, before the break up of Gondwana (the supercontinent comprising most of the southern hemisphere plus Arabia and India). Rainforests covered most of Australia for 40 million years after the split but climate changes and, later, human intervention reduced them to small patches. In these vestigial forests are found some of the very oldest plants, including ancient types of ferns and Jurassic–era araucarians, our most primitive conifers.

LIKE THAT?
TRY THIS

**61. Katoomba
Scenic Railway**
*New South Wales,
Australia*

In the fragrant Blue
Mountains, board the
world's steepest
passenger railway
(with an incline of
52 degrees) for a
vertiginous 310m
(1,017ft) long ride
through Jurassic
rainforest.

The 23-mile (37km) Kuranda Scenic Railway cuts through
a chunk of this evolution-charting environment, on North
Queensland's Atherton Tablelands – a fertile plateau and part
of the Great Dividing Range. The railway, started in 1887
and opened in 1891, was built to provide a supply link to the
Pacific for the tin miners toiling in the Australian interior.

Construction wasn't easy; the section from valley-nestled
Redlynch through Barron Gorge was especially difficult –
the bush was dense, the gradients vertiginous, the waterfalls
numerous and the indigenous people hostile to the project.
Some fifteen tunnels, ninety-three curves and numerous
bridges, all constructed by hand, were required to master an
altitude gain of 320m (1,050ft). After this, there was no money
left to continue the line to the pioneer village of Herberton, as
originally planned.

The Kuranda Scenic Railway is less a lifeline today, more
a tourist ride through aeons of botanical history.
Comprising some 90-year-old
timber carriages, trains leave from
the Great Barrier Reef city of
Cairns and head into Barron
Gorge National Park via ravines,
waterfalls and a profusion of flora.
At the interim station at
Freshwater a railway museum
pays tribute to the early pioneers.
At Kuranda, the 1913 Swiss
chalet–style terminus still stands.

RIGHT: The Kuranda Scenic
Railway travels via many
tunnels and bridges.

PUFFING BILLY

Victoria, Australia

The volcano that formed Victoria's Dandenong Ranges was last active 200 million years ago. But there's still plenty of smoke amid these hills. The Puffing Billy Railway opened in 1900 so that settlers in the Ranges could access the region's capital city, Melbourne. Today the railway is designed for tourists, with open-sided carriages instead of goods cars, but is still pulled by vintage steam locos, the oldest dating to 1901. Billy takes 90 minutes to cover the 15-mile (24km) haul between the suburb of Belgrave and the town of Gembrook, home to Puffing Billy Railway Station. En route it sweeps through mountain ash and eucalyptus, crosses timber trestle bridges, passes old settler stations and a steam museum, and offers far-reaching views to the Southern Ocean.

SERRA VERDE EXPRESS

Paraná, Brazil

Cut through one of the planet's oldest, most important forests,
along gravity-defying tracks through the hills.

Need to know
- *Point in time: 65 million years ago (age of Atlantic Forest)*
- *Length: 68 miles (110km)*
- *Minimum time: 3 hours*
- *Key stops: Curitiba, Marumbi, Morretes, Paranaguá*
- *Countries crossed: Brazil*

The Serra Verde Express is both a tremendous train journey and an eye-opening lesson in natural history, cutting through one of the planet's most important biomes: Brazil's Atlantic Forest (Mata Atlântica). Although the Amazon grabs most headlines when it comes to Brazilian biodiversity, the Mata Atlântica is perhaps even richer. Some areas boast 450 different tree species per hectare, with around 20,000 plant species recorded. There are also about 2,200 species of birds, mammals, reptiles and amphibians, including jaguar, ocelot, golden lion tamarin and the rare maned three-toed sloth.

It's nothing short of miraculous that all this life still exists here. The forest, which dates back to when South America split from Africa some 65 million years ago, once covered an area of approximately 560,000 square miles (1.5 million sq. km). Since the Portuguese discovered Brazil in 1500, arriving first at Porto Seguro amid the Atlantic Forest, deforestation has been rampant. Now, only around 8 percent of the original area remains.

The Serra Verde Express begins in Curitiba, capital of Paraná state, high on an inland plateau. The city was officially founded in 1693 and over the centuries grew to become a key hub for timber, grain, mate plant and coffee cultivation. By the 1860s there was talk of building a railway to the port of Paranaguá, to transport these goods to the ocean. It seemed impossible, but work began in 1880 and in just 5 years, with a crew of 9,000 men and the construction of fourteen tunnels and numerous bridges, the challenging mountainous terrain of the Serra do Mar was mastered. The line was complete.

Curitiba is a fitting start point for a *verde* (green) train. The city has long embraced eco initiatives, and has an ultra-efficient urban transport system. From Curitiba the train forges towards Piraquara, a town of natural springs within the Atlantic Forest. It then runs through the

MORE TRAINS AMID TREES

- - - - - - - - - - - - - - - -

64. Bieszczadzka Forest Railway
Southeast Poland

This 7.5-mile-long (12km) narrow gauge forestry line from Majdan once supplied timber for the Austro-Hungarian Empire. Now its sometimes-steam-hauled carriages provide lush mountain views.

65. Klevan–Orzhiv
Western Ukraine

The industrial trains running through the forests near the settlement of Klevan have ploughed a dreamy 1.85-mile-long (3km) furrow through the trees that's been dubbed the 'Tunnel of Love'.

LEFT: Brazil's Atlantic Forest is one of the planet's most biodiverse habitats.

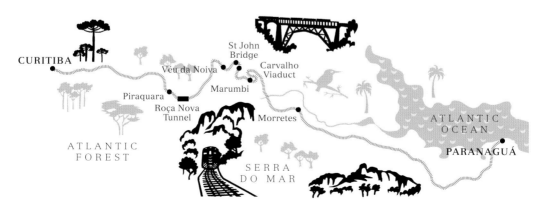

CURITIBA

St John Bridge

Véu da Noiva

Carvalho Viaduct

Marumbi

Piraquara

Roça Nova Tunnel

Morretes

ATLANTIC FOREST

SERRA DO MAR

ATLANTIC OCEAN

PARANAGUÁ

429m (1,407ft) Roça Nova Tunnel, the longest en route. At an altitude of 955m (3,133ft), it's also the railway's highest point.

Rumbling on through the lush mountains, amid palm and fig trees, the train passes the Véu da Noiva (Veil of the Bride), a 70m (230ft) cascade tumbling into the green. In the distance, the Atlantic glitters. The railway then negotiates the St John Bridge, a 55m (180ft) high metal span that proved to be one of the most challenging aspects of the build, and the last to be finished. The metal truss was constructed in Belgium, sailed over to Paranaguá and hauled up to its final position by train. Later, during Brazil's anti-Republic Federalist Revolution (1893–95), the bridge was set to be blown up to prevent rebels crossing; fortunately, there was a change of plan.

Soon after the bridge, the Serra Verde Express inches along the curvaceous Carvalho Viaduct, which takes a 45-degree turn around the Marumbi Mountains, seeming to float above the forest. Then, at Porto de Cima, the railway hits its steepest incline, dropping almost 4 metres (13ft) in height with every 100m (328ft) travelled.

There's a chance to get out at Marumbi station. You could even break the journey here for a hike in the Marumbi Mountains. After Marumbi, the train continues down to Morretes, named for the *morros* (hills) that surround the city. Riverside Morretes is vibrantly green, and renowned for its restaurants – this is the place to sample *barreado*, the local beef stew.

After about 3 hours, the train pulls in to Paranaguá, Paraná state's oldest city. Archeological evidence suggests indigenous peoples had lived here for thousands of years before the Portuguese turned up around the mid-16th century. It's a large, lively tropical port, still busy transporting goods, even if the railway that was once so economically important disgorges only tourists these days.

LIKE THAT?
TRY THIS
- - - - - - - - - - - - - - - - - - -

66. Redwood Forest Steam Train
*California,
United States*

Ride a 1880s narrow gauge log-hauling line for 3.25 miles (5.2km) through the ancient redwood stands of Roaring Camp, pulled along by 19th-century steam locomotives.

RIGHT: The train ride from Curitiba to Paranaguá is like a natural history lesson.

67
FOREST RAILWAY

Alishan, Taiwan

Though the 53-mile (86km) network of the Forest Railway in Taiwan's Alishan region was built to help loggers cut down trees, it's now the best way to appreciate this ancient forest as it stands. The Japanese, who ruled Taiwan at the time, began constructing narrow gauge railways here in 1906. All manner of engineering solutions were required to tackle the mountains, from Z-shaped switchbacks to seventy-seven wooden bridges. Alight at Shenmu Station to walk past some of the forest's sacred trees, the oldest of which are 3,000 years old. Or ride the Zhushan line (Zhaoping Station–Zhushan Station) in the early hours to reach the railway's highest point (2,451m / 8,041ft) for sunrise.

68
HISATSU LINE

Kyushu, Japan

When constructing a railway between the towns of Yatsushiro and Hayato, it would have been easier to build along the East China Sea coast. But at the beginning of the 20th century, the Japanese – who had just fought wars against China and Russia – were feeling defensive. So they hacked a line inland instead. This is a boon for today's rail travellers, as the 77-mile (124km) Hisatsu Line is now an unhurried unfurling of natural beauty, rumbling along the Kumagawa River and switchbacking into the Kirishima Mountains. Indeed, the section near Yoshimatsu is officially one of the three best views from a train in Japan.

Tourist steam trains riding the Vaser Valley Forestry Railway in Romania's swathe of the Carpathian Mountains scoop up water along the way to cool their engines.

69
VASER VALLEY FORESTRY RAILWAY

Northern Romania

Romania's Carpathian Mountains harbour some of Europe's last remaining old-growth forests. They also used to be riddled with narrow gauge forest railways, laid to transport timber out of the inaccessible valleys. Now, just one working line remains, the 13.5-mile (22km) Vaser Valley Railway, known locally as the Mocăniţa. Built in 1932, it runs from the town of Vişeu de Sus to the sawmills at Paltin, near the Ukrainian border. Lumberjacks still use the line; from spring to autumn a tourist steam train does, too. En route, river water is scooped up to cool the engine and waste wood from the mills is used for fuel.

70
WEST COAST WILDERNESS RAILWAY

Tasmania, Australia

West-coast Tasmania has few settlements or roads, but plenty of rugged mountains and old-growth rainforest – the Huon pines here can live for up to 2,000 years. In 1897, an audacious railway dared to take on this wild frontier, providing a link between the copper mines of Queenstown and the port of Strahan. Various bridges and an Abt rack and pinion system (devised by Swiss engineer Roman Abt) were required to master the severe inclines of the King River Valley and beyond. Today, the original 19th-century steam locomotives ply the 21-mile (34.5km) reconstructed route.

71
VOGELFLUGLINIE

Germany and Denmark

As birds follow a timeless migration route between Central Europe and Arctic Scandinavia, so do the trains of the Vogelfluglinie (Bird Flight Line), regardless of topography. In order for this service to connect the German powerhouse of Hamburg and the Danish capital, Copenhagen (a journey of around 5 hours),

it must navigate the Fehmarn Belt strait in the Baltic Sea. There's no tunnel or bridge, so the train drives right onto a ferry. Passengers must leave the carriages for the 11-mile (18km) crossing between Puttgarden on the German island of Fehmarn and Rødby on the Danish island of Lolland. It's one of the few train-ship experiences in Europe, although perhaps not for long: a tunnel (the Fehmarn Belt Fixed Link) is due to open in 2021.

GROTTE DE ROUFFIGNAC TRAIN

Dordogne, France

Board a tiny train for a short spin around
an ancient underground art gallery.

Need to know
- *Point in time: 13,000 years ago (age of Rouffignac rock art)*
- *Length: 0.6 miles (1km)*
- *Minimum time: 1 hour*
- *Key stops: Grotte de Rouffignac*
- *Countries crossed: France*

The Grotte de Rouffignac boasts quite the menagerie: 158 mammoths, twenty-nine bison, sixteen horses, twelve ibex, eleven woolly rhinos, six snakes and one bear. And they've all been lurking inside the cave for around 13,000 years.

This cavern is part of a 5-mile-long (8km) system of cavities, hewn from the Cretaceous limestone of southwestern France around 2–3 million years ago. The drawings inside were created by Magdalenian peoples, who were widespread across Europe during the Upper Paleolithic period, towards the end of the last Ice Age. These peoples were prolific artists, using flint or bone tools and charcoal-like manganese dioxide to adorn the cave walls.

They were also renowned for being mammal hunters; coincidentally or not, the mammoth – which so dominated their doodles – became extinct during their time.

The paintings of the Grotte de Rouffignac have been known about since at least the 16th century but it was only in the 1950s that archaeologists realised they were so old. Since 1959 visitors have been permitted to enter the caves aboard an electric train. The train limits the number of people, thus restricting human impact on this delicate environment. Tours run from mid-March to November (although dress warmly, as it's always cold inside).

The cave entrance used today is near the village of Rouffignac, and is most likely the one used by the Magdalenians themselves. The drawings are spread throughout the underground labyrinth. The hour-long train ride covers only around 0.6 miles (1km), focusing on areas where the concentration of artwork is greatest. Every now and then the train stops so that passengers can take a closer look. As well as the cave art, there is evidence that bears once lived here – claw scratches on the walls and hibernation hollows on the ground.

RIDES TO EARLY REMAINS

73. Rhine–Ruhr S-Bahn (S28)
Germany

Take the Mettmann–Düsseldorf local railway to meet ancient ancestors. It runs via Neanderthal, where the first 'Neanderthal man' fossils were found; they're now in Mettmann's museum.

74. Train des Merveilles
Alpes-Maritimes, France

From Nice, ride for about 60 miles (100km) through the Roya Valley to Tende, where thousands of Neolithic and Bronze Age engravings are carved into the rocks.

75. Channel Tunnel Rail Link
Kent, United Kingdom

While digging for the High Speed 1 line at Ebbsfleet, Kent, a 400,000-year-old elephant skeleton surrounded by flints was unearthed, shedding new light on Palaeolithic Britain.

FAR LEFT: Visitors can access the Grotte de Rouffignac by electric train.

LEFT: The cave paintings of Rouffignac were created around 13,000 years ago.

DANUBE VALLEY RAILWAY

Baden–Württemberg and Bavaria, Germany

Navigate a scenic section of Europe's
second-longest river by rail.

Need to know
- *Point in time: 11–15 million years ago (Danube formed)*
- *Length: 208 miles (335km)*
- *Minimum time: 5.5 hours*
- *Key stops: Regensburg, Ingolstadt, Donauwörth, Ulm, Immendingen, Donaueschingen*
- *Countries crossed: Germany*

LIKE THAT? TRY THIS
----

77. Murg Valley Railway
Baden-Württemberg, Germany

Inch through an ancient Black Forest gorge. The 36-mile (58km) line between the towns of Rastatt and Freudenstadt involves ten tunnels, eight bridges and spectacular views.

RIGHT: The railway cuts through the Jurassic limestone landscapes of the Upper Danube Valley.

The Danube, Europe's second-longest river, rises in Germany's Black Forest and empties into the Black Sea, 1,777 miles (2,860km) away. It came into being around 15 million years ago: as the Alps lifted, drainage patterns changed and this nascent waterway broke for the east. The Danube isn't just hydrologically interesting, though; it's long been a vital resource, frontier and superhighway. It still is.

Today, much of the Danube's German course can be navigated by train. Plans to build such a river-hugging line were first mooted in the mid-19th century, largely for military reasons. The railway was a target during the Second World War, and Nazi forces destroyed many bridges as they retreated in 1945. But the Donautalbahn (Danube Valley Railway) was soon running again.

Travelling upstream, the Donautalbahn's first stage, through Bavaria, links the medieval town of Regensburg with Ulm, crossing the Danube five times. Along this stretch is the Danube Gap, where the river inches through the Jura Mountains, and the city of Ingolstadt, which features in Mary Shelley's *Frankenstein*.

Soon after, the train visits pretty Donauwörth, then chugs through forested hills to Ulm, where Albert Einstein was born and where the spire of Ulm Minster soars 161.5m (530ft) high – the world's tallest church steeple.

The Donautalbahn's Baden–Württemberg section is the most picturesque, especially the section through the Upper Danube Nature Park's Jurassic limestone crags. Between Immendingen and Tuttlingen is the Danube Sinkhole where the Danube's waters flow underground, leaving the riverbed partially dry for up to 200 days a year.

The railway ends in Donaueschingen, where the Danube is born. A small karst spring, enclosed in an ornate pool at Fürstenberg Palace, is the official source of the mighty river.

78
DON DET–DON KHON

Southern Laos

Transportation is difficult in landlocked, mountainous Laos. Even the venerable Mekong River – formed around 8 million years ago – isn't much help, with its seasonal water-level fluctuations. But there have been tiny attempts at rail travel: amid the Si Phan Don (Four Thousand Islands) archipelago, the French tried to establish a line in 1893. The Don Det–Don Khon narrow gauge railway was just 4.3 miles (7km) long and once spanned these two tropical, palm-tickled Mekong isles. By 1950 it had all but been abandoned, but you can still walk its route, from the old concrete piers through paddy fields and over the 170m (558ft) long viaduct, beyond which a plinthed locomotive slowly rusts in the humid air.

79
BRIENZ–ROTHORN RAILWAY

Bernese Oberland, Switzerland

Created after the last Ice Age, Lake Brienz is a startling hue of blue – and is best viewed aboard the Brienz–Rothorn Railway. This 4.7-mile (7.6km) line, opened in 1891, carries the only daily steam service in Switzerland; on Wednesday afternoons during the summer drivers even cook sausages in the loco's steam kettle on a special 'Steam Sausage Express' service. All trips on this line start from mountain-nestled Brienz, with the engine fixed at the back, pushing the carriages slowly up via wooden chalets, pine forests and wildflower meadows. The top of 2,350m (7,710ft) Mount Rothorn is where three Swiss regions meet: Bern, Obwalden and Lucerne. From here, admire a perfect panorama of Lake Brienz and an ocean of alpine peaks.

ORURO–UYUNI

Southwest Bolivia

You can catch a train from the Bolivian city of Oruro to the altiplano outpost of Uyuni – a journey of around 195 miles (315km). But when you explore the outskirts of Uyuni, the prospects for further rail travel look pretty bleak indeed. Here sits the Cementerio de Trenes, a bizarre graveyard of rusting rails and graffitied locomotives that were abandoned when the mining industry collapsed in the 1940s. And they don't stand a chance of revival. The cemetery sits on the edge of the dazzling Salar de Uyuni salt flats (formed around 10,000–13,000 years ago), leaving the locos to be gnawed by the corrosive air. Somehow these ghostly relics convey the history of the railway here far better than an indoor museum ever could.

TRAIN DE CHARLEVOIX

Québec, Canada

The St Lawrence River, which flows through an ancient geological depression from the Great Lakes to the Atlantic, is one of North America's key thoroughfares. From First Nations peoples to fur-trading voyageurs, humans have long travelled its banks. Now a tourist train does the same, plying the 78 miles (125km) between Québec City and the mountain resort of La Malbaie. The Train de Charlevoix follows an old loggers' line, stopping at coastal villages, serving up fancy food, and keeping so close to the mighty waterway's edge that it feels like a cruise. Look out for seabirds and whales en route.

CHAPTER TWO
THE DAWN OF TIME

Ride from the birth of civilisation to AD 600, discovering long-gone empires, religious roots, archaeological treasures and ancient cultures.

CAIRO–ASWAN

Nile Valley, Egypt

Ride back to the time of the pharaohs alongside
one of the world's longest rivers.

Need to know
- *Point in time: 3100* BC
  *(Early Dynastic Period
  started)*
- *Length: 546 miles
  (879km)*
- *Minimum time:
  10–12 hours*
- *Key stops: Cairo, Giza,
  Asyut, Qena, Luxor,
  Esna, Edfu, Kom
  Ombo, Aswan*
- *Countries crossed:
  Egypt*

ALTERNATIVE ANCIENT EGYPT

- - - - - - - - - - - - - - - - - -

83. Cairo–Alexandria
Northern Egypt

Navigate the Nile Delta
by train: a 2.5-hour ride
links the Egyptian
capital Cairo (with its
antiquities museum) to
the Mediterranean port
of Alexandria, founded
by Alexander the Great
c. 331 BC.

Train carriage? Or time machine? Hard to say. Because
riding the railway along the Nile can feel like trundling back
to an era when pharaohs were in charge. Africa's longest
river seems unaffected by modernity. Gaze out onto palm
trees, ox-carts, lateen-sailed feluccas and the occasional
camel, and you'll feel as if the past 5 millennia haven't
happened at all.

The Nile is the lifeblood of Egypt. Without its waters and
fertile floodplain, this thirsty desert nation could not have
thrived. This has long been the case. Permanent settlements
began to develop along the river from about 6000 BC. By
around 3100 BC Upper and Lower Egypt had been unified,
creating arguably the world's first nation-state and
launching the civilisation that dominated the Mediterranean
until the arrival of Alexander the Great. To ancient
Egyptians, the Nile was a vital resource, but also integral
to their beliefs. The river divided the land of the living (to
the east) from the land of the dead (west), and colossal
monuments were built by its banks.

Much later, the Nile was a magnet for railway builders,
too. In 1851, Egypt's rulers enlisted British railway engineer
Robert 'Rocket' Stephenson to construct a line from
Alexandria to Cairo, through the Nile Delta. Opened in
stages between 1854 and 1856, this was Africa's first
railway. Originally it crossed the Nile at the city of Kafr
el-Zayyat via a train ferry. After Egypt's heir presumptive
drowned when his carriage fell into the water here in 1858,
Stephenson built a swing bridge to replace the ferry.

The line south from Cairo took longer to construct. But
by 1898 it was possible to travel upriver by train from Cairo
to the frontier city of Aswan, a journey of 546 miles (879km).
Today, this is a convenient way to access the sites in Egypt's
south. Most tourists travel overnight, aboard the 'deluxe'
sleeper service. If you're travelling north–south, you nod off
in the metropolis and wake up in a different world: a pinky

dawn breaking over mud-brick houses, net-flinging fishermen and the endless desert.

However, riding the sleeper means missing most of the views. Technically there are government restrictions preventing tourists using the cheaper daytime Cairo–Luxor–Aswan express. In practice, you can get around them by buying tickets online or aboard the train.

Leaving Cairo's grand Ramses Station, the railway's first task is to cross to the west bank of the Nile, via the Imbaba Bridge. The original bridge, designed by Gustave Eiffel, was opened in 1892; the current one dates from the 1920s. Once across, the train heads to Giza, where the Pyramids sit in the desert-nibbled suburbs.

BELOW: Riding alongside the River Nile, it seems little has changed for millennia.

These three massive funerary monuments, constructed from 2580 BC, include the only remaining ancient Wonder of the World.

Egyptian life unfolds as the railway continues south along the Nile's west bank to Nag Hammadi, where it crosses a swing bridge. Next is Qena, on a large bend of the Nile; this is the stop for the Graeco-Roman temple of Dendara. However, Luxor is the best place to appreciate ancient Egypt: 85 percent of the civilisation's sites lie hereabouts. Waterfront Luxor Temple, Karnak's vast complex of columns and obelisks, the Theban Necropolis and the Valley of the Kings all sit in and around the city.

The Luxor–Aswan line was originally narrow gauge. In 1896, the Egyptian military mounted a campaign in Sudan, and a supporting railway was needed quick smart. The line was converted to standard gauge in the 1920s. Now it takes 4 hours to trundle from Luxor to Aswan, via Ancient Egyptian relics at Esna, Edfu and Kom Ombo.

The gateway to southern Egypt since antiquity, Aswan simmers amid sandy mountains on the Nile's first cataract. The whole city feels like a timewarp, with its palm trees, crumbling ruins and drifting felucca sailboats. Head to the Old Cataract Hotel (built by pioneering British travel agent Thomas Cook in 1899), and toast your train trip with a drink on the balcony overlooking the timeless river.

MEDITERRANEAN SEA

Alexandria
Kafr el-Zayyat
CAIRO
Giza
River Nile
Asyut
Qena
Nag Hammadi
Valley of the Kings
Luxor
Esna
Edfu
Kom Ombo
ASWAN
RED SEA

RIGHT: The railway along the Nile links Cairo to southern sites, such as Karnak's Great Hypostyle Hall.

DOĞU EXPRESS

Turkey

The 1,208-mile (1,944km) Doğu Express links the metropolis of Istanbul to wild far-eastern Turkey at a rather un-express-like pace. Indeed, this train service takes about 40 hours to amble to its final stop, the city of Kars near the Armenian border in Eastern Anatolia. Throughout Classical antiquity and beyond this mountainous region was fought over by a succession of empires. For instance, after following a stretch of the River Euphrates the train calls at the city of Erzurum, probably founded around 4000–5000 BC and variously ruled by Persians, Byzantines, Sassanids, Mongols and many others. Erzurum's Archaeological Museum and Seljuk monuments tell some of the story.

KHYBER MAIL

Indus Valley, Pakistan

Discover the once-great railway line that wheezes through the heartland of one of the world's oldest civilisations.

Need to know
- *Point in time: 3300–1300 BC (period of Indus Valley civilisation)*
- *Length: 1,069 miles (1,721km)*
- *Minimum time: 32.5 hours*
- *Key stops: Karachi, Hyderabad, Rohri, Multan, Lahore, Rawalpindi, Peshawar*
- *Countries crossed: Pakistan*

The Indus Valley civilisation was one of the world's first advanced societies. Archaeological sites on the Indus River's fertile floodplains date it to around 3300 BC, possibly earlier. Trade was vital to the civilisation's success, aided by major technological strides including, perhaps, the first use of wheeled transport.

Flip to the 19th century and new transport tech entered the Indus Valley again. In 1851, the British began building a railway north from the Arabian Sea port of Karachi. By the time the colonialists left in 1947, newly independent Pakistan had over 5,000 miles (8,000km) of tracks. The pre-eminent service was the Khyber Mail, which became the unifying backbone of this nascent nation.

Seventy years on, the Khyber Mail is a shadow of its former self. Pakistan's economic and political troubles have hit hard. But for now the train soldiers on – mostly, though rarely on time.

At the time of writing, the UK Foreign and Commonwealth Office advises against travel to large parts of Pakistan due to a high risk of terrorism – a shame, because this is a classic ride. From Karachi the train wends up the valley, through Sindh province, crossing the Indus via the bridge at Kotri. It then ambles through the cotton fields and orange groves of Pakistan's Punjab. Soon it passes the significant Indus Valley archaeological site of Harappa; sadly, the ancient mounds here were ravaged in the 1850s when thousands of bricks were removed to provide railway ballast.

After the culture-rich city of Lahore, the train veers northwest, grinding through Rawalpindi and over the Indus via the Old Attock Bridge. It finishes in Peshawar, from where the border with Afghanistan is only a few miles west.

Northwest Pakistan

The pass over the Khyber Mountains is one of history's most tactically significant. Darius I, Alexander the Great and Genghis Khan all marched over this notch between Afghanistan and Pakistan. Briefly, a railway attempted the same. In 1925, the British completed a 32-mile (52km) line from the frontier town of Peshawar to 1,065m (3,494ft) Landi Kotal, the pass's highest point. The line fell out of regular use, but in the 1990s vintage steam locos began taking tourists on this rugged ride – involving ninety-two bridges and four height-gaining reversing stations. Sadly, flood damage brought the service to a halt in 2006.

LEFT: The Khyber Mail and the Khyber Pass Railway both served Peshawar.

LITTLE TRAIN OF PELION

Thessaly, Greece

Take a narrow gauge train up through the olive groves of the
Pelion Penisula to reach the summer retreat of the Greek gods.

Need to know
- *Point in time:*
  510–323 BC *(Classical period of Greece)*
- *Length: 17.5 miles (28km)*
- *Minimum time: 1.5 hours*
- *Key stops: Áno Lehónia, Áno Gatzea, Miliés*
- *Countries crossed: Greece*

BELOW: The Evaristo de Chirico Bridge is linear, but the tracks run across in a curve.

Mount Pelion is legendary. According to the ancient
Greeks, the 1,651m (5,417ft) high peak was plonked atop
Mount Ossa on the Pelion Peninsula by two giants who
planned to use it as a leg-up to Mount Olympus. It was also
said to be the birthplace of the half-human, half-horse
centaurs. Its slopes supposedly provided wood to build the
Argonauts' ship, on which they sailed to find the Golden
Fleece. It was even thought to be the summer retreat of
the twelve Olympian gods and goddesses. Suffice to say,
Pelion looms large in the mythology of this intellectual
heavyweight of a civilisation.

You don't need giant steps or godly powers to help you
up the mountain these days. Between 1894 and 1903, a 60cm
(24in) narrow gauge line – one of the narrowest in the world

PELION PENINSULA

VÓLOS

MOUNT PELION

MILIÉS

Evaristo de Chirico Bridge

ÁNO LEHÓNIA

Áno
Gatzea

PAGASETIC GULF

Taxiarchis Stream

– was laid here. The 37-mile-long (60km) railway led from
the port of Vólos, on the Pagasetic Gulf, to the village of
Miliés, 400m (1,312ft) up on Pelion's flanks. It was
masterminded by Italian engineer Evaristo de Chirico,
father of the Vólos-born surrealist artist Giorgio de Chirico.
Giorgio observed his father at work and became fascinated
by this curious new form of transportation; tiny trains are
often hidden in his paintings.

The train played a key role in the development of the
undulating Pelion Peninsula, enabling local markets to grow,
people to move and culture to spread. It was closed in 1971,
usurped by roads. But it has opened again as a heritage line,
running once a day on weekends between Easter and
October (daily July–August). The Little Train of Pelion no
longer covers the full original route. It starts from the
station at Áno Lehónia, a short bus ride from Vólos, and
follows the final 17.5 miles (28km) up to Miliés.

In its early days, the train was nicknamed Moutzouris
(Smudgy), on account of the black smoke pumped out by
the original steam locomotives. These have since been
converted to diesel, and now haul just three passenger cars,
rather than the twenty-five-plus wagons that used to be
bursting with local people and produce. It's not the most
comfortable ride – seats are wooden and hard – but it's
a wonderful way to climb up into the lush, hidden valleys.
The peninsula is quite unlike the old islands-and-beaches
perception of Greece. It's hilly and green, cloaked in dense

MORE ANCIENT
GREECE RIDES

88. Katakolon Train
Peloponnese, Greece

Limber up on the 8-mile
(13km) train ride from
the port of Katakolon
to the ruins of ancient
Olympia, where the first
Olympic Games were
held in 776 BC.

**89. Athens–
Thessaloniki**
Greece

A new 310-mile (500km)
high-speed line
between Athens
(founded 3000 BC) and
Thessaloniki (315 BC)
will soon slash the
journey time between
Greece's two most
important cities.

LIKE THAT? TRY THESE
- - - - - - - - - - - - - - - -

90. Mount Lycabettus Funicular
Athens, Greece

Survey the sites of Athens, including the ancient Acropolis, from the city's highest hill, Mount Lycabettus. A 210m-long (690ft) inclined railway runs to the top.

91. Odontotos Rack Railway
Peloponnese, Greece

Opened in 1896, the 14-mile (22km) narrow gauge line between the towns of Diakopto and Kalavrita slices though Vouraikos gorge, legendarily cracked open by the Greek god Hercules.

forest, olive groves, herbs and fruit trees – a breath of cool, fresh, fragrant air on a sweaty summer's day.

Of course, those hills provided a technical challenge for Evaristo and his crew. In order to master the 2.8-percent gradient and plunging ravines that lie between Áno Lehónia and Miliés, they built a series of tunnels, buttresses and handsome multiple-arch viaducts of marble and grey limestone; the bridge of Kalorema is particularly impressive. There was certainly an effort to build sensitively – the line blends well into the natural environment. The views are wonderful, too, extending over the spring-dotted hillsides to the glittering Pagasetic Gulf.

The terrain gets increasingly dramatic as the railway approaches Miliés. A few hundred metres before the terminus, the train reaches an iron trestle bridge known as the 'Bridge de Chirico', which spans a deep gorge above the Taxiarchis stream. It has an unusual design: the bridge itself is linear, but the tracks run across in a curve.

The train lingers in Miliés (which means 'apple trees'). This gives passengers a few hours to wander around the village square, browse the shops and visit the 18th-century church before boarding the train back down. Alternatively, you could stretch your legs, walking across the pedestrian catwalk of the Evaristo de Chirico Bridge and back to Áno Lehónia, a hike of around 5.5 hours.

RIGHT: The Little Train of Pelion has one of the world's narrowest railway gauges.

FAR RIGHT: Bridges on the Pelion line are built to blend into the natural environment.

GREAT ORME TRAMWAY

North Wales, United Kingdom

Take a vintage cable-hauled train up a coastal headland
that was mined back in the Bronze Age.

Need to know
- *Point in time: 4,000 years ago (copper mined at Great Orme)*
- *Length: 1 mile (1.5km)*
- *Minimum time: 20 minutes*
- *Key stops: Victoria Station, Halfway Station, Great Orme Summit*
- *Countries crossed: United Kingdom*

RIGHT: Trams have hauled up the Great Orme headland since 1902.

ALTERNATIVE TRAMWAY

93. T1 Tram
Istanbul, Turkey

The vintage T1 Kabataş–Bağcılar tram links many great sites of ancient Constantinople, including the astonishing Hagia Sophia, a basilica-cum-mosque built AD 532–37, and now a museum.

Oh, how the Bronze Age copper miners of north Wales would have appreciated this tiny little train. Around 4,000 years ago, prehistoric people started hand-digging precious metal out of Great Orme, a large limestone headland near the seaside town of Llandudno. But it wasn't until 1901, long, long after the mining had ceased, that work started on a narrow gauge single-track tramway, to transport people and goods up the 207m (679ft) high mound.

The Great Orme Tramway was opened in 1902. Now, it's Britain's only remaining cable-operated street tramway, and one of only three in the world. It was built in two halves, which operate independently of each other; two trams run on each of the two halves at the same time. It works on a counterbalancing funicular system, with the descending tram providing some of the power to haul up the ascending one. The original four Victorian tramcars are still in use.

The tramway's lower section starts from Victoria Station (built 1904). It climbs steeply through the streets, partly up the middle of the road, with Llandudno Bay sweeping behind. Passengers get out at recently refurbished Halfway Station, where there's an exhibition about the line and two winchmen controlling the powerful motors. From Halfway it's a short walk to the Great Orme Bronze Age Copper Mines, where you can explore the ancient tunnels. Also nearby is the 6th-century church of St Tudno – the tramway used to carry up the coffins for burial (mourners had to pay full fare for the deceased!).

The upper section of the tramway is less steep, inching up the grassy slopes, past grazing sheep and Kashmiri goats (a herd has roamed here since the mid-19th century). Views from the summit are spectacular, stretching as far as the Lake District and the Isle of Man on a clear day.

94
TREN TURISTICO DE LA SABANA

Central Colombia

Colombia's national rail network stopped running in the 1990s. But the 33-mile (53km) 'Savannah Railway', which has linked capital Bogotá and the colonial town of Zipaquirá since 1898, lives on – in style. The handsome steam and diesel locos of the Tren Turistico de la Sabana run north from Bogotá's neoclassical Sabana Station into the green Andean hills. Troupes of musicians and vendors hawking empanadas wander through the carriages. At Zipaquirá there's a chance to explore the main plaza and visit the UNESCO World Heritage–listed salt mines (home to a Roman Catholic Salt Cathedral), which were being quarried by the pre-Colombian Muisca culture as long ago as the 5th century BC.

95
ISTANBUL METRO

Istanbul, Turkey

Building a metro in Istanbul is a frustrating task. In this most historically significant of cities, so long a cultural crossroads, every dig of the spade turns up yet another fascinating relic of the past. The Tünel, Istanbul's first underground line, opened in 1875, making it the world's second oldest. It still makes its short uphill jaunt between the neighbourhoods of Karaköy and Beyoğlu. However, a more modern, rapid-transit metro was begun in 1989 and is still being built. The discovery of the odd Roman cistern or Byzantine shipwreck tends to cause delays, while the unearthing of a Neolithic settlement in the port area of Yenikapı in 2009 managed to rewrite history books, pushing Istanbul's known history back by around 6,000 years.

96
ATHENS METRO

Athens, Greece

The Athens Metro is more subterranean museum than subway. Begun in the 1990s, in preparation for the city's 2004 Olympic Games, excavation work soon unearthed a host of treasures dating to the days of ancient Greece. Many of these items are visible at Metro stations, displayed pretty much where they were found. At Syntagma station passengers commute past glass-cased *amphorae* (two-handled jugs), a pre-Mycenaean cemetery and Roman baths. At Monastiraki station (right beneath the Acropolis) you can see the former stone embankments of the Iridanos River, which was turned into a sewer in the 2nd century AD.

BELOW: Canary Wharf's Crossrail station is just one part of this huge infrastructure project.

CROSSRAIL

Southeast England, United Kingdom

Prepare to ride Crossrail, the huge transportation project that's also become a game-changing archaeological dig.

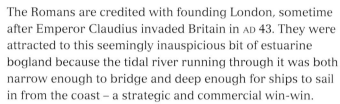

Need to know

- *Point in time: AD 43 (Romans invaded Britain)*
- *Length: 73 miles (118km)*
- *Minimum time: 1 hour 40 minutes*
- *Key stops: Reading, Heathrow, Paddington, Tottenham Court Road, Liverpool Street, Canary Wharf, Romford, Shenfield, Abbey Wood*
- *Countries crossed: United Kingdom*

The Romans are credited with founding London, sometime after Emperor Claudius invaded Britain in AD 43. They were attracted to this seemingly inauspicious bit of estuarine bogland because the tidal river running through it was both narrow enough to bridge and deep enough for ships to sail in from the coast – a strategic and commercial win-win.

Roman 'Londinium' began as a small settlement on the north bank of the Thames. In a matter of decades it had been razed (by Boudicca, queen of the Iceni tribe) and rebuilt, this time bigger and within stone walls. Over subsequent millennia such bouncebackability has become something of a local trademark – with every invasion, outbreak or natural disaster, London picks up the pieces and carries on. It's now one of the most populous and important cities in the world. And Crossrail is currently digging through the many layers of its rich and varied past.

Crossrail, one of Europe's largest infrastructure projects, is hoping to ease the congestion problems of this heaving, historic metropolis. Begun in 2009, and with full line completion due in 2019, it involves the construction of 73 miles (118km) of new railway lines running east-west from the town of Reading in Berkshire to the town of Shenfield in Essex. There are also branches off to Heathrow Airport and Abbey Wood, in the borough of Greenwich. En route, Crossrail will run through the City of London, the square mile that constituted the majority of the capital from its Roman beginnings to the Middle Ages.

It's a huge undertaking, requiring ten new stations and the boring of 26 miles (42km) of new tunnels. But it's also the country's biggest archaeological dig, bringing to the surface a host of ancient artefacts and game-changing remains that were buried as the capital continued to grow on top of them.

The oldest item unearthed to date is a rare piece of amber, found deep under the dock bed at Canary Wharf,

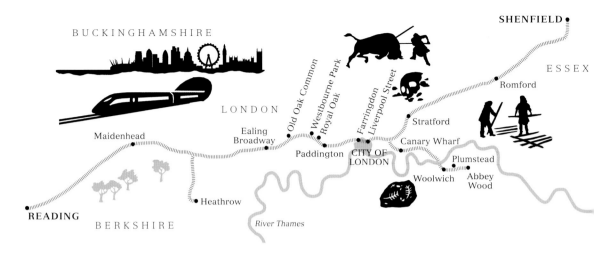

London's financial heartbeat. This lump of fossilised tree resin is around 55 million years old and may be able to help research into ancient plant species and global warming. Meanwhile, a 68,000-year-old waterway found near the River Westbourne at Royal Oak nods to ancient fauna. The bones of bison and the now-extinct aurochs (a very big, wild cow) were found here and may even bear the marks of human hunters.

Tunnelling in North Woolwich, near London City Airport, uncovered what is being described as a Mesolithic tool-making factory. Around 150 pieces of flint, including some blades, were found, suggesting humans were living in the Thames Valley around 9,000 years ago. At Plumstead, the

discovery of 3,500-year-old wooden stakes could nod to Bronze Age hunters building timber pathways across the area's marshes.

Liverpool Street provided particularly rich pickings. Archaeologists found twenty disembodied Roman-era skulls arranged along a Roman road. They also unearthed the former Bedlam Burial Ground, from which they identified the DNA of the bacterium that caused the 1665 Great Plague. Finds at Farringdon were similarly ghoulish: an emergency burial site containing victims of the Black Death, the plague that killed an estimated 200 million people in Europe in the mid-14th century.

There's a pleasing continuum to some of the discoveries. At Westbourne Park, in the borough of Kensington and Chelsea, the Crossrail crew found remains of Victorian engine sheds used for Isambard Kingdom Brunel's visionary Great Western Railway (GWR), which is regarded as the most complete early main line railway in the world. Unseen for 100 years, these offer insights into the early development of rail transport. At Old Oak Common in nearby Hammersmith and Fulham, the GWR locomotive repair depot (built 1906 and decommissioned in 2009) was excavated prior to demolition. Interesting historical items are bound for museums while the site will eventually house the new Crossrail train depot. And so the wheel of London history turns again.

BELOW: London is a great layer cake of history, as the Crossrail builders are currently discovering.

Q TRAIN – BROADWAY EXPRESS

New York City, United States

Ride the Big Apple's Q Train for an adventure through Spanish, Greek, Irish, Russian and Native American culture.

Need to know

- Point in time: 12,000 years ago (Lenape peoples inhabited New York City area)
- Length: 18 miles (29km)
- Minimum time: 1 hour 5 minutes
- Key stops: Astoria/96th Street, Times Square, Union Square, DeKalb Avenue, Brighton Beach, Coney Island
- Countries crossed: United States

ALTERNATIVE UNDERGROUNDS

99. Metro C Line
Rome, Italy

While excavating a line extension beneath the Piazza Venezia, engineers unearthed a grand two-storey cultural centre built during the rule of Emperor Hadrian (AD 117–138).

100. Marmaray Tunnel
Istanbul, Turkey

Istanbul (founded 660 BC) has always been a continental crossroads. Since 2013, an 8.5-mile (13.6km) tunnel under the Bosphorus Strait has connected Europe and Asia by rail.

Opened in 1904, New York's Subway is now the most extensive in the world. A subterranean spaghetti of transportation, it wiggles over a distance of 233 miles (375km), along twenty-four lines, between 469 stations, 24 hours a day, 365 days a year.

It's a network that serves the United States' most populous and multicultural city. Countless immigrants have entered the country here and many have stayed. A ride along the subway's Q Train or 'Broadway Express' is an underground journey through that story of immigration and a nod to the Lenape people, the true native New Yorkers.

The Lenape first inhabited this land by the Hudson River around 12,000 years ago when it was a wilderness of forest and swamp. Some of the thoroughfares created by these early peoples are still used. The Wickquasgeck Trail was the primary Lenape trading route, a 15-mile (24km) north-south path across Manhattan. Today, it's become Broadway.

Up to 2016, the Broadway Express started in the Greek neighbourhood of Astoria, Queens. From 2017, the Q's new start point is 96th Street in Manhattan's Spanish Harlem. However, the line still ploughs under historic Broadway, stopping at Central Park, the former Irish-American hub of Hell's Kitchen, glitzy Times Square, Koreatown, Herald Square (for the Empire State Building), Union Square and Canal Street, the heart of Chinatown.

Here, you could switch briefly onto the R Train to follow Broadway to the tip of Manhattan and visit the National Museum of the American Indian (alight Whitehall Street) to learn more about the Lenape. Alternatively, keep following the multicultural Q, which dips under the East River to reach Brooklyn. It passes through Prospect Park, the Jewish enclaves of Midwood and Flatbush, and the Russian neighbourhood of Brighton Beach (nicknamed 'Moscow on the Hudson'). The train terminates at Coney Island, famed for its funfair and iconic hotdog diner Nathan's, set up in 1916 by a Polish immigrant.

BELOW: Coney Island looks somewhat different from when the Lenape people roamed what's now New York City.

SETHU EXPRESS

Tamil Nadu, India

Make a Hindu pilgrimage to a holy temple via the
long, sea-straddling Pamban Bridge.

Need to know
- *Point in time:
  500–300 BC (Hindu
  Ramayana written)*
- *Length: 375 miles
  (603km)*
- *Minimum time:
  11.5 hours*
- *Key stops: Chennai,
  Villupuram,
  Tiruchirappalli,
  Manamadurai,
  Ramanathapuram,
  Rameswaram*
- *Countries crossed:
  India*

The town of Rameswaram is one of the key Hindu pilgrimage
sites in India. And the Pamban Bridge, which links Pambam
Island (on which Rameswaram sits) to the Tamil Nadu
mainland, is one the country's most impressive pieces of
railway engineering.

Rameswaram's importance dates back to around
500–300 BC, when the *Ramayana* was written. This ancient
epic documents the life of legendary Prince Rama; among
other episodes, it describes how the prince once instructed
his army of monkey men to build a bridge from Rameswaram
over to Lanka (modern-day Sri Lanka) to rescue his wife Sita
from the demon-king Ravana. The boulders that still pepper

LIKE THAT?
TRY THIS

- - - - - - - - - - - - - - - - -

**102. Haridwar–
Allahabad**
Northern India

Travel 450 miles (724km)
between these two
sacred River Ganges-
side cities where,
according to ancient
Hindu mythology,
Vishnu spilled drops
of *amrita* (the nectar
of immortality).

RIGHT: The long Pambam
Bridge links Pambam island
to the Indian mainland.

the Gulf of Mannar are said to be the remains of Rama's bridge. The *Ramayana* also tells how Rama worshipped a sand *lingam* (symbol of the Hindu god Shiva) to pay penance for killing Ravana, who was also a Brahmin (priest). The current Ramanathaswamy Temple in Rameswaram, dating from the 16th and 18th centuries, is said to contain that same mound of sand.

Engineers have yet to create an India–Sri Lanka causeway. But they have managed to leash Pamban Island to the rest of Tamil Nadu via the Pamban Bridge. Construction of this 2,065m-long (6,775ft) cantilever span began in 1902. Railway men who had worked on the Himalayan lines were brought in to construct it. Prefabricated parts were sent over from Britain and 143 concrete pillars were erected. A Scherzer rolling bascule (split and lift mechanism) was incorporated halfway along, so the section could lift and ships could pass through.

The Pamban Bridge eventually opened in 1914. Over its 100-plus years it has withstood the fury of cyclones and the corrosive salty environment. Indeed, it continues to convey masses of Hindu pilgrims, who flock here from all over the country. The Sethu Express provides a direct connection between Chennai, capital of Tamil Nadu, and Rameswaram's holy sites, with extra services laid on at peak pilgrimage times.

MORE INDIAN ESCAPADES

103. Bharat Darshan
India

Board a private sleeper train for a multi-day Hindu pilgrimage. Stops vary by departure but include sacred sites such as Tirupati (where Lord Rama once lived).

104. Kolkata–Puri
Eastern India

This 310-mile (499km) journey connects the bustle of Kolkata (West Bengal) to Puri (Odisha), home of the Jagannath Temple, a major Hindu pilgrimage site.

105
JANAKPUR RAILWAY

India and Nepal

Nepal's only passenger railway, the 40-mile (64km) narrow gauge line between Jainagar City (India) and the town of Bijalpura, is no more. It ceased sometime in 2014; vintage locos now rust by the tracks. In its day, this train was chock-full, heavy with pilgrims disembarking midway at the triple-holy city of Janakpur. This was allegedly one-time home of Buddha and the Jain teacher Mahavira, and was mentioned in the Hindu *Ramayana*. The huge Rajput-style Janaki Mandir Hindu temple is the big draw. The good news: the line is being rebuilt, and India and China are both keen to help develop a Nepalese rail network. Watch this space.

TEL AVIV–JERUSALEM

Central Israel

Twist and turn through the Biblical Judean Hills
to reach the tomb of Jesus.

Need to know
- *Point in time:* AD 30–33 *(purported death of Jesus)*
- *Length: 51 miles (82 km)*
- *Minimum time: 1 hour 40 minutes*
- *Key stops: Tel Aviv, Lod, Jerusalem*
- *Countries crossed: Israel*

TOMB-SEEKING TRACKS

- - - - - - - - - - - - - - - - -

107. Tacna–Arica Railway
Peru and Chile

The Chinchorro peoples are best known for mummification, having mastered the practice in 5000 BC. The railbus of the 39-mile (63km) Tacna–Arica line traverses the Chinchorro's heartland; mummies are displayed at a nearby museum.

ABOVE RIGHT: Tel Aviv's old port district of Jaffa is rich in bohemian cafe culture.

RIGHT: The train plunges through biblical landscapes to reach the holy city of Jerusalem.

In order to take this historic journey slowly, you need to get in quick. In 2018, a high-speed line is set to open between Israel's second-largest city, Tel Aviv, and its capital, Jerusalem. This will slash the journey time to just 28 minutes. Until then, however, the ride remains a more leisurely, anticipation-building, 100-minute jaunt.

Mediterranean-lapped Tel Aviv has been inhabited since the Bronze Age. However, these days it feels more cosmopolitan and modern; it has a youthful feel and a centre packed with cool cafes and Bauhaus-era architecture. For a taste of the old, take the train east.

First the train whizzes across farmland to the 19th-century railway station at Lod. Mentioned in the Bible, Lod was the birthplace of St George. After George famously killed a dragon, he was killed himself (in AD 303) for refusing to renounce his Christianity; his remains were returned here, and are now ensconced in a beautiful church.

After Lod the terrain gets more testing, and the train is forced to slow as it twists and turns amid the gorge-sliced Judean Hills. This arid, rugged range is rich in biblical resonance. For instance, the line enters the Valley of Rephaim, an ancient route through the mountains where King David supposedly clashed with the Philistines. It also skirts the Brook of Sorek, allegedly where Delilah persuaded Samson to divulge the secret of his strength.

There's a stop at Jerusalem Biblical Zoo, which has its own little train, running amid a collection of animals mentioned in the Bible. Then the line terminates at Jerusalem's Malha Railway Station. Jerusalem is one of the world's holiest cities, sacred to Christians, Muslims and Jews. Jesus is said to have been executed here around AD 30–33. In the old town, the Via Dolorosa allegedly follows his path to crucifixion; it finishes at the Church of the Holy Sepulchre, in which lies his tomb.

RELIGIOUS RIDES

108. Tbilisi–Yerevan
Georgia and Armenia

Armenia was the first country to officially adopt Christianity, in AD 301. And this biblical connection isn't lost on those taking this 10.5-hour sleeper train west-east: you'll see sunrise creep over Mount Ararat, the peak where Noah's ark allegedly still rests.

109. Downpatrick and County Down Railway
Northern Ireland, United Kingdom

Only a 4-mile (6.4km) section of this railway remains. It runs between Downpatrick (burial place of St Patrick, Ireland's patron saint, who died in AD 461) and Inch Abbey.

110. Pilatus Railway
Lake Lucerne, Switzerland

The world's steepest rack railway ascends Mount Pilatus, on which – via some convoluted mythology – the ghost of Pontius Pilate is said to reside.

111. Caspian Odyssey
Europe and Asia

This journey aboard a luxurious Golden Eagle train from Yerevan (Armenia) to Almaty (Kazakhstan) includes a train-ferry over the Caspian Sea. The scope of this sea was hotly debated in antiquity, not least by Alexander the Great (356–323 BC).

After leaving Tel Aviv and cutting through biblical hills, the Tel Aviv–Jerusalem train (previous page) arrives in the city of Jerusalem, sacred to Christians, Jews and Muslims.

ROME–SYRACUSE

Southern Italy

Board a train on board a ferry that connects the
Eternal City with ancient Sicily.

Need to know
- *Point in time: 214–212 BC (Siege of Syracuse)*
- *Length: 517 miles (832km)*
- *Minimum time: 12 hours*
- *Key stops: Rome, Formia, Naples, Maratea, Villa San Giovanni, Messina, Syracuse*
- *Countries crossed: Italy*

There's a lot to like about this direct train ride between the Italian capital and the island of Sicily. It's scenic all the way, largely hugging the country's sunny southwest coast, zipping amid village-scattered hillsides, historic towns and lemon groves. It also manages to combine the romance of rail travel with the thrill of a mini Med cruise. In order to cross the Strait of Messina, which separates Sicily from the Italian mainland's toe, the carriages are driven straight onto a ferry. The passage takes 30 minutes, during which you can either wander up on deck for a breath of sea air or stay in your carriage, nestled in the ferry's hold, for the experience of riding a train on a boat.

The service starts from Rome's Termini station, heading south through the countryside of Lazio and Campania, and flirting with the Mediterranean at the hill-flanked beach resort of Formia. This ancient city, founded by the Greeks, is dotted with Roman remains including the fancy holiday villas of the political elite and the old harbour of Giànola. From Formia, the train continues to Naples, capital of the south. Gritty, atmospheric, untouristy, delicious (stop for authentic Neapolitan pizza if you've time), Naples sits on its eponymous bay with Mount Vesuvius looming menacingly behind.

The train arcs around the bay for a bit before cutting inland, rather than negotiating the vertiginous Amalfi Coast. It hits the sea again at the city of Salerno

MORE ROMAN
RAILWAYS
- - - - - - - - - - - - - - - - - - - -

**113. Rome–Ostia
Antica**
Lazio, Italy

A 19-mile (30km) journey
connects Rome with the
well-preserved ruins of
its ancient seaport, Ostia
Antica, at the mouth of
the Tiber River.

114. Koblenz–Trier
*Rhineland-Palatinate,
Germany*

This 70-mile (113km)
riverside rail trip passes
vineyard-lined slopes
and 2.6 mile-long (4.2km)
Kaiser Wilhelm Tunnel
to reach the Roman-
founded city of Augusta
Treverorum (now Trier).

**115. Messina–
Palermo**
Sicily, Italy

Follow the Roman's
strategic Via Valeria
road on a 140-mile
(225km) train trip along
Sicily's north coast.
Finish in capital
Palermo, a cultural
crossroads for over
2,500 years.

116. Rome–Pisa
Western Italy

The coast-hugging
2-hour 45-minute trip
from Italian capital
Rome to Pisa with its
leaning tower, via the
seaport of Civitavecchia,
roughly follows the
Roman Via Aurelia
road (built 241 BC).

and heads along parts of the Cilento Coast. Now a protected
nature reserve, the Cilento is home to glorious coves, olive
groves and historic narrow-alleyed towns.

From here on, the train scarcely leaves the sparkling sea,
trundling along the shorelines of Basilicata and Calabria,
two of the least-developed regions of Italy. It passes the
grotto-riddled cliffs around Maratea, the lemon-growing
town of Diamante and the Norman castle of Belvedere.
South of the Savuto River, it inches along the Calabrian
peninsula's narrowest point, much of it reclaimed from
malarial swamp in the past century. Views continue to be
spectacular: the Aeolian Islands and Sicily are in sight.

In sight, but just out of reach . . . A bridge to Sicily has
been mooted by everyone from the Romans to former Italian
Prime Minister Silvio Berlusconi – but it hasn't happened yet.
So for now crossing the Strait of Messina still requires a boat.
At the port of Villa San Giovanni, train tracks on the dock are
aligned with those in the ferry's belly, and on the loco goes.

The boat-train service between southern Italy and Sicily
launched in 1899. During the First World War, one ferry hit

ABOVE: The Rome–
Syracuse train takes a ferry
across the Strait of Messina.

a mine; in 1943, another was sunk by the Germans, although it was later raised and put back into service for several decades. Now budget cuts are the problem most likely to scupper it, but at the time of writing the boat-train continues. After its passage across the water, it docks in the Sicilian seaport city of Messina, lines up its tracks and disgorges its rail cargo once more.

From Messina the train traces Sicily's east coast via the resorts of Taormina and Catania, Mount Etna simmering behind. It finally stops at Syracuse, a gorgeous golden-hued tangle of alleys, strewn across a natural harbour and on to Ortygia island. Settled by the Greeks in 733 BC, Syracuse quickly became one of the biggest, most important cities in the Western world. However, its fortunes changed in 214 BC when the Romans attacked; the invaders eventually triumphed after a 2-year siege, gaining control of the whole of Sicily. Even the ingenious weaponry designed by ancient Greek scientist Archimedes couldn't save Syracuse in the end. Although perhaps some version of Archimedes' fabled 'iron claw' – which could allegedly lift ships right out of the water – could come in handy for shifting today's trains?

LIKE THAT?
TRY THESE

117. Capri Funicular
Capri, Italy

The glamorous Italian island of Capri was made fashionable by Emperor Caesar Augustus (27 BC–AD 14). The 15-minute funicular from Marina Grande helps you explore his beloved holiday retreat.

118. Cart tracks
Pompeii, Italy

When Vesuvius erupted in AD 79 and buried Pompeii, one of the innovations preserved in ash were grooved tracks in the roads – an early prototype railway, perhaps?

119. Palermo–Agrigento
Sicily, Italy

Take a plodding 85-mile (137km) train ride across Sicily from capital Palermo to Agrigento's awesome Valley of the Temples, founded as a Greek colony in the 6th century BC.

120. Funicolare Centrale
Naples, Italy

The hills of historic Naples (according to legend, founded 680 BC) are tackled by this inclined line, which climbs 170m (558ft). It is one of the world's busiest funiculars.

LEFT: Syracuse was under siege for two years in the third century BC.

121
EGNATIA RAILWAY

Greece and Turkey

In around 200 BC the Romans built
the Via Egnatia, a road linking
what is now the coast of Albania
to Byzantium (now Istanbul).
In 2019, the European Union is
planning an 'Egnatia Railway',
roughly aping a 350-mile (565km)
section of the ancient highway
through northern Greece. The new
line will link northwest-coast
Igoumenitsa to the port of
Alexandroupolis on the Greco-
Turk border. It will run via the
Pindos Mountains and
Thessaloniki (Greece's second-
largest city), close to the
archaeological remains of Pella,
birthplace of Alexander the Great.
Sadly, as one strand of Egnatia-by-
rail opens, another closes: the
'Friendship Train Express', which
ran from Thessaloniki to Istanbul,
was discontinued in 2011.

122
HADRIAN'S WALL
COUNTRY LINE

Northern England, United Kingdom

You can't ride a train alongside
Hadrian's Wall, which was built
by the eponymous emperor in
AD 122. However, the 60-mile
(97km) Newcastle–Carlisle route
('Hadrian's Wall Country Line')
offers access to the stone rampart
that once marked the Roman
Empire's northern extreme. It also
happens to be one of the world's
earliest passenger railways – the
first-ever train ticket was sold at
Brampton station in 1836. Handy
station stops include the pretty
town of Haltwhistle, from where
it's a short walk along Haltwhistle
Burn to reach the Wall, and
Corbridge, where you can
wander through a once-bustling
Roman settlement.

123
ROME–BRINDISI

Southern Italy

The Romans built the Via Appia (Appian Way), their first road, in 312 BC; eventually it extended from Rome to Brindisi, on the Adriatic coast. Today, the direct 5-hour rail journey between the two cities picks up the sandal-prints of long-gone legionaries. It visits the town of Capua, where the main street (Corso Appio) still follows the Roman road. It heads east to the ancient crossroads town of Benevento, with its Arch of Trajan and Roman theatre. And it joins a coastal offshoot of the Via Appia at the historic harbour town of Bari. It finishes in Brindisi, the Roman 'gateway to the east'. Here, two marble columns (one mostly destroyed) mark the Via Appia's end.

124
CIRCUMVESUVIANA RAILWAY

Campania, Italy

When Mount Vesuvius blew its top in AD 79, it buried the towns of Pompeii and Herculaneum (Ercolano) under its deadly pyroclastic flow. The volcano remains feisty: it's erupted around thirty times since the 1st century AD and will likely do so again. So don't put off a ride on the Circumvesuviana Railway's 29-mile (47km) Naples–Sorrento line. It leaves from the lively port of Naples and calls at both of the ill-fated Roman cities, where you can walk amid villas, bathhouses and brothels excavated from beneath the ash. The railway continues round the Bay of Naples to the lemon-scented clifftop town of Sorrento, with Vesuvius brooding behind.

RIGHT: The train serves the city of Split, where Emperor Diocletian built his retirement palace.

ZAGREB–SPLIT

Croatia

Take a Roman rail ramble though Dalmatia, ending
at Diocletian's dramatic seaside palace.

Need to know
- *Point in time:
  AD 284–305 (reign of
  Emperor Diocletian)*
- *Length: 265 miles
  (426km)*
- *Minimum time:
  6 hours*
- *Key stops: Zagreb,
  Ogulin, Knin, Split*
- *Countries crossed:
  Croatia*

Diocletian is the darling of Dalmatia. Born near Spalatum
(modern-day Split, in Croatia's Dalmatia province) in AD 244,
he rose from humble beginnings to become the 51st Roman
Emperor. He also managed to steady the empire after a
period of tumult and near-collapse. It must have been a
tough job, and by AD 305 Diocletian was ready to step down.
For this purpose he built a vast fortress-palace retirement
home of white stone, Italian marble and Egyptian columns
on the shores of the Adriatic Sea. Today, the city centre of
Split spills around and about the remains of this dazzling,
UNESCO World Heritage–listed complex.

The vibrant Croatian capital, Zagreb, sits near another of the country's Roman relics. Andautonia, founded on the banks of the Sava River in the 1st century AD, is just southwest of the city. This was once the administrative and cultural hub of the Zagreb region, evidenced by what remains today: the colonnaded main street, extensive baths, and fancy frescoed villas with underfloor heating.

The rail line between Zagreb and Split is a scenic way to combine these historic sites and cross the country. In summer a slow sleeper train makes the journey – but that would be missing the point. Better to board a day train to watch as the lush fields, neat vineyards, sparkling lakes, meandering rivers, craggy limestone mountains and, as the train nears Split, glorious coast slowly glide by.

It's not the most straightforward terrain. The track frequently has to cut through tunnels and bend around hillsides, but slick tilting trains make the ride as smooth as possible. En route, the train passes the town of Ogulin, home to a 16th-century tower. It also calls at history hotspot Knin, variously the site of a Roman camp, capital of the medieval Kingdom of Croatia and an ethnic Serb stronghold during the 1990s war in the Balkans.

**MORE CULTURAL
JOURNEYS**

**126. Macomer–Bosa
Green Train**
Sardinia, Italy

This scenic 28.5-mile (46km) narrow gauge mountain train trundles past conical stone *nuraghi*, enigmatic megalithic relics unique to Sardinia, built from around 1800 BC.

**127. Arbatax–Mandas
Green Train**
Sardinia, Italy

This 99-mile (159km) ride from Arbatax harbour, on Sardinia's east coast, into the highlands reveals more *nuraghi*, plus craggy peaks, poppy fields and vineyards.

**128. Petit Train
de La Rhune**
*Pyrénées-Atlantiques,
France*

This metre gauge rack railway (built 1924) runs to the top of La Rhune mountain in the heart of the Basque region. Basque culture originated here 7,000 years ago.

129. Euskotren
Northern Spain

Explore 7,000 years of Basque culture aboard 'The Mole' railway, nicknamed for its many tunnels. The 14-mile (22km) San Sebastián–Irun ride nudges the foothills of the Pyrenees.

LEFT: Explore the cobbled streets of Zagreb, only 6 hours by train from Split.

130
RHODOPE NARROW GAUGE LINE

Southwest Bulgaria

The 78-mile (125km) narrow gauge railway between the Bulgarian towns of Bansko and Dobrinishte is one of the slowest, yet most scenic, in the Balkans. It takes 5 hours to traverse the valleys and ravines of the Rila and Rhodope ranges, and the alpine views are divine. Which is unsurprising: the fabled Rhodopes were allegedly created when Queen Rhodope of Thrace offended the Greek gods, and Zeus turned her into the mountains. En route the line forges through Velingrad Gorge, the spa town of Velingrad and onto the Plain of Thrace. It also masters the 1,267m (4,157ft) high Avramovo Saddle via sixteen tunnels, two spirals and a 180-degree turn.

131
LATORCA

Hungary and Ukraine

Trace in reverse the route taken by the Huns, the warrior-tribe most notoriously led by Attila 'the Scourge of God' in the 5th century AD. It's believed that the Huns migrated west from the Asian steppes via the Caspian Sea, Dnieper River and Carpathian Mountains to set up camp in what's now Hungary. The Latorca service runs from Hungarian capital Budapest to Ukrainian capital Kiev, a city of broad boulevards and gilded domes on the Dnieper. On its 24-hour run, the train passes magnificent mountains, traverses the immense Puszta flatlands (Attila's spiritual horse-riding home) and crosses the River Tisza, in which Attila was allegedly buried in a coffin of lead, silver and gold.

GDANSK–TRIESTE

Poland, Czech Republic, Austria and Italy

Travel across Europe, from the Baltic coast to the
Adriatic Sea, to follow the ancient amber trail by train.

Need to know
- *Point in time: 1600 BC
  (amber trade thriving)*
- *Length: 1,200 miles
  (1,930km)*
- *Minimum time:
  24 hours*
- *Key stops: Gdansk,
  Kalisz, Vienna, Trieste*
- *Countries crossed:
  Poland, Czech
  Republic, Austria, Italy*

Amber was big business in the ancient world. This
fossilised tree resin, abundant in the Baltic region, was in
demand across Europe and beyond. The Egyptians believed
it helped preserve their mummies. The Romans and Greeks
extolled its medicinal properties. It was made into jewellery,
burned for its fragrance, buried with the dead. Thus, from
at least 1600 BC, an 'Amber Road' developed to transport
this precious substance from the
continent's northern shores to
the Mediterranean.

To recreate an Amber Road
by rail, start in the Polish port of
Gdansk. This was the centre of
the European amber trade and
still has a thriving amber economy
with a dedicated museum and
countless workshops. The nearby
town of Pruszcz Gdanski has a
reconstruction of a 2,000-year-old
amber-trading post.

From Gdansk, take the train
south via Bydgoszcz to Kalisz,
reputed to be Poland's oldest
city (Graeco-Egyptian geographer
Ptolemy mentioned it in the 2nd
century AD). Although this
accolade is questionable, Kalisz
has certainly been a key trading
post for centuries and the Kalisz
Regional Museum contains many
prehistoric artefacts found in
the region.

From here you could detour
to Wielun for the annual summer
Amber Festival (complete with

Roman chariot racing). Otherwise continue south to the city of Katowice and across the Czech Republic to the glorious Austrian capital, Vienna, where there are fine amber exhibits in the Kunsthistorisches Museum Wien. It's also possible to take the S7 suburban train to the Danube-side Roman ruins of Carnuntum, where traders from the north would have exchanged their Baltic amber for wine and trinkets from the south.

From Vienna, head to journey's end, the classy Italian city of Trieste, which is just along the Adriatic coast from what remains of Aquileia. At this ancient Roman artisanal hub, founded in 181 BC, raw amber was worked into spectacular things, some of which are displayed at the on-site museum.

BELOW: The Polish city of Gdansk was the capital of the ancient amber trade.

BEIJING–BADALING

Northwest China

Visit the Great Wall of China on the country's
very first railway – while you still can.

Need to know
- *Point in time: 221–206 BC (Great Wall first built)*
- *Length: 38 miles (61km)*
- *Minimum time: 1 hour 20 minutes*
- *Key stops: Beijing North, Changping, Qinglongqiao, Badaling*
- *Countries crossed: China*

BELOW: Trains swiftly leave behind Beijing's sprawl, bound for the Great Wall.

For 2,000 years, a succession of Chinese dynasties continued to build and better the Great Wall of China. The first cohesive barrier to guard against the Mongol hordes was constructed by Emperor Qin Shi Huang from around 221 BC. By the end of his reign, it stretched 3,100 miles (5,000km). Up until the end of the Ming Dynasty, in the 17th century, the wall was still being refined – today's huge, impregnable-looking rampart, studded with watchtowers, was refined by them. But none of those paranoid bulwark-builders factored in the assault of modern technology. They were on the lookout for invaders trying to get in over the wall, not underneath it.

The first railway to tackle the Great Wall of China was the country's first Chinese-built railway. The initial section of the Jingbao Railway was constructed from 1905 to 1909

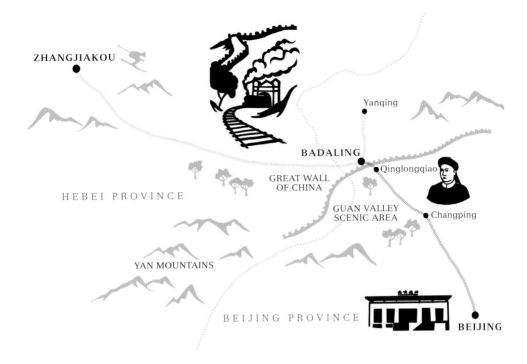

to link capital Beijing to the city of Zhangjiakou, in northwestern Hebei province. It was the handiwork of trailblazing engineer Zhan Tianyou, who had quite the task on his hands. Between the two termini lie the rugged Yan Mountains, along which the Great Wall runs.

To master the Nankou–Badaling section of the wall, where gradients are severe, Zhan built a herringbone railway at Qinglongqiao, 35 miles (56km) north of Beijing. Here, trains powered by two double-traction engines pulled into the station forwards, then pulled out again backwards, gaining height over a shorter distance.

Tianyou also created a series of four tunnels, including the 1,092m-long (3,583ft) Badaling Tunnel. The workmen had no machinery, so every scrap of dirt was dug out by hand. However, Zhan Tianyou's shaft construction method, which involved burrowing from both sides and from a central well simultaneously, speeded things up. The project was completed ahead of schedule and under budget.

Zhan Tianyou became a national hero, and is known as the 'Father of China's Railroad'. His tomb and his likeness in bronze now stand at Qinglongqiao's original 1908 station. At Badaling, at the highest point on the line some 38 miles (61km) northwest of Beijing, there is a Zhan

MORE CHINA TRAIN TRIPS

134. Beijing–Zengzhou
China

Zip 497 miles (800km) from capital Beijing across the Yellow River valley to Zhengzhou, the cradle of Chinese martial arts and, around 1000 BC, the world's biggest city.

135. Kunming–Guilin
Southwest China

The ancient tribal areas of Yunnan and Guangxi are becoming more accessible, with a high-speed line slashing this 553-mile (890km) journey from 20 hours to five.

Tianyou Museum where you can see many of the great man's mapping instruments, books and manuscripts.

More than 100 years after its completion, the Jingbao Railway is still a popular way to reach the best-preserved section of the Great Wall of China. First built in 1505, the Badaling Great Wall is 4.7 miles (7.6km) long, up to 7.8m (26ft) high and 5.7m (19ft) wide, which enabled the army to march ten abreast. It has been a little over-preserved, and swarms with tourists on weekends and holidays, but is an undeniably impressive site. Travelling there by train, rather than tour bus, means you can explore at your own pace.

Leaving from Beijing North Station, the journey to Badaling takes around 80 minutes. En route, there are views out into the Guan Valley Scenic Area and, as you get closer, of the wall itself snaking across the forested ridges. From Badaling train station, shuttle buses connect to the tourist hub at the wall's base, where there's a museum, cinema, restaurants and cable car – alternatively, make the steep hike up.

However, times are a-changing. A new high-speed Beijing–Zhangjiakou line is scheduled to be built in time for the 2022 Winter Olympics, to link venues in the capital with Hebei's ski fields. This will replace Tianyou Zhan's pioneering route and slash the journey time. There's still the matter of getting past the Great Wall. To do this, China will build the world's deepest and largest high-speed railway station at Badaling, 102m (335ft) below the surface. Some of the world's most advanced explosion technologies are being employed: the new 7.5-mile-long (12km) tunnel will be blasted using an electronic detonator that causes barely a ripple, so as not to disturb the UNESCO World Heritage–listed rampart above.

BELOW: The Great Wall of China once measured around 3,100 miles (5,000km) long.

136
SARONIC GULF–
GULF OF CORINTH

Peloponnese, Greece

Welcome to 'The World's First Railway'! Sort of . . . The 3.7-mile-wide (6km) Isthmus of Corinth links the Peloponnese Peninsula to the Greek mainland and divides the Saronic Gulf from the Gulf of Corinth, forcing ships to sail right around the Peloponnese. This vexed the ancient Greeks so, in around 600 BC, they constructed the Diolkos ('puller of boats'), a stone-paved rutway with two parallel grooves. Using winches, some kind of wheeled contraption and a lot of hard work, it's thought that they were able to haul boats across the land, creating an almighty shortcut – and a prototype railway. Today, ill-preserved remnants of the Diolkos can be seen.

137
IZMIR–SELÇUK

Western Turkey

This wonder-full journey starts in Izmir, a mountain-flanked metropolis on the Ionian Sea. This is the site of ancient Smyrna, the history of which spans its foundation by Alexander the Great to its incineration during the Greco-Turkish War (1919–22). From Izmir, it's a 75-minute train ride to one of the Seven Wonders of the Ancient World. Greek poet Antipater of Sidon was the first to record such a list, around 140 BC. He cited only six wonders, but did include the Temple of Artemis at Ephesus (near Selçuk station). Sadly, only fragments of the temple remain, but greater Ephesus, one of the world's best-preserved Graeco-Roman cities, remains a wonder.

138
TUNIS–GOULETTE–MARSA LINE

Northern Tunisia

The 12-mile (19km) Tunis–Goulette–Marsa line was Tunisia's first railway, opened in 1872. But the ground it covers has a far more venerable history. Tunis, the capital, is part 8th-century Arabic medina, part 19th-century European-flavoured boulevards. However, take the train to the city's northern suburbs and you'll discover a different era. Ancient Carthage was founded by the Phoenicians around 813 BC and had become master of Mediterranean trade by 600 BC but was destroyed by Rome in 146 BC. Alight at Carthage Hannibal Station and walk up Byrsa Hill for views over what remains: bits of bathhouses, basilicas and the old harbour, strewn beside the sea. Note: the UK Foreign Office currently advises against all but essential travel to Tunisia.

139
OSAKA–MOZU-FURUICHI

Central Honshu, Japan

Osaka is an uber-urban metropolis of skyscrapers and neon. But a short train trip will take you back over 1,500 years. South of the centre is the tumulus site of Mozu-Furuichi Kofungun, an ancient burial ground. *Kofun* are mound tombs, built for the country's elite from AD 250 to 650. Across Japan, there are almost forty kofun over 200m (656ft) long; eleven are within Mozu-Furuichi. They are huge, mysterious and now hemmed in by the greater Osakan sprawl. Take the Hanwa Line to Mozu Station (15 minutes) to be amazed.

BELOW: The maroon-liveried Seven Stars train does a complete circuit of Japan's Kyushu island.

KYUSHU SEVEN STARS

Kyushu, Western Japan

Ride in luxurious style around Japan's most westerly
island, the historic gateway to the land of Na.

Need to know
- *Point in time: 660 BC
  (Japan founded by
  Emperor Jimmu)*
- *Length: 745 miles
  (1,200km)*
- *Minimum time: 4 days*
- *Key stops: Fukuoka,
  Yufuin, Miyazaki,
  Hayato, Sendai,
  Yatsushiro*
- *Countries crossed:
  Japan*

Kyushu, the third-largest island of Japan, is the birthplace
of the nation. According to the *Nihon Shoki* (The Chronicles
of Japan), it was from southern Kyushu that legendary
Emperor Jimmu set forth to found Japan in 660 BC. There's
no proof but there is evidence of human settlement in the
region before the 10th century BC. Also, Kyushu's
Yoshinogari site (400–300 BC) is one of the country's most
important archaeological locations.

The first written record of Na (as Japan was then known)
appeared in the 1st century AD, in the Chinese *Book of Han*.
Trading between Na and China was well underway by then,
and Kyushu would probably have been the first port of call.
The island is the closest part of Japan to the Asian mainland
– South Korea is just 80 miles (128km) away, across the
Korea Strait. As such, Kyushu has long been the gateway
for cultural and commercial interaction between this rather
closed-off nation and the rest of the continent.

So it's not surprising that, centuries later, Kyushu was
the first place in Japan to welcome the new transportation
technologies from the West. It was here, in 1868, in the city
of Nagasaki, that railways were first introduced to the
country. Scottish merchant Thomas Blake Glover set up
an 8-mile (13km) test track to demonstrate the 'Iron Duke',
a steam locomotive he'd imported from Shanghai. The
Japanese were impressed. Railways soon took off.

Kyushu now has around 1,865 miles (3,000km) of
railway. The first Kyushu *Shinkansen* (bullet train) launched
in 2004, connecting the cities of Fukuoka and Kagoshima,
but most of the island's tracks are narrow gauge lines that
weave unhurriedly amid the green hills, hot springs and
coastal villages.

So: plenty of tracks, spectacular scenery. Now fast
forward to 2013, when Kyushu claimed another rail first:
Japan's first luxury sleeper train. The Kyushu Seven Stars is
a seven-coach stunner in deep-maroon livery, comprising

**141. London–
Marseille Eurostar**
*United Kingdom
and France*

Take a direct Eurostar
from London to
Marseille (6.5 hours)
to explore the
Mediterranean port's
Le Panier district, site
of the marketplace
established by the
Greeks, who founded
the city in 600 BC.

**142. Bucharest–
Constanta**
Southeast Romania

It's 140 miles (225km)
from Romania's capital
Bucharest to its
biggest Black Sea port,
Constanta. Roman poet
Ovid died here in AD 17;
his statue now stands in
Constanta's Ovid Square.

**143. Dhaka–
Chittagong**
Bangladesh

It takes 5.5 hours to
travel by train from the
Bangladeshi capital
Dhaka to the harbour
city of Chittagong,
which according to
Ptolemy's *Geographia*
(AD 150) was at that time
the most important port
in the East.

a lounge car, dining car and five sleeping cars, with space
for just twenty-eight passengers. Every spacious, wood-
panelled compartment has artisanal furniture, unique
upholstery and en suite designer bathrooms. A piano tinkles
in the Blue Moon bar, gourmet seasonal treats are served in
the Jupiter restaurant, and big windows ensure unfettered
views. The Iron Duke experience this is not.

The Kyushu Seven Stars offers 2-day and 4-day itineraries.
The 4-day trip skirts right round the island, visiting five of the
island's seven prefectures. Journeys start from Hakata station
in Fukuoka (Kyushu's biggest city), where *Shinkansen*
services from neighbouring Honshu island terminate. From
Fukuoka the train glides east to Yufuin, a rural resort town
tucked below Mount Yufu. It's a hotbed of hot springs (*onsen*)
– a great place to take a restorative dip, a stroll along the
café-lined main street or a walk around Lake Kinrinko.

After a night on board, the train heads south along
Kyushu's east coast, offering views of the North Pacific
Ocean. It stops at the city of Miyazaki, alleged birthplace of
Emperor Jimmu, where you can walk along a causeway to
the shrines of Aoshima Island.

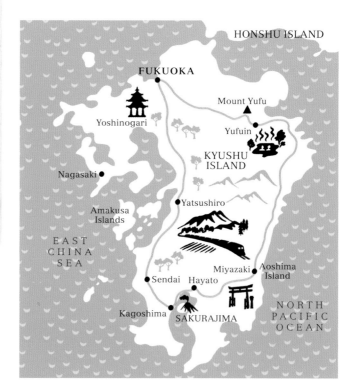

Despite the fact that this is a sleeper train, passengers spend the second night off-train in a traditional *ryokan* (inn). The next morning the journey continues from Hayato Station passing Kagoshima, Kyushu's southernmost city, guarded by Sakurajima, one of Japan's most active volcanoes. At Sendai, the Kyushu Seven Stars picks up the winding west-coast Hisatsu Orange Railway. This route connects the towns of Sendai and Yatsushiro via citrus orchards, historic towns, hot springs, Zen temples, offshore islands and the sparkling East China Sea. The train stops midway for sunset, dinner and a night's rest.

On day four, the train continues to Yatsushiro. On selected departures, passengers hop off again for a boat cruise around the leafy Amakusa (Heaven's Grass) Islands, once home to a thriving Christian population until the religion was suppressed in the 17th century. Back on the train, it's then a short ride back to Fukuoka, a full circuit of Kyushu complete.

Routes can vary: check cruisetrain-sevenstars.com for the latest info before booking.

TRADING TRAIN

144. Halstatt Salt Mine Train
Salzkammergut, Austria

Humans have extracted salt from the region of Salzkammergut since 5000 BC. Now a train takes visitors from the Bronze Age mine and up the mountain within which it lies.

The Dawn of Time   117

HEJAZ RAILWAY

Saudi Arabia, Jordan and Syria

Remember the ill-fated railway that followed an ancient trade route and was destroyed by Lawrence of Arabia.

Need to know
- *Point in time: 300 BC–200 AD (Incense Route flourished)*
- *Length: 820 miles (1,320km)*
- *Minimum time: 4 days*
- *Key stops: Medina, Tabuk, Mudarrawra, Amman, Damascus*
- *Countries crossed: Saudi Arabia, Jordan, Syria*

BELOW: The Mada'in Saleh ruins in Saudi Arabia date back to the first century AD.

The idea of a transport corridor through the Arabian Peninsula to the Levant is as old as the hills. Over 2,000 years ago, this region was a key part of the Incense Route, which saw frankincense and myrrh from Yemen and Oman hauled to the Mediterranean. This fragrant trade highway ran through Saudi Arabia's Hejaz region, via the cities of Mecca, Medina and Mada'in Saleh, before forging on to Petra and Amman in Jordan and Damascus in Syria.

When a railway plying a similar route was first opened, its aim was the movement not of perfumes but of pilgrims. The narrow gauge Hejaz Railway was built by the Ottoman Turks, who wanted to slash the travel time between Istanbul (Turkey) and Mecca. Muslim pilgrims undertaking the Hajj could only get as far as Damascus by train; from there it was an arduous, dangerous, 2-month camel ride to the holy city.

This is not a kind environment for railway construction. Rugged escarpments, soft sands, intense heat and hostile tribesmen caused problems. Many bridges were required and in many places wooden sleepers had to be replaced with iron ones after locals stole them to fuel their fires. However, a line as far as Medina opened in 1908.

The First World War derailed the route's planned extension to Mecca. During the Arab Revolt against the Ottomans (1916–18), guerrilla forces led by T.E. Lawrence 'of Arabia' repeatedly attacked the railway. It never recovered. The southern section was abandoned barely a decade after the train's first run. Bits of railway detritus still dot the desert, and the old terminus in Medina has been converted into the Hejaz Railway Museum.

The northern section has suffered, too. In Jordan, phosphate trains still use a branch line from the southern city of Ma'an to the Red Sea resort of Aqaba, but services between Amman and Damascus stopped in 2006. Sadly, Syria's civil war makes a resumption of this historic route very unlikely indeed.

ABOVE: An old Hejaz Railway steam locomotive rests in Jordan.

The Southwest Chief (next page) crosses a vast swathe of the United States, running between Chicago and Los Angeles via the resplendent Rocky Mountains.

SOUTHWEST CHIEF

United States

Imagine the world of the early Native Americans on this classic train trip between Chicago and Los Angeles.

Need to know

- *Point in time:* AD *500 (Native American farming and hunting changed)*
- *Length: 2,265 miles (3,645km)*
- *Minimum time: 42 hours*
- *Key stops: Chicago, Kansas City, Albuquerque, Flagstaff, Los Angeles*
- *Countries crossed: United States*

The Southwest Chief cuts right through the heart of the United States. It leaves Chicago, on the shores of Lake Michigan, crosses the Great Plains, hits the Rocky Mountains, traverses the red rock and desert of the wild southwest and pulls up at the Pacific in Los Angeles.

It's a route strewn with historic reminders. Alongside the tracks are rivers linked to 16th-century conquistadores, Spanish-founded cities, gunslinging cowboy towns, Civil War battlefields, Hollywood movie locations and (in San Bernardino) the first McDonald's. But there are also vast tracts of American wilderness that give an inkling of what life was like here long before Christopher Columbus landed in North America. The train's big windows and unhurried pace help convey the United States' scale and diversity, and make you ponder how ancient peoples survived before Big Macs and fries.

The first humans in the American southwest were nomadic hunter-gatherers, but the arrival of maize (around 2000 BC) initiated a shift towards agriculture. In around AD 500, selective crop breeding created more productive seeds; communities settled and the population boomed. Also around AD 500, the advent of the bow and arrow revolutionised bison hunting for Great Plains tribes. For Native Americans across the country, change was afoot.

The Southwest Chief is a fascinating way to explore the United States' indigenous history. As the train rumbles across the Midwest grasslands and desert scrub, it's easy to imagine being transported back in time. But there are also more direct links. For instance, between the cities of Gallup and Albuquerque (New Mexico) the train runs through Navajo land – a Navajo guide hops aboard to provide commentary on the region's legends and history. The route also runs through Native American settlements, such as New Mexico's San Felipe Pueblo (founded 1706), and visits La Junta, Colorado, where the

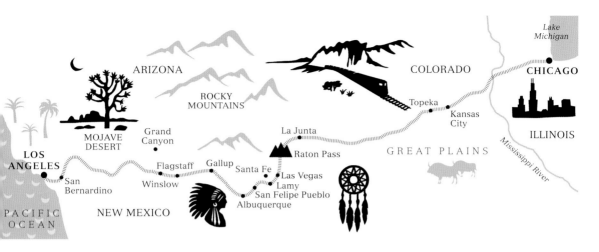

Koshare Indian Museum has a matchless display of Native American artefacts.

The railway's origin dates back to the Santa Fe Trail, the arduous 19th-century trade route between Missouri and the west. In 1859, the Atchison, Topeka and Santa Fe Railway (AT&SF) was chartered to build a track along this old road. By 1872, the AT&SF main line had reached Colorado; by 1885, it connected to Los Angeles.

BELOW: Amtrak's Southwest Chief heads west from Albuquerque.

147. Coral Coast Railway
Viti Levu, Fiji

On the Pacific archipelago of Fiji, first populated around 1500 BC, the Coral Coast Railway uses restored sugar-cane locomotives to run tours on old narrow gauge plantation tracks.

148. Suzuran Line
Hokkaido, Japan

The Ainu, the original inhabitants of Hokkaido island, may have originated around 300 BC. Investigate their history via the Suzuran Line: take a 1-hour ride from Sapporo to the town of Shirao, home to a replica Ainu village.

149. Heartland Flyer
Midwest United States

Cowboys meet 'Indians' on this 206-mile (332km) ride between Oklahoma and Texas. Native Americans inhabited the Midwest thousands of years before Europeans arrived, and Oklahoma City's American Indian Center tells their story.

150. Antananarivo–Andasibe
Central Madagascar

Explore Madagascar – first settled by seafarers from Indonesia in the 1st century AD – by 1930s Micheline. These bus-like trains occasionally run the 90-mile (145km) route from Antananarivo to Andasibe-Mantadia National Park.

Industry and expansion may have been the railway's original aim, but in the 1930s there was an injection of glamour too. The AT&SF's Santa Fe Super Chief, which made its first Chicago–LA run in 1936, was the A-lister of trains. With its red and yellow Warbonnet livery (a nod to the coloured feather headdresses worn by Plains Indian leaders), Pullman sleeper cars and gourmet meals, it became famed for its celebrity passengers. Sadly, the Super Chief stopped running in 1971. The Southwest Chief, which uses mostly AT&SF lines, is its less-starry successor. Though the food isn't quite as fancy, the views remain the same.

Those views depend on your direction of travel. Westbound, the train leaves Chicago's Union Station mid-afternoon, arriving in Kansas City around 10 p.m. Passengers wake up to see western Kansas sliding towards Colorado's Rocky Mountains. Later, New Mexico appears, and one of the journey's highlights: the dramatic Raton Pass over the Sangre de Cristo Mountains. The train hits Las Vegas by lunchtime, then Lamy (railhead for Santa Fe), Albuquerque and, by 9 p.m., Flagstaff in Arizona for the Grand Canyon. The train traverses the Mojave Desert overnight, arriving in Los Angeles for breakfast.

Eastbound, the train departs Los Angeles just after 6 p.m., reaching Flagstaff early the next morning. Passing Native American cities such as Winslow and Gallup, it pauses briefly in Albuquerque, then spends the afternoon slicing through the rest of New Mexico before hitting Colorado for sunset. The Kansas plains are dealt with overnight; dawn breaks somewhere around state capital Topeka or Kansas City. Then it's over the Missouri plains and the Mississippi River, to pull into the 'windy city', Chicago, by mid-afternoon.

RIGHT: Cloud Gate is a public sculpture in Chicago by artist Anish Kapoor.

TEHACHAPI PASS RAILROAD LINE

California, United States

The indigenous Kitanemuk people had been using California's Tehachapi Pass for millennia before Europeans arrived. But in the 19th century the Southern Pacific Railroad saw the pass's potential. Opened in 1876, the 28-mile (45km) Tehachapi Pass Railroad provided the final link in the railway line between San Francisco and Los Angeles. Hacked through granite by 3,000 Chinese labourers, the line's highlight is the 0.75-mile (1.17km) long Tehachapi Loop, a large, continuous curve that spirals over itself. Around forty freight trains complete the loop each day; the only passenger service to do so is the occasional Amtrak Coast Starlight, which is permitted to detour here only if its regular route is closed.

JASPER–RUPERT TRAIN

Western Canada

Cut across the British Columbia wilderness, where majestic mountains and forest meet First Nations and pioneer history.

Need to know
- *Point in time: 3000 BC (Tsimshian lived at Prince Rupert)*
- *Length: 720 miles (1,160km)*
- *Minimum time: 2 days*
- *Key stops: Jasper, Prince George, Prince Rupert*
- *Countries crossed: Canada*

The hardiest humans have eked out an existence in the British Columbian wilderness for thousands of years. At Prince Rupert, archaeologists have unearthed remains of houses built by Tsimshian peoples 5,000 years ago. Much later, from the 18th century, European fur traders then gold prospectors delved in. In 1914, the Grand Trunk Pacific Railway (GTP) opened, linking the Manitoba city of Winnipeg with the Pacific port at Prince Rupert, cutting across this wild frontier.

But despite the train, this chunk of British Columbia remains a sparsely populated place. Most of the townships visited by this line, from Jasper (Alberta) to Prince Rupert

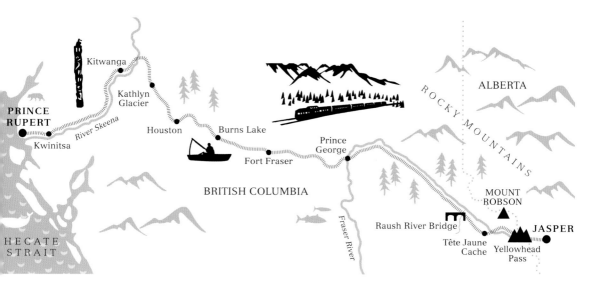

(British Columbia), count their residents in handfuls. It's a journey that showcases the majesty of Mother Nature and the resilience of the few who've semi-tamed it.

Starting in the adventure jump-off town of Jasper, the train slips through the Rocky Mountains via Yellowhead Pass. It follows the salmon-filled Fraser River, scythes through forest and offers views to Mount Robson, the Canadian Rockies' highest peak. It also passes railroad settlements such as Tête Jaune Cache, from where paddle steamers once set off down the Fraser River. Just before mile 33, there's a particularly fine photo opportunity as the train curves across the Raush River Bridge.

At the sprawling city of Prince George the train stops for the night. Passengers head to a hotel so they don't sleep through any scenery. The next morning, more magnificence unfurls. The train rumbles past Fort Fraser, the fur-trading outpost where the GTP's ceremonial 'Last Spike' was driven in 1914. Soon, Kathlyn Glacier appears, along with a sprinkle of towns with First Nations heritage (look for the totem pole at Kitwanga).

The train picks up the River Skeena (a Tsimshian word meaning 'water out of the clouds') and runs via Kwinitsa Station Railway Museum. It finishes in pretty Prince Rupert, where Tsimshian culture meets whale-watching boats, seafood shacks and tours to see grizzly bears.

LEFT: The Jasper–Rupert line links Rocky Mountains with the Pacific Ocean.

153
SANTA CLAUS EXPRESS

Finland

On this comfortable long-distance sleeper service you can nod off amid the cultured streets of Finland's capital, Helsinki, and wake up in the snow-cloaked Arctic Circle. Trains leave at around 10 p.m. and, after ploughing north through Finland for 555 miles (893km), the Santa Claus Express reaches Rovaniemi about 12 hours later. Rovaniemi, at 66°N, is the capital of Finnish Lapland and self-proclaimed home of Father Christmas – you can pay Old St Nick a visit at the Santa Claus Village. Or, instead, head to a reindeer farm to meet local Sami (Lapp) people, who've inhabited this icily incredible region since at least the 1st century AD.

154
KUNMING–HAIPHONG RAILWAY

China and Vietnam

From the Don Song culture (1000 BC–100 AD) to the minority peoples dotted there today, the Vietnam-China borderland has always been an anthropologically fascinating spot. In 1910, the French built the Kunming–Haiphong Railway, a cross-border narrow gauge line through the region. It passed minority peoples' towns and magnificent mountains, via 152 tunnels and 178 bridges – including the jaw-dropping 102m (335ft) high Inverted V Bridge over the Sicha River. Sadly, this scenic line is largely closed but a new high-speed Kunming–Hekou Railway traverses China's Yunnan province. At the Vietnamese border, passengers can taxi to Lao Cai train station and rejoin the original French line to Haiphong. This is the jumping-off point for the emerald waters, karst islands and junk-boat cruises of Halong Bay.

155
HEFEI–FUZHOU LINE

Eastern China

The 502-mile (808km) Hefei–Fuzhou high-speed line opened in 2015, reducing travel time between the two cities from 14 hours to four. But it's a pity to rush: this is one of the most picturesque railways in China. The train crosses the Yangtze River, traverses 170 bridges and passes tea plantations in the Wuyi Mountains. It also cuts through the cloud-swirled, pine-studded Huangshan (Yellow Mountains). This UNESCO World Heritage–listed and scenically spectacular range is said to be the birthplace of the Yellow Emperor, a legendary figure traditionally believed to have ruled 2698–2598 BC who is credited as the founder of Chinese civilisation.

156
VELES–BITOLA

Southern Macedonia

Rumbling across the Plain of Pelagonia now, it's hard to imagine that this was the heartland of one of the most powerful kingdoms in antiquity. During the reign of Philip II (359–336 BC), ancient Macedon controlled the whole Greek world; the city of Heraclea Lyncestis (modern Bitola) was founded by Philip. Now, the 80-mile (129km) Veles–Bitola railway traverses a charmingly retrograde rural landscape of dishevelled stations and sleepy fields. From Veles, a tumbling old city by the Vardar River, trains chug southwest into the mountains to Prilep, jumping-off point for Treskavec Monastery. They then continue over the plain to Bitola, where Ottoman townhouses, a Turkish bazaar and the ruins of Philip's old city await.

MAHAPARINIRVAN EXPRESS

Bihar and Uttar Pradesh, India

Prepare to be enlightened on this
Buddhist pilgrimage by train.

Need to know
- *Point in time: 563 BC
  (reputed birth date
  of Buddha)*
- *Length: 1,420 miles
  (2,285km)*
- *Minimum time: 8 days*
- *Key stops: New Delhi,
  Gaya (Bodhgaya),
  Varanasi (Sarnath),
  Gorakhpur
  (Kushinagar), Lumbini,
  Gonda (Shravasti),
  Agra*
- *Countries crossed:
  India*

The Mahaparinirvan Express might just be the world's most
enlightening railway ride. Also called the Buddhist Circuit
Train, it's a multi-day trip that follows in the footsteps of
Siddhartha Gautama, the founder of Buddhism.

According to the traditional account, Siddhartha was
born into the royal family of a small kingdom on the
India-Nepal border, some time in the 6th century BC.
He enjoyed a privileged upbringing, but he started to
question the meaning of life as he grew older. Eventually
he bid goodbye to his palace and became a wandering
holy man, travelling across northern India, practising
meditation, living ascetically, searching for the truth.
Finally, after sitting under a Bodhi tree for 40 days, he
found what he was seeking.

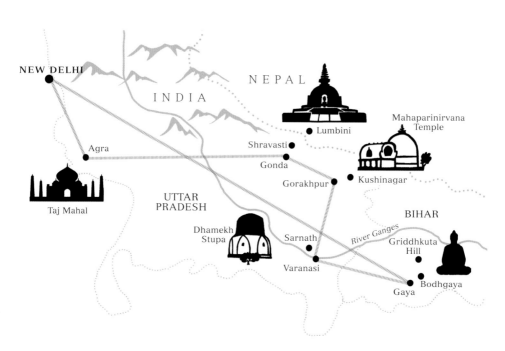

ABOVE: Varanasi is one of India's holiest cities.

The Mahaparinirvan Express is named after the *Mahaparinirvana Sutra*, a text containing an explanation of Buddha's later teachings. This spiritual train service does not transport passengers to Nirvana. Rather, it's a zigzagging loop that begins and ends in India's capital, New Delhi, and connects places with links to Siddhartha. It is a tourist train, involving multiple excursions and taking 8 days. But there's nothing to stop an independent traveller plotting their own course between the same sites, using Indian Railway's expansive network (with a few buses and taxis thrown in).

From New Delhi the Mahaparinirvan runs right across the plains of Uttar Pradesh for 620 miles (1,000km) to reach the ancient city of Gaya. This is the nearest railhead to the pilgrimage town of Bodhgaya, in which Siddhartha found enlightenment. These days, Bodhgaya is dominated by a huge cross-legged Buddha statue; nearby is the Mahabodhi Temple Complex, home to the famous Bodhi tree under which he attained enlightenment.

The tour spends a day visiting sites in Bihar state by bus, including Griddhkuta Hill, where Buddha spent months preaching. The next leg by train is from Gaya to Varanasi, on the banks of the Ganges. Varanasi is Hinduism's most sacred city, and one of the oldest living cities in the world. About 6 miles (10km) north is Sarnath, where Buddha delivered his first sermon, introducing his doctrine to the world. The spot is marked by the 34m-high (112ft) Dhamekh Stupa, the earliest bricks of which date back to 200 BC.

Next, the train rumbles on to the city of Gorakhpur, the best rail access point for the small village of Kushinagar, about 34 miles (55km) to the east. Kushinagar is where Buddha died and reputedly where he found freedom from the cycles of life and rebirth. Set amid grassy gardens and ancient ruins, Mahaparinirvana Temple contains a golden reclining Buddha statue thought to be around 1,500 years old.

From Kushinagar, it's possible to take a bus across the border into Nepal to visit the sacred site of Lumbini (note: a visa will be required). This is Buddhism's ground zero: the place where Siddhartha Gautama was born. There's a religious park filled with monasteries, including an offering-strewn shrine at the birthplace itself.

After rejoining the railway at Gorakhpur, the next stop is the city of Gonda, which is a short drive from Shravasti. Buddha spent most of his monastic life in this ancient walled city on the Gangetic plains. He preached at Jetavana Monastery, the remains of which can be visited today. A *stupa* now stands just outside Shravasti, where Siddhartha performed the 'Twin Miracle': it's said that for several days he produced flames from his upper body and water from his lower body, alternating between the two, and switching the flow from his left side to his right.

The Mahaparinirvan Express squeezes in a visit to the city of Agra – not directly connected with Buddhism, but no one wants to miss the Taj Mahal. From here it's only a few hours' ride back to New Delhi, the pilgrimage's end.

ORIENTAL DESERT EXPRESS

Eastern Morocco

Follow a long-forgotten railway into the Sahara
for a chance to meet Berber nomads.

Need to know
- *Point in time: 1300 BC (Berber nomads populated the Sahara)*
- *Length: 189 miles (304km)*
- *Minimum time: 12 hours*
- *Key stops: Oujda, Bouarfa*
- *Countries crossed: Morocco*

It seems that the Swiss are so good at railways they can even sniff them out in the Sahara . . . In the 2000s, Morocco-dwelling Swiss expat Edi Kunz discovered an abandoned single-track railway line running north-south in far east Morocco. It connects the lively bazaars of Oujda, an old trading post close to the Algerian border, and the remote settlement of Bouarfa, at the edge of the desert. In between, this long-forgotten line streaks across the wild Oriental Plateau, a region more synonymous with Amazigh (Berber) nomads than locomotives.

Morocco was a French protectorate from 1912 to 1955, and the railway was originally built to transport the French military. Later it carried coal from Bouarfa to the Mediterranean coast. Now, the colonial troops are long gone and the mines have closed but the line is running once more. Occasionally. The tracks are used a few times a week by mineral-carting freight trains, and they're usually used a few times a year for adventurous train lovers.

BELOW: Passengers riding the Oriental Desert Express in the 1960s – before it was abandoned to the Saharan sands.

ABOVE: The main square in the old trading post of Oujda.

Passengers on Kunz's private Oriental Desert Express trips ride on a diesel-pulled, air-conditioned viewing wagon. It's more like a private taxi than a train. With no one else using the line, the loco can stop whenever and wherever it wants. It might pull over so passengers can admire a herd of sheep, visit the few villages en route or take a closer look at Beni M'thar's abandoned Catholic church. Practical stops may be required, too, to help shovel sand off the tracks. The train will definitely stop for a mint tea and a chat when it sees a group of passing nomads. Still living a very traditional way of life, these hardy desert people seem barely changed from the first Amazigh, who moved westward from the Nile Valley into the region over 3,000 years ago.

159
MAURITANIA RAILWAY

Mauritania

Some of the longest trains in the world trundle across the empty deserts of Mauritania. They lug iron ore for 437 miles (704km) from the mines around Zouérat, on the Sahara's edge, to the Atlantic port of Nouadhibou. It's Mauritania's only railway, and these metal monsters – up to 1.6 miles (2.5km) long – make quite a sight amid the sand. Ordinarily out here you'd see only camel-riding nomads, distant descendants of the people of the Berber Kingdom of Mauretania (300 BC–AD 700), which gave the country its name. Sadly the trains are freight only, although it's not unusual for 'passengers' to hop on top of an ore container to hitch a ride.

CHAPTER THREE

THE MIDDLE AGES

Delve into the medieval era,
from AD 600 to 1500, to travel with
pilgrims, traders, crusaders
and lost civilisations.

BANGKOK–CHIANG MAI NORTHERN LINE

Thailand

Travel through Thailand's central plains to link
new capitals, old capitals and remote highland kingdoms.

Need to know

- *Point in time: 1296 (Kingdom of Lan Na founded)*
- *Length: 467 miles (751km)*
- *Minimum time: 14 hours*
- *Key stops: Bangkok, Ayutthaya, Lopburi, Phitsanulok, Lamphun, Chiang Mai*
- *Countries crossed: Thailand*

BELOW: The journey ends amid the lush highlands around Chiang Mai.

The train journey from Bangkok to Chiang Mai is like cramming for Thai History 101 in the space of 14 hours. It's also an easy way of getting from the country's capital to its leafy highlands.

The Bangkok–Chiang Mai Northern Line, which was first surveyed in the 1890s and officially opened in 1922, runs up the broad alluvial plain of the Chao Phraya River. It was quite a feat, hacking a railway across the fertile grassland, through near-impenetrable jungle and up into the mountains. But these tracks became the country's unifying spine, running along its history-laden central corridor.

During the latter part of the first millennium AD, Tai peoples migrated from southern China into Southeast Asia. The Khmer Empire ruled this area at that time. But in 1238 a Tai chieftain established the independent Kingdom of Sukhothai, on Thailand's central plain; its people called themselves Thai ('free'). Sukhothai thrived for over a century, until the city-state of Ayutthaya, a little way south,

became dominant in 1350 – so dominant that even the Khmers had to yield to its sovereignty. Further north, the Kingdom of Lan Na (Kingdom of a Million Rice Fields) was flourishing. It established its independence and its capital, Chiang Mai, in 1296.

And all of this Middle Ages intrigue was happening along the route of the Northern Line. The 467-mile (751km) line begins in Bangkok, which grew from a small trading post in the early days of the Ayutthaya Kingdom to become capital in 1782. There's certainly no doubting Bangkok's status now. It's a head-spinning cocktail of glass towers, traffic jams, temples, markets, malls, swanky bars and seething clubs.

Both day and sleeper services leave from Bangkok's Neo Renaissance–style Hualamphong Station, opened in 1916. First the train rolls through city districts, where shanties lean towards the tracks, before emerging into viridescent rice paddies. After about 1.5 hours the train pulls into Ayutthaya, aforementioned former capital. It's said that, at its peak, the ancient city had so many gilded temples it dazzled from miles away. Today, the original city lies in atmospheric decay (it was sacked by the Burmese in the

ABOVE: Now a bustling capital, Bangkok began life as a small trading post.

18th century), its red-brick ruins hinting at past glories. Hire a tuk-tuk or bike at the station to explore.

From Ayutthaya, the Northern Line continues towards Lopburi, one of Thailand's oldest cities. It was designated second capital of the Ayutthaya Kingdom but is a little shabby today. However, it does have an 800-year-old Khmer temple, which is most notable for the hordes of macaque monkeys that have made it their home.

Further north, the train stops at Phitsanulok. Pilgrims disembark here for Wat Phra Si Ratana Mahathat, the city's important Buddhist shrine, but this is also the nearest railhead for Sukhothai (36 miles / 58km northwest). The partially reconstructed ruins of the old kingdom of Sukhothai spread over a huge area, although a dense cluster – including the remains of the royal palace and twenty-six temples – lie within the old rectangular city walls.

As the railway line clatters up through the verdant mountains to Chiang Mai, the terrain becomes increasingly dramatic, the air increasingly cool. Before the railway was completed, Lan Na was a remote, inaccessible Shangri-La; it wasn't until 1932 that the whole area officially became a province of Siam (as Thailand was then known). It still feels like a land apart, with its jungly lushness, Burmese-influenced cuisine and distinct dialect, handicrafts and traditions.

Though much modernised, Chiang Mai retains an air of the ancient, especially in its moated old quarter of low-rise wooden houses and serene temples. The city is also the gateway to wilderness further north. You can trek into the hills to meet some of Lan Na's tribal peoples, who live much as they did before the first trains arrived.

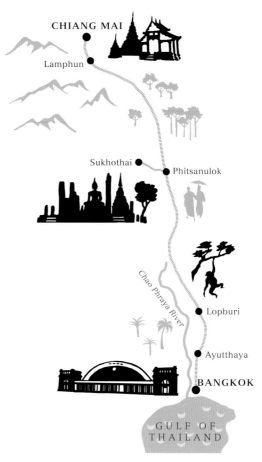

CHIANG MAI

Lamphun

Sukhothai

Phitsanulok

Chao Phraya River

Lopburi

Ayutthaya

BANGKOK

GULF OF THAILAND

RIGHT: Wat Arun, the Temple of Dawn, dominates the banks of the Chao Phraya in Bangkok.

161
BANGKOK–UBON RATCHATHANI

Eastern Thailand

This 357-mile (575km) train journey starts in the current Thai capital Bangkok. It runs via former capital Ayutthaya, then heads east towards the heartland of the Khmer Empire, the region's dominant force before that era. The journey's final destination, Ubon Ratchathani, is deep in Thailand's eastern Isan province, where many of the county's Khmer relics can be found. Stop en route at Nakhon Ratchasima station to visit Phimai, an elaborate temple complex built from the late 11th century; it marks the end of the ancient Khmer highway from Angkor in Cambodia. Or hop off at Sisaket, gateway to many ruins, including the Shiva-dedicated *stupas* of Prasat Wat Sa Kamphaeng Yai.

162
BATTAMBANG BAMBOO TRAIN

Northwest Cambodia

There are relics around the city of Battambang – notably, the Khmer temple of Wat Ek Phnom – providing evidence that the region has been inhabited since the 11th century. However, a more curious relic is the defunct Battambang–Phnom Penh rail line, which now carries a unique form of transportation. Bamboo Trains (comprising wooden palettes on metal frames, with tiny engines) haul produce and people to villages a few miles down the tracks. During the 20-minute ride they plough through the undergrowth and career over bridges; if two trains meet, the one with less cargo is temporarily dismantled so the other can pass.

JR NARA LINE

Honshu, Japan

Connect Kyoto and Nara, two former Imperial
capitals, for a glimpse into the Japanese past.

Need to know
- *Point in time:* AD 794
  *(Japanese capital
  moved to Kyoto)*
- *Length: 22 miles
  (35km)*
- *Minimum time:
  50 minutes*
- *Key stops: Kyoto,
  Tofukuji, Inari, Uji,
  Nara*
- *Countries crossed:
  Japan*

In 50 minutes you can take a train through one of the most
formative periods of Japanese history. Buddhism arrived
via China in the 6th century, bringing big changes. When
Japan's first permanent capital was established at Nara in
AD 710, Buddhism became the court's religion. Nara's Todaiji
temple was built in 752; its Big Buddha Hall remains the
world's largest wooden building.

But Nara's tenure was brief. In 784 the capital moved,
first to Nagaoka, then in 794 to Kyoto; Kyoto remained the
Imperial seat until 1868, when that role was taken by Tokyo
(then called Edo). The JR Nara line runs between Kyoto and
Nara, offering a short, thick slice of history.

Kyoto is Japan's most intoxicating city. The centuries seem to vanish amid its teahouses and tight alleys, where you might glimpse a geisha. However, the JR Nara Line starts at the futuristic station. First stop is Tofukuji, a Zen temple founded in 1236. It has impressive gates and halls, but is best in autumn, when the maples flanking Tsutenkyo Bridge burst into fall flame. Next is Inari, home to 8th-century Fushimi Inari Shrine, where a snaking procession of more than 5,000 red *torii* gates leads up the mountain behind.

Halfway to Nara, the train calls at Uji. The city's Ujigami Shrine is believed to be the oldest extant shrine in Japan, dating to 1060. Uji was also one of the first places in Japan to start cultivating green tea, and is renowned for its superior brews and green-tea noodles.

In less than an hour the train arrives at Nara Station. As well as Todaiji Temple, there's Kasuga Taisha (the most revered Shinto shrine) and a museum of Buddhist art. There's also the site of Heijo Palace, the emperor's residence when Nara was capital. No original structures remain but the vastness of the area hints at its past glory.

FASCINATING FOUNDATIONS

164. Eizan Kurama Line
Honshu, Japan

Take a 30-minute electric train ride from Kyoto to the mountain village of Kurama. It's home to a Buddhist temple founded in the 8th century.

165. Yangon Circular Railway
Myanmar (Burma)

Take the commuter train around Myanmar's biggest city, founded in the 11th century. Carrying 150,000 people a day, it offers a great insight into local life.

166. Levanto–La Spezia
Liguria, Italy

A scenic 11-mile (18km) railway connects the five cliff-teetering villages of the Cinque Terre, the oldest of which, Monterosso, was founded in AD 643.

167. Florence–Pisa
Tuscany, Italy

It's 47 miles (76km) from Florence, 'Birthplace of the Renaissance', to Pisa, home to the Leaning Tower – which was already leaning on its completion in 1372.

ABOVE: Hop off at the Fushimi Inari Shrine, where more than 5,000 red torii gates lead up the mountain.

LEFT: The Ginkaku-ji Temple is just one of the many sacred sites in Kyoto.

IRON SILK ROAD

Central Asia

As railway-building booms in China and beyond, it's increasingly possible to trace the original Silk Road route by train.

Need to know
- *Point in time: 1450s (Silk Road trade route declined)*
- *Length: Around 4,000 miles (6,400km)*
- *Minimum time: 4–5 days*
- *Key stops: Moscow, Astana, Almaty, Ürümqi, Turpan, Lanzhou, Xi'an*
- *Countries crossed: Russia, Kazakhstan, China*

Around 200 BC the Chinese officially made contact with the West and, for the next 1,500 years, the Silk Road unfurled across Central Asia. This legendary trading route had many strands, but essentially connected Chang'an (today Xi'an) in China with Constantinople (now Istanbul) in western Turkey. Camel caravans loaded with paper, spices, gunpowder and the eponymous silk forged westwards. Arts, architecture, philosophy, technology and religion flowed both ways.

However, by the 13th century, the Silk Road was waning. The Mongol Empire collapsed and China's new, paranoid, Great Wall-building Ming Dynasty essentially closed shop. In 1453 the Byzantine Empire fell to the Ottomans who curtailed trade west through its empire. Merchants took to the seas. The Silk Road was dead.

Now it's being reborn. The Iron Silk Road – or Trans-Asian Railway – is a project to build a web of high-speed railways between China and Europe through Asia. China's ambition is that, by 2020, the network will interlink forty

LEFT: St Basil's Cathedral dominates Moscow's Red Square.

MORE SILK ROAD RAILWAYS

169. Khunjerab Railway
Northern Pakistan

By 2030, a 424-mile (682km) railway may run through the Karakoram Mountains to the Khunjerab Pass, once a key thoroughfare on the Silk Road route into China.

170. Golden Eagle Silk Road
Russia, Uzbekistan, Turkmenistan, Kazakhstan and China

Follow the Silk Road in style aboard the opulent Golden Eagle train. This 21-day rail trip links Moscow and Beijing, via cities such as Merv, Bukhara, Turpan and Xi'an.

171. Bilaspur–Mandi–Leh Railway
Ladakh, India

If built, this proposed line in the Himalayas, which apes an important Silk Road strand, would feature the world's highest train station, at 5,359m (17,582ft) high Taglang La.

countries; it's hoped London–Beijing overland will take 2 days, rather than fifteen, as it does now.

The Iron Silk Road isn't yet complete, but segments can already be followed. Since the 1950s, Moscow and Beijing have been connected by the iconic Trans-Mongolian Railway, via Mongolian capital Ulaanbaatar. More recently, an alternative link between the two capitals has become possible via a more central corridor. From Moscow, rail passengers can travel through Kazakhstan and along the route of the ancient Silk Road in China, either all the way to Beijing or terminating in Xi'an. A less direct alternative runs via Uzbekistan's capital Tashkent, which connects to great Silk Road cities such as Samarkand and Bukhara.

Currently, it takes 2.5 days to get from Moscow to Astana in Kazakhstan, via scrappy towns, wooden villages and *babushkas* selling snacks on station platforms. Gradually, the terrain becomes hillier and then opens on to the endless steppe. Oil-rich Astana, Kazakh capital only since 1997, is an anomaly rising from the plains, dominated by shiny futuristic skyscrapers. Almaty, a little further south, is a more characterful metropolis, with tree-lined boulevards and views to the snowy Tien Shan Mountains.

The onward train crosses more Kazakh-steppe before entering China via the windswept Dzungarian Gate. This straight valley is one of the only ways through the near 2,000-mile (3,200km) mountain chain separating China from the west, so has long been a portal for migration, trade, invasion – and now trains.

From here, the railway leads over the semi-desert to Ürümqi, capital of China's Xinjiang province and once a key stop for ancient trade caravans; it's now home to a Silk Road Museum. More interesting is Turpan, a little further east. Backed by the crimson-hued Flaming Mountains and once the domain of steppes nomads, it was claimed by the Chinese in the 1st century AD and provided a vital stepping stone for westward expansion. Most atmospheric is the nearby ruined clifftop fortress of Jiaohe. It was founded in 108 BC and became an important Silk Road outpost until it was sacked by Genghis Khan in the 13th century. The train also passes Jiayuguan, the wild, westernmost extent of the Great Wall of China, and Lanzhou, where the Silk Road meets the Yellow River.

Xi'an was the end – or beginning – of the Silk Road, and the heart of ancient China. It was from Xi'an that the first Chinese missions were sent west, marking the birth of the Silk Road over 2,000 years ago. However, the city's finest hour was under the Tang Dynasty (618–907), when the population boomed, immense walls were built and Western products filled the markets. Today, you can walk Xi'an's gargantuan ramparts and visit the nearby Terracotta Warriors, the army of sculptures buried with Emperor Qin Shihuang over 2,000 years ago. And you can squint through the smog at the hubbub of traffic, trying to imagine that the cars are camels instead.

RIGHT: The Iron Silk Road takes a central route along the ancient trading highway.

174
SOUTHERN XINJIANG RAILWAY

Western China

Kashgar was once the trade nexus of the East. When Venetian merchant Marco Polo visited the city in 1275 he called it the 'starting point from which many merchants set out to market their wares all over the world'. The 899-mile (1,446km) Southern Xinjiang Railway follows a key strand of the Silk Road, between Kashgar and Turpan, along the southern slopes of the Tien Shan mountains. Old Kashgar has been subsumed, its ethnically Uighur roots diluted by an influx of Han Chinese. But traces of the past remain, in the mosques and muezzin calls, the chaotic bazaars and massive Kashgar Sunday Market, where merchants still do a roaring trade.

175
ORIENT SILK ROAD EXPRESS

Uzbekistan

Link the most magnificent reminders of the Silk Road via the Orient Silk Road Express. This private train runs a 10-day tour of Uzbekistan's ancient cities. It visits Shakhrisabz, birthplace of brutal Turco-Mongol prince Tamerlane (1336–1405) and home to the ruins of his palace. It crosses the Kyzylkum Desert to reach Bukhara with its glittering domes and intricately tiled monuments. It goes to Khiva, an *Arabian Nights*-style fortress of mosques and mausoleums. And it heads to Samarkand, to admire the 15th-century Bibi-Khanym Mosque and enormous Registan Square.

HEART OF PERSIA

Iran

Loop between the most majestic cities of
ancient Persia aboard a magnificent train.

Need to know
- *Point in time: 633–656
  (Muslims conquered
  Persia)*
- *Length: Around
  2,500 miles (4,020km)*
- *Minimum time:
  14 days*
- *Key stops: Tehran,
  Mashhad, Yazd,
  Isfahan, Shiraz,
  Kashan, Shustar, Susa*
- *Countries crossed:
  Iran*

**LIKE THAT?
TRY THIS**
- - - - - - - - - - - - - - - - - -

**177. Prague–
Karlovy Vary**
Czech Republic

In 147 miles (236km),
travel from the Czech
capital to the spa town
of Karlovy Vary, named
after Holy Roman
Emperor Charles IV who
founded the city in 1370.

Iran oozes history. It was home to one of the world's oldest
civilisations, and has been the seat of mighty empires – not
least the Achaemenids, who in 480 BC ruled over a greater
percentage of the world's population than any other empire,
ever. But it was from the 7th century, when Muslims
defeated the ruling Sassanids, that a big cultural shift
occurred. The subsequent Islamisation led to a golden age
for Persian science, literature, philosophy and art.

The Heart of Persia railway journey aboard the Golden
Eagle is a comprehensive loop of this strategic crossroads
of a country, in five-star style. Immaculate attendants, silken
upholstery, polished wood and a piano tinkling in the
lounge car all nod to the most romantic days of rail travel.
Meanwhile, ancient Iran glides past the picture windows.

The Golden Eagle's two-week Iran itinerary tends to run
three or four times a year. It starts in capital Tehran, where

the National Museum gives a handy primer, displaying artefacts stretching back 35,000 years. Then a catalogue of great sites and cities unfolds.

The train visits Mashhad, where Imam Reza (765–818), eighth Shia Imam, is buried in the world's largest mosque by area, and where Ferdowsi (940–1020), 'Father of Persian Literature', rests in a white marble tomb. It continues to the desert city of Kerman, a major trade hub when Marco Polo stopped by in 1271, and still home to an old adobe (mud-brick) centre with a bustling bazaar. The train heads to mountain-backed Isfahan, former capital and still the very height of Persian elegance, with its huge squares, preened gardens, graceful bridges and glittering, mosaic-tiled mosques. And then there's Shiraz, 'city of poets', a cultural hub for over 2,000 years and one of the major cities of the medieval Islamic world. All in all: exquisite train, gorgeous country, monumental history. Very civilised indeed.

RIDES TO FINE FOUNDATIONS

178. Kiev Funicular
Ukraine

The funicular up Volodymyrska Hill links Kiev's Upper Town and its lower commercial district of Podil, where some buildings date to the city's founding in the 9th century.

179. Tel Aviv–Acre
Israel

In 1099 the First Crusader army occupied Jaffa (old Tel Aviv). Up the coast is Acre, which fell to Crusader forces in 1104 and still has its Crusader castle.

180. Sofia–Mezdra
Bulgaria

Take a train through the Balkan Mountains, which created a natural fortress for the Bulgarian Empire (founded 681).

LEFT: For the height of Persian elegance, take a luxury train to Isfahan.

181
WEST RHINE RAILWAY

Rhine Valley, Germany

The West Rhine Railway meanders alongside its namesake river for 115 miles (185km) between the cities of Cologne and Mainz. Prettiest is the Koblenz–Bingen stretch, through the UNESCO World Heritage–listed Middle Rhine. Here, the river is fringed by cobbled villages, serried vines and more than forty medieval castles, nodding to the valley's strategic importance over the centuries. Disembark at Bacharach for 12th-century crag-top Stahleck Castle; rebuilt in the 20th century, it's now a hostel. Get off at Sankt Goar to visit ruined Rheinfels (founded in 1245), the biggest castle on the Rhine. Or stop at Oberwesel for Castle Schönberg – the original 1100s castle burned down, but the remains have been reborn as a sumptuous hotel.

182
TRAM 28

Lisbon, Portugal

Clatter up the steep, tightly-packed streets of the Alfama, the Portuguese capital's oldest district, aboard a classic yellow tram. The medieval Alfama was largely modelled by the Moors, who ruled Lisbon from 714 to 1147. Somehow it stood fast when the 1755 Lisbon earthquake flattened most of the city. The 1930s Remodelado streetcars of Line 28 take about 40 minutes to rattle along their full route. From Praça do Martim Moniz, they run through the Graça district into the Alfama, via the massive Moorish castle. They then hit the elegant plazas of downtown Baixa, the cultural hub of Chiado and the bar-filled Bairro Alto before halting just beyond Estrela's baroque basilica.

183
VARANASI–KHAJURAHO EXPRESS

North India

It's a good job there hasn't been a railway to Khajuraho for very long. Because this erotic ancient site only survived due to its inaccessibility, safe from the disapproving eyes of prudish invaders. Built by the Chandella dynasty on the remote, dust-blown plains of Madhya Pradesh around 950–1050, the temples of Khajuraho are a *Kama Sutra* carved in stone. Saucy nymphs, fornicating couples, orgies and bestiality are all on display. In 2008, a branch line from the town of Jhansi to Khajuraho opened. This enables direct train travel on certain days of the week; the journey from the holy Hindu city of Varanasi to the raunchy temples takes around 11 hours.

184
FERROVIE DEL SUD EST

Puglia, Italy

Several little train lines wiggle around Italy's stiletto heel, courtesy of Ferrovie del Sud Est (South-East Railways). These lines are lovely ways to link Puglian towns via endless orchards and olive groves. The region was first settled by the Mycenaean Greeks but its most singular relics are its less ancient *trulli*, distinctive drystone-walled buildings with conical roofs. Alberobello is full of them, the oldest dating back to the 14th century. Visit the town via the 70-mile (113km) Bari–Taranto railway, which also stops at Martina Franca, a supremely photogenic walled hilltop town. From here, pick up the 64-mile (103km) Martina Franca–Lecce line to visit the beautiful baroque town at its end.

Take the Cusco–Machu Picchu line (next page) through the heart of the Sacred Valley to access the heights of Peru's long-abandoned Incan city. On the Belmond Hiram Bingham, it's 1920s glamour all the way.

CUSCO–MACHU PICCHU

Southern Peru

Take a train from the Inca Empire's most
important city to its most magical ruin.

Need to know
- *Point in time: 1200–1572 (reign of the Inca Empire)*
- *Length: 54 miles (86km)*
- *Minimum time: 3 hours*
- *Key stops: Poroy, Ollantaytambo, Aguas Calientes*
- *Countries crossed: Peru*

The Cusco–Machu Picchu train neither starts in Cusco nor
ends at Machu Picchu. But ultimately this train through
the Sacred Valley *does* connect the former capital of
the Inca Empire with its most spectacularly sited ruin.

The Inca seemingly emerged from nowhere around 1200,
after their founder-king Manco Cápac allegedly sprang from
Lake Titicaca. Over the following 300-plus years this
precocious civilisation grew to rule the largest empire South
America has ever known. At its zenith, Inca territory
stretched around 3,400 miles (5,500km) from north to south.
However, by the mid-16th century, after the Spanish
conquistadores arrived and flexed their unfriendly muscles,
the Inca had been almost wiped out.

But those bellicose conquistadores never found Machu
Picchu. The secretive citadel, tucked into the misty folds of
the Andes, was too well hidden. It was the Inca themselves

who abandoned the city around 1540. Machu Picchu was then virtually forgotten for over 350 years until 1911, when American explorer Hiram Bingham 'rediscovered' it and brought it to the world's attention.

In a way, Hiram Bingham continues to do so today. The most luxurious train service running PeruRail's Cusco–Machu Picchu route bears the explorer's name. With its smart livery, polished brass and gourmet meals served on white linen, the Belmond Hiram Bingham brings 1920s-style glamour to the Peruvian highlands. It's also the most expensive option. The two alternatives are the mid-range Vistadome train, which is far less plush but offers big panoramic windows and complimentary snacks, or the budget Expedition train, on which the windows are still sizeable but the snacks aren't free. There's also a no-frills train for locals, but foreigners aren't allowed on it.

Although the price tag and decor vary across the three options, the views out of the window remain the same – all three run on the same narrow gauge tracks through the Sacred Valley. These days the journey departs from the station of Poroy, 8 miles (13km) west of Cusco. This has

ABOVE: Cusco was the capital of the Inca Empire.

been a necessity since 2009, when landslides damaged the zigzagging section of track in between. Still, Cusco is the route's spiritual railhead. This high-altitude city, at a breathy 3,400m (11,200ft) above sea level, was the heart of the Inca Empire. Today it's a glorious layer cake of Inca and colonial architecture.

Travellers must take a bus or taxi to board the train in Poroy (KM13 of the line). From here the train winds upwards, eventually reaching a high plateau of fields and villages where locals tote maize and children in their bright *k'eperina* shawls. Then it descends via switchbacks into the Urubamba Valley to join the churning river where it hits the valley floor near Ollantaytambo (KM67). This old cobblestoned town is dominated by the remains of an enormous Inca fortress.

At KM82, the train passes fresh-legged trekkers: the 4-day Inca Trail to Machu Picchu starts from this railhead. Then the valley becomes narrower all the way to the bustling town of Aguas Calientes (KM111), journey's end. Sort of . . .

Machu Picchu itself is a 3-mile (5km) bus ride away. And, with its stone ruins tumbling down an improbable, peak-flanked slope, what a finale it is. Even today no one really knows what the citadel was for: Collecting cocoa? Safeguarding virgins? Performing sacred rituals? Whatever Machu Picchu's purpose, it's perhaps the world's most magnificent and mysterious terminus.

TREN DE LA LIBERTAD

Northern Andes, Ecuador

Explore a region once ruled by the Inca, on an abandoned train line that was restored in the 21st century.

Need to know
- *Point in time: 1450–1500 (Ecuador conquered by the Inca)*
- *Length: 34 miles (54km)*
- *Minimum time: 8 hours 15 minutes*
- *Key stops: Otavalo, San Roque, Andrade Marín, San Antonio, Ibarra, Hoja Blanca, Salinas*
- *Countries crossed: Ecuador*

BELOW: The Train of Liberty calls at the town of Ibarra, famed for its super sorbets.

Before the 15th century, the region that's now Ecuador was populated by jostling tribes. Then the empire-building Inca showed up. The locals were finally subdued by Inca ruler Huayna Cápac in Otavalo in 1495. It's said the waters of nearby Laguna Yahuarcocha are tinged red because of the bodies Cápac dumped there after an especially bloody massacre. There followed centuries of exploitation of Ecuador's Andean peoples, first by the Inca, then by the Spanish. Defiantly, the train that now runs through the area is called the Tren de la Libertad – the Train of Liberty.

The railway through Ecuador's northern highlands once distributed the region's textiles: wool, cotton, alpaca blankets and bright tapestries. It slipped out of use as the Pan-American Highway made road transport more appealing. But over the past few years, 34 miles (54km) of the line has reopened between the market town of Otavalo and the former salt-mining centre of Salinas. Now it transports tourists rather than textiles.

Otavalo's huge market, and specifically the Plaza de Ponchos, still offers a dazzling display of indigenous weaving and is a good place to browse for a new blanket. Every Friday, Saturday and Sunday, the train ploughs north from this high-altitude hub (2,535m / 8,317ft), crossing trestle bridges, sliding through hand-hacked tunnels and inching through literally breathtaking Andean landscapes. This is a region of looming mountains, brilliant-green hills and fields of maize, agave and sugar cane. The train's wooden sash windows roll down, so it's easy to get a closer look.

En route, the train stops at the highland village of Andrade Marín to visit the textile museum and at San Antonio for its woodcarving workshops. Ibarra, the regional capital of Imbabura Province, is the place to indulge in *helados de paila*: fruity sorbets stirred in big copper pans. At the terminus at Salinas, a welcoming committee of traditional *bomba* dancers awaits, followed by a tasty local lunch.

BELOW: The train leaves from Otavalo, home to one of Ecuador's most colourful markets.

188
O AND V TRAINS

South Korea

The Baekdudaegan mountain range of South Korea isn't just scenically spectacular. It's the spiritual spine that unites the country and, according to Zen master Doseon Guksa (826–98), distributes the country's *gi* (life energy). The circular, 160-mile (257km) O Train loops around the central inland region, starting from capital Seoul and stopping at the so-called 'healing city' of Jecheon (known for its oriental medicines), Taebaek (for the azalea-cloaked peak of Taebaeksan) and the Buddhist temples of Yeongju. At Buncheon Station, the O Train links with the V Train for a dramatic, hour-long, valley-slicing ride to Cheoram Station through the mystical, energy-giving Baekdudaegan range.

189
SACHKHAND EXPRESS

India

In Sikhism, the religion based on the teachings of Guru Nanak (1469–1539), there are five *Takhts* (thrones of authority). Chief of these is in the Punjabi city of Amritsar, housed in the dazzling Golden Temple complex. Here, the Akal Takht Sahib (Eternal Throne) sits opposite the Hari Mandir (House of God), a gilded shrine afloat in a central pool. Two of the other Takhts are near Amritsar. One is in Patna, in distant Bihar state. And one is 1,294 miles (2,082km) to the south, in the ancient city of Nanded in Maharashtra. The Sachkhand Express provides a direct, if long, connection: Sikh pilgrims can travel from Amritsar, down half the length of India to Nanded's Takht Hazur Sahib to pay their respects.

KOYA LINE

Honshu, Japan

Koyasan is one of Japan's holiest mountains. More than a hundred temples are scattered on its misty slopes. It's been a spiritual centre ever since the Buddhist monk Kobo Daishi erected a shrine here in the early 9th century, simultaneously founding Japan's Shingon sect. The easiest way to make a pilgrimage is via the 40-mile (64km) Koya Line, which links the urban clamour of Osaka to Gokurakubashi ('Bridge to Paradise') Station at Koyasan's base. As the train rumbles south, it crosses rivers, slips through tunnels, climbs a narrow gorge and offers views of the sacred Kii Peninsula. From Gokurakubashi, a cable car completes the journey to the mountaintop.

BORDEAUX– SAINT-ÉMILION

Southwest France

The 28-mile (45km) vineyard-dotted train journey between the boozy city of Bordeaux and little Saint-Émilion is intoxicating. First, learn about grapes at Bordeaux's Cité du Vin museum. Then head for the medieval fortified village of Saint-Émilion, renowned for its wines. It was founded by Aemilianus, an 8th-century monk who retreated to a cave here. The village's most important brotherhood, though, is the Jurade. Created in 1199, its job is to assess the quality of Saint-Émilion's wine. Judge for yourself at the Maison du Vin tasting lounge.

TRANSYLVANIA CIRCUIT

Transylvania, Romania

Take a terrifying train journey into the lair of Dracula,
via medieval villages and mighty mountains.

Need to know

- *Point in time: 1431–1476 (life of Vlad the Impaler)*
- *Length: Around 642 miles (1,033km)*
- *Minimum time: 18 hours*
- *Key stops: Brasov, Sighisoara, Medias, Cluj-Napoca, Oradea, Arad, Sibiu*
- *Countries crossed: Romania*

BELOW: Bran Castle is claimed to be former home of Vlad the Impaler – Count Dracula.

The word 'Transylvania' paints a vivid picture. It evokes dark, creepy forests, sinister rock-perched castles and, of course, vampires. This region of Romania was the home of Count Dracula in Irish author Bram Stoker's 1897 Gothic novel. And in the 15th century, it was home to the man who supposedly inspired him: Vlad Dracula, 'Vlad the Impaler' – a prince with a fondness for skewering his enemies on stakes.

Using local trains, you can make a spookily spectacular Transylvania circuit linking medieval Dracula-ish towns and traversing the Carpathian Mountains. Start in the hill-encircled city of Brasov, which has a wonderful Gothic and baroque centre. Brasov is a short bus ride from the village of Bran and 'Dracula's Castle'. Actually, Bran Castle (built 1377) has only tenuous links to Vlad, but its turrets and ramparts, nestled in the Bucegi Mountains, look suitably vampiric.

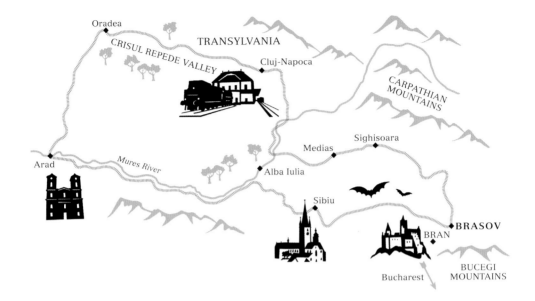

LIKE THAT?
TRY THESE

- - - - - - - - - - - - - - - - -

193. Petrin Hill Funicular
Prague, Czech Republic

This 5-minute funicular runs uphill from picturesque Malá Strana (Lesser Town). It passes through Charles VI's Hunger Wall (built 1360–62), part of Prague's medieval fortifications.

194. Gediminas Hill Funicular Railway
Vilnius, Lithuania

It takes just 35 seconds for this little funicular to run up the hill to the Vilnius Castle complex, built and added to from the 10th to the 18th centuries.

From Brasov, take the train northwest to the city of Sighisoara. It was here, amid the muddle of ancient houses and Saxon citadel, that Vlad was born in 1431. Further northwest is Transylvanian capital Cluj-Napoca, full of baroque buildings and bohemian cafes. In Stoker's novel, protagonist Jonathan Harker arrived in Cluj-Napoca (then called Klausenburg) by train and stayed at its Royal Hotel. The old Hotel Transilvania claims to have inspired it.

The line west from Cluj-Napoca cuts through the rolling green Crisul Repede Valley to reach Oradea, a city of fine secessionist and art nouveau architecture near the Hungarian border. Next, veer south to Arad, a key trading hub on the Mures River. Visit Arad's Vauban fortress and Orthodox monastery before riding west to Sibiu, the most fairy-tale town in Transylvania. Founded by German settlers in the 12th century, it's a charming jumble of towers, squares and cobbles. In the crypt of Sibiu's Evangelical Cathedral is the tombstone of Mihnea the Bad, Vlad's son, who was stabbed to death here in 1510.

195
JITONG RAILWAY

Inner Mongolia, China

In parts, the wild, remote steppe of Inner Mongolia doesn't feel much changed since Genghis Khan was galloping across it in the 13th century, master of the newly formed Mongol Empire. However, since 1995 it's the trains of the Jitong Railway that have been galloping here, originally powered by steam. The line, which runs for 587 miles (945km) between the industrial cities of Jining and Tongliao, was the world's last steam-operated main line. This industrial region is rich in coal, so it made sense to buy some QJ Class 2-10-2 coal-fired locomotives and use the local resources to run the railway. That lasted until 2005, when diesel finally took over.

196
DUBAI METRO

Dubai, United Arab Emirates

The first written mention of Dubai appears around 1095 when this sandy spot on the Persian Gulf was just a little fishing village. Who knew it would become a forward-thrusting metropolis of metal and glass? Among other developments, Dubai has made big strides in transportation. It no longer relies on *abras* – though you can still catch one of these traditional wooden boats to cross the Creek. Now, it has the longest fully automated metro network in the world – 47 miles (75km) without a single driver. Moreover, several metro stations are modern art spaces, with light displays, sculptures and 3D shows. Train carriages wrapped in e-paper technology can also become moving works of art.

AALBORG–RIBE

Jutland, Denmark

Explore the legacy of history's most fearsome
seafarers by taking the train.

Need to know

- *Point in time: 793–1066 (Viking era)*
- *Length: 210 miles (338km)*
- *Minimum time: 4 hours 30 minutes*
- *Key stops: Aalborg (Lindholm), Hobro, Århus, Vejle (Jelling), Ribe*
- *Countries crossed: Denmark*

MORE VIKING ADVENTURES

198. Copenhagen–Roskilde
Denmark

Follow the Vikings from the exhibits in Copenhagen's National Museum of Denmark to the 11th-century Viking ships in Roskilde's Viking Ship Museum, a 35-minute ride away.

From the late 8th century, warriors began sailing from Scandinavia to launch raids on foreign soil, plundering and pillaging as they went. These Norsemen (Northmen) hailed largely from Denmark, Norway and Sweden. They weren't one ethnic group, but were united in their style of attack, their uncivilised ways and their pagan beliefs. Ordinarily they were clansmen and farmers. But put them in a longship with the promise of loot and adventure, and they became something else – thieves, vandals, killers. They were given the Old Norse name for 'pirate': *vikingr*.

The Viking age is generally considered to have begun with the first raid on England's Lindisfarne monastery in 793, ending in 1066, when King Harold defeated Harald Hardrada (the last great Viking king) at Stamford Bridge near York, before being defeated himself at the Battle of Hastings, a few weeks later. However, while these era-defining actions occurred on British soil, Denmark is the Vikings' spiritual home.

A train tour of Jutland is particularly rich in Norse heritage. Begin in the lively university city of Aalborg, which sits on the narrowest point of the Limfjord, a channel separating the Jutland Peninsula from the island of North Jutland. For the Vikings, the Limfjord was like a storm-trooping superhighway, linking the easterly Kattegat sea to the North Sea, providing a quick route to the west. The Vikings founded settlements here from around 700, and evidence can be seen at Aalborg's Lindholm Høje, the biggest ancient burial ground in Scandinavia. Almost 700 graves and 150 stone ships have been discovered, dating from the Iron Age and Viking period.

From Aalborg's handsome 1902 station, take a train south across big-sky Danish landscapes to the market town of Hobro, at the head of Mariager Fjord. This is a jumping-off point for the remains of Fyrkat, a Viking ring castle dating from 980. You can explore its circular ramparts,

longhouse foundations and visitor centre, built in the style of a Viking farm.

Fyrkat's purpose was to control the main route between Aalborg and Århus, and the latter is the next stop. Århus, Denmark's second city, began life as the fortified Viking settlement of Aros in the 8th century. Today, the old city sits beneath the new, which can be experienced at Århus's Viking Museum. The underground treasure trove is built on the site of an archaeological excavation, at the same level as ancient Aros.

From Århus, a direct train runs south towards the forested hills of Vejle, another fjord-head town on Jutland's east coast. An important trading stop in the Middle Ages, it's also the railhead for the UNESCO World Heritage–site of Jelling. There are huge burial mounds here, and two fascinating rune stones. One was erected by King Gorm the Old, the other (in 965) by his son Harald Bluetooth, inscribed with the words: 'Harald who won for himself all of Denmark and Norway and made the Danes Christian.' It marks a big moment: the Vikings were finding Christ.

LEFT: Århus is certainly more civilised than its former incarnation, the Viking town of Aros.

Having trundled west across Jutland from Vejle, the rail odyssey ends at Ribe, Denmark's oldest town. The Vikings established a market here around 700, trading crafts for coins (Ribe had its own mint). Sited by the Wadden Sea, it was also the perfect launch pad for longship attacks. These days, Ribe's medieval old town of wonky half-timbered houses retains a time-warp feel. It has a fine old cathedral and a good collection of Danish works in the art museum. But most atmospheric is the VikingeCenter, where the 8th century is brought to life, complete with a sword-wielding warrior or two.

BELOW: Ribe, Denmark's oldest town, lies on the Wadden Sea – the perfect launch pad for Viking attacks.

SØRLAND RAILWAY

Southern Norway

Trace Norway's Viking past aboard the 373-mile (600km) Sørland Railway between the cities of Oslo and Stavanger. The must-visit in Oslo is the Viking Ship Museum, which contains two of the world's best-preserved wooden Viking vessels, both dating from the 9th century. Then book a window seat for the 8-hour train ride to Stavanger on the North Sea to look out on alpine hills, green valleys and glorious coast. In Stavangar, visit the Archaeological Museum. Then head out to Hafrsfjord to see the enormous 'Swords in Rock' monument. It commemorates the Viking naval battle of 872 that paved the way for the unification of Norway.

FAR NORTH LINE

Scotland, United Kingdom

The United Kingdom's northernmost railway, which runs for 160 miles (257km) from Inverness to Wick and Thurso (close to John o'Groats on Britain's northeastern tip), cuts through the land of the ancient Picts. These tribal peoples of the north resisted the Romans, fought the Vikings and finally joined with the Scots in 843. The Picts' only written legacy is their carved stones, some of which can be accessed from the Far North Line: the Eagle Stone (via Dingwall Station), the Nigg cross-slab (Invergordon) and the eighteen stelae at Dunrobin Castle. There's history at both ends too. Craig Phadrig hill in Inverness was once the fort of a Pictish king. In Thurso, the Caithness Horizons Museum reveals more of the Pict story.

HEART OF WALES LINE

Wales and England, United Kingdom

Chug across the Welsh Marches and over the English border,
right through the dyke designed to keep out invaders.

Need to know
- *Point in time: 757–96 (reign of King Offa of Mercia)*
- *Length: 121 miles (195km)*
- *Minimum time: 4 hours*
- *Key stops: Swansea, Llanelli, Carmarthen, Llandovery, Llandrindod Wells, Knighton, Craven Arms, Shrewsbury*
- *Countries crossed: United Kingdom*

Back in the 8th century, you might have got your ears chopped off (or worse) for straying over the Mercia-Wales border. Relations were not good between what was then England's largest kingdom and the Welsh to the west. So bad were they in fact, that Mercian King Offa built a 150-mile-long (240km) defensive dyke to keep out the Celts.

Thankfully, crossing between the two nations is now much less fraught with danger. Indeed, there's a lovely little railway that glides right through the historic frontier-land of the Welsh Marches with the minimum of fuss but the maximum of pleasure.

The Heart of Wales Line opened fully in 1868 to link a string of remote, valley-nestled communities. It is part of the United Kingdom's main rail network but, as the train

trundles gently between rolling hills and rural halts (most of which provide ideal gateways for hikes and exploration), it feels more like an adventure than a bog-standard A to B.

From bayside Swansea, Wales's second city, the line soon skirts the sandy Loughor Estuary, veering northeast through unspoiled Welsh countryside. En route there are lush slopes fluffed by sheep and examples of engineering elegance (especially eighteen-arch Cynghordy Viaduct). There are stiff climbs, such as the haul up to isolated Sugar Loaf Station and its eponymous peak. There are Victorian spa towns, nature reserves and the looming Black Mountains.

The line crosses the England-Wales border at the market town of Knighton – in Welsh, Tref-y-Clawdd (Town on the Dyke). Knighton is home to the Offa's Dyke Centre, and remains of the ancient earthwork can be seen nearby.

The line terminates in Shrewsbury, county town of Shropshire. In Offa's day this strategic spot on the River Severn would have been a fortified settlement protecting the Mercian boundary. History still seeps through Shrewsbury, from its 11th-century abbey and castle to its half-timbered medieval streets.

ALTERNATIVE UK RAILWAYS
- - - - - - - - - - - - - - - - - - -

202. London–Canterbury
England, United Kingdom

Travel across the Weald like Chaucer's pilgrims in *The Canterbury Tales* (written 1387–1400), who set off from London to visit Thomas Becket's shrine in Canterbury Cathedral.

203. Swanage Railway
Dorset, United Kingdom

Ride a nostalgic steam train for 6 miles (10km) from seaside Swanage to atmospherically ruined Corfe Castle. The castle was built in the 11th century but part destroyed during the English Civil War.

204. Bury St Edmunds–Lincoln
Eastern England, United Kingdom

Start in Bury, where a key Magna Carta meeting was held in 1214. End in Lincoln, where an original 1215 copy of this revolutionary bill of rights is on display.

LEFT: The Heart of Wales Line cuts through remote countryside, including the valleys around Llandovery.

205
TRAIN DES PIGNES

Provence, France

This 94-mile (151km) narrow gauge railway first opened in the 1890s; it got its moniker from the *pignes* (pine cones) used as steam-engine tinder. These days it's hauled by diesel on its scenic journey between the Côte d'Azur city of Nice and the town of Digne-les-Bains in the Alpine foothills. En route, it twists along the Var Valley, which is littered with medieval villages. Cream of the crop is Entrevaux, with its citadel perched above the Var River and its walled old town, entered via gate and drawbridge. These were sensible precautions against the Moorish Saracens raiding Lower Provence between the 8th and 11th centuries.

206
NORWICH–GREAT YARMOUTH

Norfolk, United Kingdom

Berney Arms is a most curious station. Located on the 20-mile (32km) Norwich–Reedham–Great Yarmouth line, it sits alone on Halvergate Marshes, amid the Norfolk Broads. It was humans digging peat from the 12th to the 14th centuries that created the Broads' riverine channels. And it was a human digging in his heels in the 1840s that created Berney Arms. Thomas Berney agreed to sell his land to the railwaymen – but only if a station was put there in perpetuity. So it was, far from civilisation. Now it's a request-only stop on selected services, used by hikers and determined drinkers bound for the equally isolated Berney Arms pub, a mile away across the fields.

BELOW: The fall of Granada's Alhambra in 1492 marked the end of Moorish Spain.

AL-ANDALUS

Southern Spain

Board a luxurious train to explore the Moorish
marvels of the sunny Spanish south.

Need to know
- *Point in time: 711–1492
  (era of Moorish Spain)*
- *Length: Around
  600 miles (965km)*
- *Minimum time: 7 days*
- *Key stops: Seville,
  Jerez, Ronda, Granada,
  Linares-Baeza,
  Córdoba*
- *Countries crossed:
  Spain*

Al-Andalus was the name of Moorish Spain, the territory
created after the Arabs conquered Iberia in the 8th century.
Al-Andalus is also the name of a train running trips that
explore the Moors' lasting legacy.

Al-Andalus the train is a slice of belle époque glamour.
Its four lounge carriages are dazzlingly refurbished 1920s
and 1930s originals, and one of the sleeping carriages
formerly conveyed British royals between Calais and
southern France. However, the history outside the piano
bar is even more striking.

ABOVE: Córdoba, one of the train's key stops, was the capital of Al-Andalus for three centuries.

The trip starts amid the heat and orange trees of Seville, the once second city of Al-Andalus. It's still dominated by the 104m-high (342ft) Giralda, built as a minaret in the 12th century but later converted to a Christian bell tower. Likewise, the Moors' magnificent Alcázar palace has been augmented over the centuries, although it remains the height of *mudéjar* architecture.

After leaving Seville, more of Andalucía beckons: the sherry-soused streets of Jerez, the historic port of Cádiz (founded by Phoenicians in 1100 BC), the foothills of the Sierra Nevada, visits to the gorge-top city of Ronda and the Renaissance towns of Úbeda and Baeza. But the masterpieces of the Moors lie in Granada and Córdoba.

The hill-nestled city of Granada was the last bastion of Al-Andalus. In 1491–2, Catholic forces laid siege to its fortified Alhambra palace and Sultan Boabdil's eventual surrender here marked the end of Moorish Spain. The Alhambra complex remains spectacular, harbouring exquisitely crafted mansions, baths, barracks, mosques and gardens.

Córdoba was, for three centuries, the capital of Al-Andalus. In the city centre is the Mezquita, the Moors' finest mosque, with a fountain-filled ablutions garden and mesmerising hypostyle hall supported by 856 columns and red-white striped arches. In the 16th century, with Spain thoroughly Christianised, a cathedral nave was plonked in. But the Moorish majesty, if not the Moors themselves, remains.

EL TRANSCANTÁBRICO CLÁSICO

Northern Spain

Trace the medieval Camino de Santiago pilgrimage trail
aboard Spain's most luxurious train.

Need to know
- *Point in time: 830 (first church built in Santiago de Compostela)*
- *Length: 400 miles (644km)*
- *Minimum time: 8 days*
- *Key stops: León, Villasana de Mena, Bilbao, Santander, Oviedo, Luarca, Ferrol, Santiago de Compostela*
- *Countries crossed: Spain*

The pilgrims hiking the long-distance Camino de Santiago (Way of St James) trail across northern Spain don't experience much luxury. Just as they have since the Middle Ages, they carry their own belongings, eat cheaply at local inns and sleep in no-frills *albergues* (pilgrim hostels). Travellers covering the same region via the Transcantábrico train suffer no such privations.

For centuries the Camino de Santiago has drawn both peasants and kings to the Galician city of Santiago de Compostela. It's said that James the Apostle came to Galicia to preach the word of Jesus in the 1st century AD. He returned to the Holy Land but, after his death and subsequent martyrdom, the saint's bones allegedly returned to northeast Spain. A church was built in 829 to house the exalted relics. Within 300 years, Santiago was medieval Europe's principal pilgrimage site.

There are many Ways of St James. The Camino Francés (which starts in St-Jean Pied de Port in France) is the most popular, but there are others, including the Camino del Norte

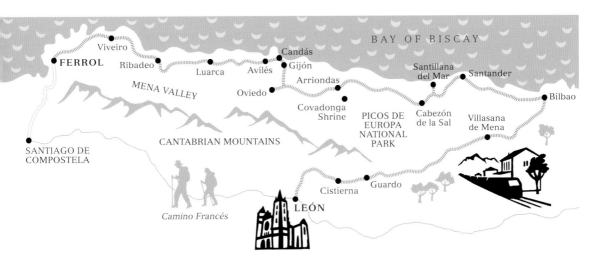

209. Florence–Rome
Italy

Make a pilgrimage along part of the Via Francigena by train. Travel via Assisi, in the footsteps of Francis of Assisi (1181–1226), to Rome's Vatican City.

210. Mariazell Railway
Austria

This 57-mile (91km) narrow gauge railway in the Styrian Alps runs to the Catholic pilgrimage centre of Mariazell, home to a miraculous Madonna icon since 1157.

211. Vall de Núria Rack Railway
Catalonia, Spain

The 12th-century Núria shrine sits high in a glacial valley in the Pyrenees, accessible only by the 8-mile (12.5km) rack railway from the town of Ribes de Freser.

212. Mount Rigi Railway
Lake Lucerne, Switzerland

Europe's first cogwheel railway (opened 1871) starts from the resort of Vitznau. It finishes at Rigi's summit, a pilgrimage spot since around 1400, thanks to its healing spring.

along Spain's north coast. Though the Transcantábrico's Clásico journey doesn't precisely follow any one of these routes, it gives a great sense of the whole region's historical significance.

The Transcantábrico doesn't follow regular train tracks, either. Instead, it utilises some of Spain's last remaining 1-metre (3ft 3in) FEVE railway lines. These run independently of the main broad gauge network and constitute Europe's largest narrow gauge train system.

The Clásico journey begins in León, a major city on the Camino Francés. Before boarding, admire the astonishing stained glass of the Gothic cathedral and the New Testament frescoes in the Basílica de San Isidoro. León's Hostal de San Marcos, a former 12th-century monastery where pilgrims sought sanctuary en route to Santiago, is now a luxury hotel.

The train offers five-star style, too. Accommodation is in hardwood-panelled suites, each with a separate bedroom, bathroom and lounge. Each night the train pulls into a quiet siding and passengers sleep on board. Most lunches and dinners are taken off-train, to showcase the region's gastronomic excellence, but breakfast is served in the dining car. Four of the public saloons, including the tea room and bar, are refurbished 1920s Pullman carriages. There's also a library and even a lively little nightclub car.

From León, the train heads east across the high plateau of Castilla y León into Basque country. Then it does an about-turn, veering westwards along the north coast (just like the Camino del Norte) to the Galician city of Ferrol. Sadly, the narrow gauge line doesn't connect from here to Santiago, so the last leg of the pilgrimage is completed by coach.

There are many highlights. The train cuts through the Cantabrian Mountains via the lush Mena Valley. It stops at the exciting cities of Bilbao (home to the Frank Gehry-designed Guggenheim Museum) and Santander. And it calls at Cabezón de la Sal, gateway to the magnificent medieval town of Santillana del Mar.

There's an off-train excursion into the Picos de Europa National Park to see the Covadonga Shrine – commemorating a Moorish defeat in 722, it's considered the birthplace of Christianity in Spain. The train also visits the Asturian capital Oviedo, where three 9th-century churches nod to when this was the country's only Christian enclave. Then there's the old town of Avilés, the sweeping

beach at Gijón, the pretty whitewashed town of Luarca and the scenic run into Ferrol.

Finally, there's Santiago itself, a UNESCO World Heritage–listed maze of alleyways with a flamboyant baroque cathedral. Inside is the reputed tomb of St James and a steady stream of pilgrims who've come – via all manner of transportation – to pay their respects.

ABOVE: The Clásico journey ends in Santiago de Compostela, where St James's tomb lies in the baroque cathedral.

213
PORTO–LISBON

Western Portugal

The 208-mile (335km) Porto–Coimbra–Lisbon journey offers a trio of treasures by train. In the 11th century, Porto became capital of the County of Portugal, the forerunner of the modern country. It's now a hill-tumbling hub of port-wine lodges at the mouth of the Douro River. An hour south by train is Coimbra, which became Portugal's first capital in 1131. Home to the country's oldest university and a youthful student population, it has both baroque palaces and buzzing cafés. Lisbon, 2 hours further south, took over as capital in 1255. It's an engaging city of characterful neighbourhoods and the best *pasteis de nata* (egg custard tarts) in Portugal.

BELMOND GRAND HIBERNIAN

Ireland

Green hills, crystal lakes, castles, folktales and whiskey – find
the essence of the Emerald Isle aboard a luxury train.

Need to know
- *Point in time: 800
  (Book of Kells written)*
- *Length: Around
  750 miles (1,200km)*
- *Minimum time: 5 days*
- *Key stops: Dublin,
  Cork, Killarney,
  Galway, Athlone,
  Westport*
- *Countries crossed:
  Ireland*

BELOW: An off-train
excursion visits legend-
shrouded Blarney Castle.

Ireland's *Book of Kells*, created around the 9th century,
was once called 'the chief treasure of the Western world'.
It's ravishing – an illuminated manuscript of the four
Gospels decorated with elaborate insular majuscule script,
Christian iconography, Celtic knots and mythical creatures,
all hand-etched in dazzling pigments. Displayed in Dublin's
Trinity College Library, in some ways it encapsulates the
beauty, spirituality and mysticism of Ireland itself.

The Belmond Grand Hibernian aims to do the same.
Launched in 2016, it is Ireland's first luxury train, with
smart carriages named after Ireland's counties and a
design aesthetic that's part Georgian Dublin, part ancient
folklore. The train's 5-day Legends and Loughs itinerary

LEFT: The Belmond Grand Hibernian offers luxurious access to Connemara.

RELIGIOUS RIDES

215. Wells–Walsingham Light Railway
Norfolk, United Kingdom

Tiny steam locos on 260mm-gauge (10.25in) track run for 4 miles (6km) to Walsingham, a pilgrimage village since 1061 when a local had a vision of the Virgin.

216. Schafberg Railway
Austria

This steep, steam-powered cog railway climbs 1,190m (3,904ft) up Schafberg Mountain. It starts in the town of St Wolfgang, founded when the saint built a church here in 976.

217. Montserrat Rack Railway
Catalonia, Spain

Ease your pilgrimage to the mountaintop monastery of Montserrat (founded 1025) via the 3-mile (5km) rack railway, crossing Pont del Centenari bridge.

218. Maastricht–Aachen
Netherlands and Germany

Aachen (Germany) was once the capital of the Carolingian Empire (600–888): relics of King Charlemagne's palace form the core of the cathedral. Maastricht (Netherlands) is a 1-hour ride away.

traces a broad loop from the capital, visiting Ireland's greatest sites and greenest countryside en route.

The train sets off from Dublin, that handsome, garrulous city on the River Liffey founded by Vikings around the 8th century. Embarkation point is Heuston Station, opened in 1846 and now named for Irish Republican Sean Heuston who was executed after the 1916 Easter Rising against the British.

From Dublin, the Grand Hibernian heads southwest, rocking through emerald scenes towards the country's second city, Cork. Here, a colourful harbour, youthful vibe and whiskey-tasting at the Jameson distillery await. Day 2 offers side-trips to kiss the fabled stone at Blarney Castle and sail on the Lakes of Killarney.

Day 3 focuses on waterside Galway, which grew from a small 12th-century fort to become capital of the Gaelic west. This is the place to sink a few stouts, seek out live music and enjoy the *craic*. Day 4 moves toward the lively Clew Bay town of Westport, via Ashford Castle (a medieval stronghold turned five-star hotel) and wild, wonderful Connemara National Park. On Day 5 the Grand Hibernian returns to Dublin.

HARAMAIN HIGH SPEED RAIL

Western Saudi Arabia

Admire the line that will speed Hajj pilgrims
between the sacred Muslim cities of Medina and Mecca.

Need to know
- *Point in time: 632 (death of Muhammad)*
- *Length: 282 miles (453km)*
- *Minimum time: 2 hours*
- *Key stops: Medina, King Abdullah Economic City, King Abdulaziz International Airport, Jeddah, Mecca*
- *Countries crossed: Saudi Arabia*

LIKE THAT? TRY THIS

- - - - - - - - - - - - - - - -

220. Ankara–Konya
Central Turkey

High-speed trains whizz from Ankara to Konya almost as fast as Konya's dervishes whirl. Find them at the shrine to Rumi, the poet who founded Sufism in 1273.

The new Haramain High Speed Rail is set to link the two most sacred Muslim cities. Construction of the 282-mile (453km) line between Medina and Mecca began in 2009, and was set for completion by 2012. Now, a 2018 opening looks likely, with contract disputes and the difficulties of building across hot, inhospitable, windblown desert blamed for delays.

However, this line can't come quick enough. Since the death of the Prophet Muhammad in 632, Mecca's Kaaba, a small stone building within the city's Al-Masjid al-Haram mosque, has been the holiest site in Islam. One of the Five Pillars of Islam is the Hajj – the pilgrimage to the Kaaba – which every Muslim is expected to undertake at least once in their life. Fifty years ago, around 100,000 pilgrims a year visited Mecca. Now the number is more like 3 million, putting huge pressure on transport infrastructure.

Because of the expected high usage of the Haramain railway, its stations have been very carefully designed. For starters, they will be vast. Designed by architects Foster and Partners, the four stations will in total cover an area more than thirty times the size of London's Trafalgar Square and will initially accommodate 60 million passengers each year. They will also have an Islamic design aesthetic, incorporating metal *mashrabiya* latticework and significant colour palettes: the gold used at Mecca Station will mirror the gold leaf of the Kaaba; vibrant green at Medina Station will reference the city's Mosque of the Prophet.

For Muslims, the line will be a boon. Non-Muslims are forbidden from entering central Mecca or Medina, where Muhammad is buried. However, the Haramain line will also connect King Abdulaziz International Airport to the Red Sea port of Jeddah, which *is* open to non-Muslim visitors. Jeddah's Al Balad district, a hubbub of souks and old coral-block buildings, is the best place to get a feel for Saudi Arabia's rich past.

RIGHT: The new high-speed line will help millions of Muslim pilgrims make their pilgrimage to Mecca.

CHINON–ROUEN

Northern France

Follow the life and death of Joan of Arc,
teenage heroine of medieval France.

Need to know
- *Point in time: 1412– 1431 (life of Joan of Arc)*
- *Length: Around 265 miles (426km)*
- *Minimum time: 5 hours 30 minutes*
- *Key stops: Chinon, Tours, Blois, Orléans, Paris, Rouen*
- *Countries crossed: France*

France has an excellent rail network, which can be used to follow Joan of Arc – peasant girl turned saint, heroine and enduring national icon.

In 1412, when Joan was born, France and England were fighting the so-called Hundred Years' War (1337–1453). As a teen, Joan had beatific visions telling her to oust the invaders. So in 1429 she went to the Loire Valley town of Chinon and persuaded French Crown Prince Charles to give her an army to free besieged Orléans.

Our rail journey begins at the mighty ruins of the Château de Chinon, where you can wander the remains of the great hall in which Joan met Charles, and the medieval old town below. From Chinon, Joan marched northeast along the Loire, just as the railway does. She paused in the city of Tours, where she was given a suit of armour. Tours is still outfitting passers-by: the half-timbered old centre is packed with clothes shops, as well as bistros serving hearty Touraine cuisine.

Next, Joan (and the train) hit the city of Blois. This is where she crossed the river – though the current stone bridge dates from the 18th century. Joan was also blessed by the Archbishop of Reims at the Château de Blois. This castle has been much altered, but still dominates the city.

Joan proceeded to liberate Orléans. She celebrated in St Croix Cathedral, since rebuilt; now Joan's tale is told in the cathedral's stained glass. The house where Joan stayed was destroyed by Nazi bombs but has been faithfully reconstructed.

Finally, continue north, via Paris (which Joan tried but failed to free), to end in the Norman city of Rouen. Joan was burned at the stake here in 1431, aged just nineteen – a flower bed in the Place du Vieux Marché marks the spot. A Joan of Arc Museum opened in the former Archbishop's Palace in 2015, where part of her trial took place.

TRAIN DU PAYS CATHARE ET DU FENOUILLÈDES

Pyrenees, France

The Cathars sprung up around 1100. A dissident religious sect, they dared question the theology of Rome, so Pope Innocent III ordered their annihilation. The Cathars sought refuge (unsuccessfully) in castles built among the foothills of the Pyrenees – and this 37-mile (60km) railway explores that region. First opened in 1904, the line now carries the tourist 'Train Rouge', climbing from the town of Rivesaltes, near Perpignan, to the mountain village of Axat. It negotiates forests, vineyards, viaducts and tunnels. And it passes medieval eyries where the Cathars once tried to hide: ruined Fenouillet Castle and rock-top Puilaurens, which fell to the pope's crusaders in 1255.

LEFT: Joan of Arc was executed in the city of Rouen in 1431.

The Middle Ages   **181**

223
BATTLEFIELD LINE

Leicestershire, United Kingdom

It's 22 August 1485. King Richard III and Henry Tudor (his rival for the English crown) face off in Bosworth Field, along with 20,000-plus fighting men. Hostilities begin soon after dawn. By noon, Richard is dead. The Tudor era has begun. But it's hard to imagine all that bloodshed aboard the 5-mile (8km) steam-hauled Battlefield Line. The railway runs from the village of Shackerstone along the canal through peaceful Leicestershire countryside to Shenton Station at the foot of Ambion Hill. Ambion was thought to be the location of the Battle of Bosworth Field, and there's a Heritage Centre here. However, historians now think the skirmish happened a few miles further south.

224
LENNAKATTEN VINTAGE RAILWAY

Uppsala, Eastern Sweden

No prizes for guessing the winner of 984's Battle of Fýrisvellir, a fight for the Swedish throne between Styrbjörn the Strong and Eric the Victorious. The battle took place on the marshy Fýrisvellir Plain, now site of Uppsala, one of Sweden's oldest cities and an important centre for trade and *ting* (governing assembly) gatherings in the Middle Ages. Uppsala is also the starting point of the scenic, steam-pulled, 20-mile (33km) Lennakatten Vintage Railway. Trains run in summer, heading east from Uppsala, across the plains to the little town of Faringe, with stops at lakeside villages – Marielund, Fjällnora and Almunge – en route.

BELOW: The Coastal Pacific cuts through the world-class vineyards of the Blenheim region.

COASTAL PACIFIC

South Island, New Zealand

Roll along the dramatic Pacific shore where Polynesian
seafarers first arrived 800 years ago.

Need to know

- *Point in time: 1250–1300 (Polynesians arrived on New Zealand)*
- *Length: 216 miles (347km)*
- *Minimum time: 5 hours 30 minutes*
- *Key stops: Picton, Blenheim, Kaikoura, Christchurch (Addington)*
- *Countries crossed: New Zealand*

New Zealanders have a phrase describing something that's really good, instead of merely average. They say: 'Sweet as'. Well, the Coastal Pacific train, which hugs the northeast shore of South Island, is 'sweet as' indeed.

It took time to build something this special. The Main North Line, the track along which the Coastal Pacific now runs, was begun in the 1870s but took 75 years to complete. The first section, between the port of Picton and the town of Blenheim, opened in 1875. Slowly, the railway inched south but construction was stalled by the outbreak of the First World War and the Great Depression. Work resumed by 1935. Then labour shortages during the Second World War caused another hiatus, although the realisation that a railway

MORE MAORI
HERITAGE

**226. Weka Pass
Railway**
*South Island,
New Zealand*

This 8-mile (13km) line
links Waipara and
Waikari. It cuts through
the Weka Pass, which is
etched with ancient
Maori rock art.

**227. Auckland
Western Line**
Auckland, New Zealand

Maori first settled in
what's now Auckland
around 1350. The
Western Line runs via
Mount Eden and Mount
Albert, where Maori
earthworks can be seen.

could help save limited resources such as petrol spurred on
the project. The line linking Picton with Christchurch, South
Island's largest city, finally opened in 1945.

Today, many rail passengers using this stretch of the
Main North Line buy a combination ferry-train ticket and
begin their journey on North Island, starting with a 3-hour
ferry trip across the Cook Strait. This scenic sailing leaves
the harbour at Wellington, New Zealand's capital, and
crosses open water before sidling between headlands and
into Queen Charlotte Sound to reach Picton. It makes you
think of the first, intrepid Polynesian seafarers – the
ancestors of the Maori – who somehow happened upon
New Zealand in their canoes, around 1250. As it happens,
one of the country's earliest archaeological sites, Wairau
Bar, is just south of Picton. In 1939, a schoolboy discovered
a burial site here containing forty-four human skeletons,
dating from 1285 to 1300. DNA analysis suggests some
of these individuals were early Polynesian settlers.

New Zealand's first arrivals did tend to stick to shore,
which is mostly what the Coastal Pacific does. The train
runs daily, October–April, leaving from Picton's 1914
weatherboarded station, right
by the dock. It curves through
the valley and is soon swaying
through the vine-streaked
Marlborough region. First stop
is Blenheim, Marlborough's main
town and a hub for gourmet
dining and wine tastings – there
are more than twenty vineyards
within easy striking distance.

After Blenheim the train heaves
up a pass through the hills; snow
peaks begin to rise in the distance.
It crosses the Awatere Bridge,
skims Lake Grassmere and, about
90 minutes after leaving Picton,
reaches the sea. For the next
60 miles (97km) or so, the Coastal
Pacific passes rocky headlands,
sandy beaches, swooping seabirds
and sunbathing seals. Happily,
the carriages have huge picture
windows and roof skylights;

there's also an open-air carriage where you can breathe in the sea air and take photos unimpeded by glass.

The best bet for seeing marine life, though, is to disembark at the mountain-backed town of Kaikoura, whale-watching capital of New Zealand. The HQ for whale tours is Kaikoura's old station building. This is where the Main North Line was officially opened in 1945; a plaque commemorating the eight men killed during the line's construction can still be seen.

After Kaikoura, more spectacular shoreline follows before the tracks veer inland, swapping the sea for verdant valleys. The train terminates in Addington, a Christchurch suburb once home to the huge New Zealand Railways depot, where many locomotives were built. It's a short bus or taxi ride into the city centre, which is rebounding creatively from the devastating earthquake of 2011. A transitional Cardboard Cathedral has been built to serve the congregation of the damaged 19th-century original, while shops and cafés have opened in colourful shipping containers. But then New Zealand has been a land of survivors for nearly 800 years.

BELOW: The temporary Cardboard Cathedral stands in the earthquake-rocked city of Christchurch.

VERDE CANYON RAILROAD

Arizona, United States

Trundle slowly through a Wild West chasm that's full of
fantastic flora, fauna and Native American history.

Need to know

- *Point in time: 650
  (Sinagua peoples
  moved into Arizona)*
- *Length: 20 miles
  (32km)*
- *Minimum time:
  4 hours (round trip)*
- *Key stops: Clarkdale,
  Perkinsville*
- *Countries crossed:
  United States*

When Spanish explorers first ventured into the peaks of
central Arizona, they called them the Sierra Sin Agua:
'mountains without water'. Centuries later, archaeologists
borrowed this name for the Native Americans who
inhabited the region from around 650 to 1425. However,
the Sinagua peoples in Arizona's Verde Valley had water
in ready supply.

The Verde Canyon, at the edge of the dramatic Mogollon
Rim, is a rare riparian sliver amid the high desert. Its rusty
sandstone cliffs and black basalt formations are cut through
by the Verde River, which feeds a diverse ecosystem.
Cottonwoods and sycamores line the banks. Prickly pear
cacti flower crimson each autumn; marigolds and larkspur

bloom in spring. Wildlife is abundant, from coyotes and bobcats to songbirds and raptors. From December to March in particular, the canyon is a hotspot for bald eagles.

The Verde River is not the only thing to wiggle through this canyon. A 38-mile (61km) branch railway was built here in 1912 to transport smelted copper from the mines at Jerome to Drake station on the Santa Fe main line. Since 1990, a 20-mile (32km) segment of the route has operated as the Verde Canyon Railroad.

The journey starts from Clarkdale, which was one of the first modern mining towns, laid out in 1914. Its original downtown area is now on the National Register of Historic Places. Clarkdale's current railway depot was built in the 1990s but the rolling stock has richer pedigree. The trains are pulled by 1950s FP7 diesel locomotives, while the oldest passenger carriage in the fleet is the 1936 *Santa Fe Bell*. It still has its original leather-topped bar, dating from its tenure running the Atchison, Topeka and Santa Fe Railroad between Chicago and Los Angeles.

ABOVE: Heritage locomotives serve Arizona's Verde Canyon Railroad.

**LIKE THAT?
TRY THIS**

- - - - - - - - - - - - - - - - - -

**229. Missouri
River Runner**
Missouri, United States

Ride from Kansas City
to St Louis via lands
once roamed by the
Mississippian culture.
Their mound site of
Cahokia (800–1600) is
just over the river from
St Louis.

Passengers can ride First Class, Coach or Caboose
(a luxury private-hire carriage). All classes can access
open-air carriages that are shaded from the elements but
offer full exposure to the landscapes. Expert staff talk about
the canyon's geology, biology and anthropology en route.

The area's human history is apparent before you board.
Tuzigoot National Monument, a pueblo built by the Sinagua
people between 1125 and 1400, sits on a Verde Valley
outcrop just east of Clarkdale. Here you can see the remains
of the ancient village, which once had eighty rooms and
housed around 250 people. This is the biggest and best-
preserved of the Sinagua ruins in the Verde Valley but there
are many more, some of which are visible from the train.

The Verde Canyon Railroad is certainly designed for
sightseeing, trundling along at a lazy 12 miles per hour
(19kph) on its out-and-back excursion. From Clarkdale
(Milepost 38), the train first passes the slag heap from the
old copper mine. Near Milepost 37, Sinagua cliff dwellings
can be seen up on the canyon sides; there's also an old wall,
built to conceal Sinagua hunters from their prey. Near
Milepost 33, the railway negotiates its highest bridge, the
Superintendent Of Bridges (SOB) trestle, where you can see
the whole train as it arcs across.

The tracks skirt a prehistoric lake bed favoured by bald
eagles before spanning Sycamore Creek and slicing through
the Coconino and Prescott National Forests. At Milepost 29,
there's an area of Native American dwellings and
petroglyphs. Peculiar rock formations follow, before the
train enters a 207m (680ft) long tunnel near Milepost 22.
There's one more bridge, then the train reaches Perkinsville
ranch (founded 1900). Parts of the movie *How the West Was
Won* (1962) were filmed here.

Perkinsville's old wooden train depot is now used as
a barn. But the train still pulls up so the engines can be
disengaged and shunted to the opposite end for the return
trip to Clarkdale – a chance to relive the Verde Valley's
history all over again.

RIGHT: The Verde Canyon
Railroad offers views of high
cliffs and dramatic desert.

METRO LINE 2

Mexico City, Mexico

Ride Mexico City's subway to get a feel for the Aztec's
lake-island capital, now buried beneath the modern metropolis.

Need to know

- *Point in time: 1325–1521 (Tenochtitlán was the Aztec capital)*
- *Length: 13 miles (21km)*
- *Minimum time: 36 minutes*
- *Key stops: Cuatro Caminos, Tacuba, Hidalgo, Zócalo, Pino Suárez, Chabacano, Tasqueña*
- *Countries crossed: Mexico*

BELOW: Mexico City's Monument to the Revolution is on Metro Line 2.

Tenochtitlán was a knockout. It was founded in 1325, allegedly on the orders of the god Huitzilopochtli, who told the migrating Aztecs to settle where they saw an eagle on a cactus eating a snake. This they did, building an impressive city of plazas, temples, canals, causeways and *chinampas* (floating gardens) on a rocky lake-island in the Valley of Mexico. At its zenith Tenochtitlán was home to 300,000 people. Then Spanish conquistador Hernán Cortés turned up.

Cortés conquered Tenochtitlán in 1521 – and did a thorough job of destroying it. The buildings were razed and a new city constructed on top. No remnants of the Aztec's awesome capital remained. Or so everyone thought, until Mexico City – the metropolis that sprang from Tenochtitlán's ashes – began building a metro.

Talismán

Tacuba Cuitláhuac
CUATRO   Popotla
CAMINOS   *Hidalgo*

Bellas
Artes

Moctezuma

Revolución   Zócalo

MEXICO
CITY

Pino
Suárez

Line 4

Niños
Héroes

Line 1

Chabacano

Villa de Cortés

Line 2

Zapata

Line 3

TASQUEÑA

Light Rail Line

XOCHIMILCO

Construction started in 1967; by 1972, three lines had opened and many archaeological discoveries had been made. For example, when excavating Pino Suárez station, workmen found a circular pyramid dedicated to Ehécatl, Aztec god of wind. They left it in place, and the station was built around it. The Metro has turned up some more unusual relics, too. While excavating Talismán station, a 12,000-year-old mammoth skeleton was unearthed.

In 1978, it wasn't railwaymen but electricians who made a major find. Digging near the Zócalo, Mexico City's huge main square, they stumbled upon the Aztecs' Templo Mayor, the vast, multi-tiered, double temple dedicated to Huitzilopochtli and rain god Tlaloc. This was the fulcrum of the Aztec world, hidden buried beneath the centre of the modern city.

Despite all this underground intrigue, Mexico City's Metro is one of the biggest in the world. It has nearly 200 stations, lines totalling over 141 miles (227km) and carries 1.6 billion passengers every year. It's also a dynamic history lesson; the names of its stations often commemorate people key to the country's past. Moctezuma station is named for the mighty Aztec emperor defeated by Cortés. Niños Héroes (Heroic Children) station is dedicated to the brave cadets who defended Chapultepec Military Academy during the 1846–48 Mexican-American War. Zapata station honours Emiliano Zapata, hero of the 1910–20 Mexican Revolution.

Metro Line 2 offers a particularly satisfying connection to the past. From Cuatro Caminos, it heads east to Tacuba station, which sits on the site of Tlacopan, a city-state once ruled by the Aztecs. Cuitláhuac station is near one of Mexico City's main thoroughfares (Avenida México–Tacuba), which mirrors one of Tenochtitlán's causeways. Near Popotla station are the remains of a Montezuma cypress under which Hernán Cortés is said to have sat and cried after a setback in 1520.

Revolución station, a few stops on, is near the triumphal 67m (220ft) tall Monument to the Revolution. Next is Hidalgo, named for the architect of Mexico's 1810 War of Independence.

Zócalo station is at the very heart of both Aztec and modern Mexico City. This is the stop for the huge central square, where a gigantic Mexican flag is raised and lowered each day. It's also the stop for visiting the cathedral, the National Palace and the ruins of the Templo Mayor. A subterranean walkway leads from Zócalo to the next station, Pino Suárez, past the Aztec temple unearthed by those early Metro-builders.

From the city centre, Line 2 heads south, passing a station named after Cortés himself to finish at Tasqueña. From here, if you like, you can continue on the Light Rail Line to the colourful, watery suburb of Xochimilco, Mexico City's 'Little Venice'. Built on the site of a pre-Columbian lake-town, Xochimilco was once connected to Tenochtitlán by a canal. Now it's the last reminder of the canals and *chinampas* that used to riddle Tenochtitlán and the Mexico Valley over 500 years ago.

231
YUCATÁN HIGH-SPEED RAIL

Yucatán, Mexico

During the later Maya period, from around 600 to 1200, Mexico's culture-rich Yucatán Peninsula was abuzz. Marvellous temple cities such as Chichén Itzá, Uxmal and clifftop Tulum peaked in population and architectural splendour. This was the place to be. Now it's possible that a new wave of activity might hit the region. The Mexican government has proposed a high-speed rail network for the Yucatán (which currently has no railways at all). According to plans, trains travelling at up to 110 miles per hour (around 180kph) would link the regional capital Mérida and the Caribbean port of Punta Venado, also connecting key Maya sites. However, though originally slated for completion in 2017, construction has yet to begin . . .

LEFT: Mexico City today – but who knows the full extent of the Aztec remains beneath?

The Middle Ages   193

DAKAR–BAMAKO EXPRESS

Senegal and Mali

Reminisce about this train that crawled across the once gold-rich plains of West Africa – and hope it may do so again.

Need to know

- *Point in time: 1230–1600 (period of Mali Empire)*
- *Length: 768 miles (1,235km)*
- *Minimum time: 46 hours*
- *Key stops: Dakar, Thiès, Diourbel, Guinguinéo, Kaffrine, Tambacounda, Kidira, Kayes, Diamou, Kati, Bamako*
- *Countries crossed: Senegal, Mali*

LIKE THAT? TRY THIS

- - - - - - - - - - - - - - - - - - -

233. Meknès–Fès
Morocco

Ride a train that links two of Morocco's imperial cities in 45 minutes. Meknès (founded in the 11th century) has magnificent monuments and mosques. Fès (founded 789) has a labyrinthine medieval medina.

LEFT: The Dakar–Bamako Express – a local lifeline – ground to a halt in 2009.

What will be the fate of the Dakar–Bamako Express? Until recently, a train service ran haphazardly between the capitals of Senegal and Mali. Second-hand rolling stock wheezed along French-laid rails, connecting the Atlantic port at Dakar to Bamako on the River Niger. The scheduled journey time was just under 2 days, but delays of 4, 8, even 12 hours weren't uncommon. Trains were filthy and dilapidated. It was advisable to buy your own mattress for the journey, and to board quickly to secure a compartment with a functioning door. The border crossing at Kidira could take several hours.

Despite all this, the train was a local lifeline. It was also a unique way to grind across the West African plains, past the mud-brick villages and station hawkers, the red earth and yellow savannah, the monkeys in the baobab trees. However, with its infrastructure in tatters and its coffers empty, the misnamed 'Express' ground to a halt in 2009.

There used to be plenty of money in this part of West Africa. The Mali Empire (1230–1600) was the largest ever to flourish in the region. At its peak, it stretched from the Atlantic coast of modern-day Senegal across Mali to Niger, taking in southern Mauritania, Guinea, even northern Ghana. It thrived thanks to trade in copper, salt and gold – in the early 14th century the Mali Empire was the source of almost half the gold in the Old World.

Now it looks like the wealth the railway so dearly needs might be materialising. In 2016, the governments of Senegal and Mali entered an agreement with a Chinese contractor to reinvigorate the line. The deal would include the modernisation of stations and a track upgrade, so the speed of passenger trains could be increased from 12 miles per hour (19kph) to 62 miles per hour (100kph). Who knows? The Express may run again . . .

234
FUJIKYU RAILWAY

Honshu, Japan

Mount Fuji looms large in the
Japanese psyche. The perfectly
conical volcano is considered
sacred, proliferates in Japanese art
and even features on the 1,000 yen
note. It dominates this little train
journey too. The 16-mile (26km)
Fujikyu Railway is the closest you
can get to Mount Fuji by rail.
It runs between the city of Otsuki
and the lakeside town of
Kawaguchiko, although many
disembark at midway Mount Fuji
station. From here, climbers keen
to conquer the mountain catch the
Fuji Tozan Bus to the start of the
trailheads, aiming to emulate the
unnamed monk who supposedly
first summited the peak in 663.

235
BEIJING–HANGZHOU

Eastern China

In 609 the cities of Beijing and
Hangzhou – along with five of
China's great rivers – were finally
connected by the 1,104-mile
(1,776km) Grand Canal. Begun
between the 4th and 5th centuries
BC, it became the world's longest
manmade channel. Now, the train
ride between the cities (via
Shanghai) plots a similar course
through this fertile region. Get off
at Xuzhou, where the waterway
visits the Western Han Dynasty
Terracotta Warriors Museum.
Or stop in Suzhou to see the canal
at its prettiest, crossed by stone
bridges and lined with red
lanterns. In lakeside Hangzhou see
the waterway come to an end and
visit the Grand Canal Museum.

236
REISSZUG

Salzburg, Austria

You can't ride Salzburg's Reisszug but you can certainly appreciate it. The small, private funicular railway that transports goods from the city's Nonnberg Nunnery to the courtyard of hilltop Hohensalzburg Castle is the world's oldest funicular. Built around 1495, the Reisszug originally ran on sleigh-style runners but wooden rails were soon adopted. The lift was hauled up on hemp rope by humans or oxen, and had to pass through five concentric walls, each with a solid wooden door, to reach the castle's inner sanctum. The rails are now steel but little else has changed. The Reisszug follows the same route and to this day is used to carry supplies.

237
FLYING DUTCHMAN FUNICULAR

Western Cape, South Africa

When Portuguese explorer Bartolomeu Dias came sailing around the bottom of Africa in 1488 – the first European ever to do so – he surely would have appreciated the Flying Dutchman. This short funicular makes light work of Cape Point, one of the continent's most southerly and most treacherous extremities. It takes just 3 minutes to whisk passengers up 87m (285ft) from the Cape's lower station to the upper lighthouse. From here, you can enjoy big views of the bush-blanketed hills, crashing waves and hazardous rocks. You may even spot the ghost of the original *Flying Dutchman*, the 17th-century galleon shipwrecked offshore, for which the funicular is named.

CHAPTER FOUR

TOWARDS THE MODERN WORLD

Journey into the age of discovery and enlightenment, from AD 1500 to 1800, when new frontiers were explored and railways were just around the corner.

PALACE ON WHEELS

Northern India

Explore marvellous Mughal architecture and resplendent
Rajput cities in the style of a *maharaja*.

Need to know

- Point in time: 1526–1857 (reign of Mughal Empire)
- Length: 1,225 miles (1,972km)
- Minimum time: 8 days
- Key stops: New Delhi, Jaipur, Sawai Madhopur, Chittorgarh, Udaipur, Jaisalmer, Jodhpur, Bharatpur, Agra
- Countries crossed: India

India's Rajput *maharajas* (princes) used to travel in high style. The most important of them had private railway carriages, bespoke 'palaces on wheels' bedecked with tapestries, frescoes, golden embroidery and *mashrabiya* latticework. Indian independence in 1947 effectively ended the era of the Rajput states, so these carriages became redundant. That is, until India's first luxury tourist train gave them a new lease of life.

The Palace on Wheels launched in 1982, with a steam locomotive hauling original maharajas' coaches. These days the engine is diesel and the carriages are better-equipped replicas, with en-suite bathrooms and air-con. However, they're just as sumptuous. The Sirohi carriage, for example, is decorated with coloured glass and semiprecious stones, like the famous Gold Fort near Pratapgarh. The Jaisalmer

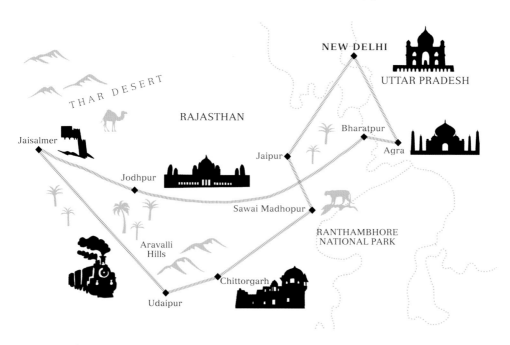

ABOVE: Staff pose proudly with their Palace on Wheels, during a loop through Rajasthan.

carriage has a ceiling of carved *jharokhas* (wooden windows) inspired by that desert city's mansions. Every carriage also has its own *khidmatgar* (personal attendant), while cuisine fit for royalty is served in chandelier-swung dining cars. There are now several luxury trains in India but the Palace on Wheels is the granddaddy of them all.

The train's classic itinerary is 'A Week in Wonderland', a loop from capital New Delhi though the regal state of Rajasthan. Modern Rajasthan encompasses most of ancient Rajputana, the territory once ruled by patrilineal Hindu clans dating back to the 6th century. However, it was the Rajputs' relations with the Mughal Empire that gave the region its richest legacy. The Muslim Mughals, led by Mongol warlord Babur, defeated the Kingdom of Delhi in 1526 and proceeded to dominate the subcontinent until 1857. The Rajputs resisted the Islamic invaders, but they also came to an accord with them. This composite culture resulted in some of India's most magnificent architecture.

Chaotic Delhi is where the Mughal Empire began. The city is home to some of the Mughals' most striking

monuments: the bulky Red Fort; Jama Masjid, India's
largest mosque; the elegant Persian tomb of Emperor
Humayun. The Palace on Wheels leaves from the city's
Safdarjung Station, after passengers have received their
ceremonial welcome – a glass of wine, a garland around
the neck, a *tika* mark on the forehead.

First the train heads southwest to Jaipur. The rose-
washed 'Pink City' was founded in the 18th century by
Maharaja Jai Singh II, former resident of nearby Amber
Fort (a spectacular sandstone stronghold). Jai Singh was
obsessed by science, as the huge astronomical instruments
of his Jantar Mantar observatory attest.

Next the train calls at the city of Sawai Madhopur. This is
jumping-off point for safaris in Ranthambhore National
Park, a jungly wilderness dotted with Mughal ruins and wild
tigers. Akbar (Mughal emperor, 1556–1605) started the
tradition of *shikar* (royal sport hunting) in the 16th century,
and the big cats were the main prize. Now tourists 'hunting'
with cameras are helping tigers' survival.

Further southwest the train stops at mighty Chittorgarh
Fort, then the gleaming-white lakeside city of Udaipur.
Udaipur's City Palace (built from 1553) is the most glorious
fusion of Rajasthani and Mughal styles, while its 18th-
century Lake Palace, rising wedding-cake-like from Lake
Pichola, is India's most photogenic. Jaisalmer, a walled
citadel in the Thar Desert, is more like a sandcastle, swirled
with *Arabian Nights* mystique.

From Jaisalmer the train returns east, first to the 'Blue
City' of Jodhpur. Once the domain of the Marwari Rajput,
Jodhpur is dominated by gargantuan Mehrangarh Fort.
Finally, before looping back to Delhi, the train reaches Agra
in Uttar Pradesh, home to the Mughals' impressive Red Fort
and a scatter of mausolea, not least the dreamy marble
Taj Mahal. Built 1631–48 by Emperor Shah Jahan, it is
a well-nigh perfect relic of the Mughal reign.

ABOVE RIGHT: The Palace
on Wheels calls at Jaipur,
home to the Hawa Mahal
(Palace of the Winds).

242
KONKAN RAILWAY

Western India

Completed in 1998, the 461-mile (741km) Konkan Railway connects the megalopolis of Mumbai with the port of Mangalore in Karnataka. It's an engineering masterstroke: more than 2,000 bridges and around ninety tunnels were required to forge a route between the Arabian Sea and the Sahyadri Hills. Along the way are rivers, valleys, mountains, mango trees, coconut palms and tiny villages. The railway also enters the heartland of Portuguese India; the Iberian nation ruled parts of the subcontinent from 1505 until 1961. In 1510, Old Goa became the capital of the Portuguese viceroyalty. Disembark at Karmali Station to wander the abandoned convents and churches of Old Goa, once considered the 'Rome of the East'.

THE BLUE TRAIN

South Africa

Glide between Pretoria and Cape Town, passing ancient landscapes aboard one of the world's most glamorous trains.

Need to know
- *Point in time: 1652 (Cape Town founded)*
- *Length: 994 miles (1,600km)*
- *Minimum time: 27 hours*
- *Key stops: Pretoria, Matjiesfontein, Kimberley, Cape Town*
- *Countries crossed: South Africa*

BELOW: Southbound Blue Trains visit Kimberley's Big Hole diamond mine.

Wood panels, white linens, gold taps. A butler to every three passengers. As much South African wine as you can drink. As many Cuban cigars as you can smoke. No expense is spared aboard the cobalt-coloured carriages of the Blue Train, which glides between South Africa's capital Pretoria and the southwest city of Cape Town.

The Blue Train has always been glamorous. In the 1920s, its predecessors – the Union Limited and the Union Express – were designed to carry the moneyed elite who had become rich from the country's goldfields. Early onboard luxuries included card tables and hot water. After being commandeered by the military during the Second World War, the trains were refurbished and, over time, became today's 'Ritz on rails'.

LEFT: Northbound Blue Trains stop at Matjiesfontein, so passengers can take tea at the Victorian-era Lord Milner Hotel.

But though the carriages exude early-20th-century romance, the view out of the window feels older and more wild. Cape Town was founded by the Dutch in 1652 and, while the settlement grew, the Cape Fold Mountains and the vast semi-desert of the Great Karoo presented a formidable barrier to explorers venturing further inland. That landscape has now been mastered by the railway (Cape Town and Pretoria were linked in 1893), but it feels no less challenging. The train's huge windows look out onto endless, grassy veld punctuated by pronking springbok, herds of wild ostrich, waterfalls tinkling down raw rocks, bush-cloaked mountains and big starry skies.

The southbound train stops at the town of Kimberley for a visit to the Big Hole mine, dug during the 1870s diamond rush. The northbound train pauses at Matjiesfontein, a Victorian time-warp town; there's a chance to explore its peculiarly British streets and take a glass of sherry in the 19th-century Lord Milner Hotel.

As an aside, while the Blue Train is the ultimate indulgence, the less flashy Shosholoza Meyl train runs virtually the same route (Johannesburg–Cape Town) for around a twentieth of the price.

OLD MINES AND EARLY SOCIETIES

244. Douglas–Port Erin
Isle of Man

The British purchased sovereignty over the Isle of Man in 1765. This 15-mile (25km) narrow gauge steam railway runs from its capital Douglas to Port Erin.

245. Algeciras–Bobadilla Railway
Southern Spain

The Spanish headland of Gibraltar was ceded to Britain in 1713. In 1890, the Algeciras–Bobadilla Railway to gorge-top Ronda was built so that British officers could escape the heat.

246. Bangkok Skytrain
Thailand

Zip around frenetic, temple- and traffic-filled Bangkok – Thai capital since 1767 – aboard this 22-mile (36km) network of elevated trains.

247. Washington DC–Williamsburg
United States

It's a 165-mile (265km) journey from the United States' capital to its most famous old town, colonial Williamsburg, founded in 1699.

South Africa's luxurious Blue Train route (previous page) begins – or ends – in the city of Cape Town, founded by the Dutch in 1652. Here, Table Mountain looms over the city's cosmopolitan streets and ocean shores.

248
PARIS–MOSCOW EXPRESS

France, Germany, Poland, Belarus and Russia

In 1693, English pacifist William Penn became the first to propose the idea of a pan-European parliament. Having earlier founded the state of Pennsylvania and advocated unification of the American colonies he suggested that a similar 'United States of Europe' could help prevent wars. The direct, once-weekly 2,164-mile (3,483km) Paris–Moscow Express feels a bit like this premise in train form. From Paris it passes through Strasbourg – appropriately, given that the rosy-stoned French city is the official seat of the European Parliament. The train also whizzes past major cities including Frankfurt, Berlin, Warsaw and Minsk before arriving in Moscow around 37 hours later.

249
CORK–COBH SUBURBAN RAIL

County Cork, Southern Ireland

Cork Harbour has witnessed many significant departures. From 1611 to 1870, thousands of Irish criminals were deported from here to penal colonies in the United States, and later to Australia. Three million emigrants also left from here, seeking a better life abroad. And on 12 April 1912, RMS *Titanic* made her last port of call in Cork Harbour; she sank 3 days later. The most significant train departure is the Cork–Cobh Suburban Rail. The 11.5-mile (18.5km) route runs east around the harbour from the lively city of Cork to the pretty island town of Cobh. Here, a museum in the old Victorian station recounts the port's maritime history.

250
COPENHAGEN–MALMÖ

Denmark and Sweden

At the beginning of the 17th
century, a journey across the
Øresund Strait would have been
a trip from Denmark to, well,
Denmark. But in 1658, the Danes
ceded the eastern shore of the
strategic waterway to Sweden,
and the Øresund marked the
border between the countries.
These days, trains glide from
Copenhagen (the Danish capital)
to Malmö (Sweden's third-largest
city) under *and* over the Strait.
Opened in 2000, the 10-mile
(16km) Øresund connection
comprises three sections: a 5-mile
(8km) cable-stayed bridge; a
2.5-mile (4km) seabed tunnel; and,
linking the two, the manmade
island of Peberholm, which also
provides a haven for wildlife.

251
RIO METRO LINE 4

Rio de Janeiro, Brazil

Rio opened an underground
system in 1979. But it was during
later excavations for Line 4, a new
10-mile (16km) subway to connect
the chic beach neighbourhood
of Ipanema to the main 2016
Olympic Park at Barra da Tijuca,
that an interesting pile of junk
was found. In the city's southern
Leopoldina area, Metro builders
found an ancient rubbish dump,
containing all sorts of treasures.
There were stone tools, thought
to be 3,000 years old. But there
were also objects discarded in the
colonial and imperial periods,
from the 17th to 19th centuries.
Artefacts included coins, pipes,
unopened perfume bottles and
even an ivory toothbrush.

TREN CRUCERO

Ecuador

Hop aboard a luxury train on a revitalised rail network
to explore huge volcanoes and impressive colonial cities.

Need to know
- *Point in time: 1534
  and 1538 (Quito and
  Guayaquil founded)*
- *Length: 277 miles
  (446km)*
- *Minimum time: 3 days*
- *Key stops: Durán
  (Guayaquil), Yaguachi,
  Bucay, Alausí, Colta,
  Riobamba, Urbina,
  Quito*
- *Countries crossed:
  Ecuador*

BELOW: Trains rumble
once more through the
Ecuadorean Andes.

The Tren Crucero is more than a train – it's a phoenix risen
from the ashes. A decade ago, Ecuador's railway network
– such a proud feat of early 20th-century engineering – lay
in tatters. Most freight and scheduled services had ceased.
Floods and landslides had damaged tracks. Engines broke
and were never mended. Stations were crumbling. In places,
locals even began building over the rails. A few disjointed
tourist trains puttered along short sections, but the future
looked black as coal.

That changed in 2008, when Ecuadorean president, and
railway fan, Rafael Correa gave the go-ahead for a huge
project to revamp the network. The 277-mile (446km) line
between capital Quito and the west-coast port of Guayaquil
reopened in 2013. An additional 34-mile (54km) section
north of Quito, between the towns of Otavalo and Ibarra,
opened in 2015. The luxury Tren Crucero now runs a 4-day
trip along the whole route, part pulled by diesel, part by
vintage steam engines. The trip also includes nights off-train
in characterful haciendas as well as bus excursions into
villages and national parks.

IBARRA

Cotacachi volcano

OTAVALO

QUITO

Cayambe volcano

Guagua Pichincha volcano

Corazon volcano

Machachi

Illiniza Norte volcano

Antisana volcano

AVENUE OF
THE VOLCANOES
(ANDES)

Cotopaxi volcano

Illiniza Sur volcano

Latacunga

Carihuairazo volcano

Ambato

Tungurahua volcano

Urbina

CHIMBORAZO
VOLCANO

Colta

Riobamba

El Altar volcano

Sangay volcano

Yaguachi

DURÁN

Naranjito

Alausí

Milagro

Bucay

Devil's Nose

Guayaquil

Sibambe

Guayas River

EMPIRE LINES
- - - - - - - - - - - - - - - - - -

253. Island Express
India

The 587-mile (945km)
Bengaluru (Bangalore)–
Kanyakumari train runs
through leafy, lovely
Kerala. It calls at
Cochin, occupied by the
Portuguese in 1503 – the
first European colony
in India.

**254. Penang Hill
Funicular**
Malaysia

Visit the capital of
Penang island, George
Town, founded 1786.
The 1,996m (6,549ft)
funicular was built in
1923, so that colonial
Brits could access
cooler hill air.

Tren Crucero's eastbound voyage is called the Train to the
Clouds, and starts in Durán, at the mouth of the Guayas
River. This is the railhead for Guayaquil, Ecuador's second
city, founded by Spanish conquistador Francisco de
Orellana in 1538. In the early 16th century Ecuador was
ruled by the Inca, but the Spanish conquered the country
in 1534, and went on to rule Ecuador for 300 years. Only
a smattering of colonial-era buildings remain in Guayaquil
(an earthquake in 1942 flattened many). But there's old-
school charm in the Barrio las Peñas neighbourhood, plus
a lively waterfront promenade.

Guayaquil isn't just the Tren Crucero's beginning, it's
also where the story of Ecuadorean railways begins.
The country's first line, opened in 1873, linked Durán to the
inland city of Milagro. This is the route the Tren Crucero
follows on Day 1, rumbling through sugar cane, banana and
pineapple plantations via Milagro to the town of Bucay.
The railway first reached Bucay in 1888 but, with the Andes
looming on the horizon, construction stalled. It wasn't until
1901 that American engineer John Harman discovered

a workable route forwards – via a mountainside overflown by condors, and a stretch known as the 'Devil's Nose'.

On Day 2, the Tren Crucero sets off along the Chanchán River to follow Harman's audacious solution. The terrain morphs from lush cloud forest to more barren highlands as the train climbs. Then, at Sibambe Station, the train hits the vertiginous hairpins of the Devil's Nose. Between here and the village of Alausí, the train ascends 500m (1,640ft) in just 7.5 miles (12km). After that it continues through the mountains, passing quinoa fields and grazing llamas en route to the city of Riobamba.

On Day 3 the Tren Crucero hits its highest point, 3,609m (11,840ft) Urbina Station, with bulbous Mount Chimborazo, Ecuador's highest peak, looming to the west. This heralds the Avenue of Volcanoes, along which twenty snow-capped, sometimes smoking volcanoes stand. They're like a ceremonial welcome, trumpeting the train's arrival in Quito – just as they did on 25 June 1908, when the Guayaquil–Quito train completed its first run.

Founded by the Spanish in 1534 atop the ruins of an Inca city, Quito has the best-preserved historic centre of Spanish America. At its heart is the Plaza de la Independencia, a wide square edged by the whitewashed cathedral and the Government Palace. There are also many churches with rich 'Baroque School of Quito' interiors.

On Day 4 the Tren Crucero travels between Otavalo and Ibarra, a journey described in Chapter 3 (p. 157). So that's almost every inch of Ecuadorean rail covered. Not bad given that at the start of the 21st century the network had almost ceased to exist.

RIGHT: From Sibambe, the train must climb the steep hairpins of the Devil's Nose.

255. Tren Urbano
Puerto Rico

The 11-mile (17km) Tren
Urbano is a quick whizz
through early New
World exploration.
En route lie some of the
oldest European
settlements in the
Americas, such as
Caparra, founded 1508.

256. Argo Wilis
Java, Indonesia

This 450-mile (725km)
journey slices scenically
through Java, from
Bandung to Surabaya.
The highlight is the
midway city of
Yogyakarta. Founded in
1755, it's Indonesia's
cultural heart.

257. San Francisco Cable Cars
United States

Spanish settlers
founded Mission
Dolores on the hilly San
Francisco Peninsula in
1776. A system of cable
cars came in 1873; only
three lines remain. Ride
the Powell-Hyde line to
Market Street, then take
a vintage streetcar south
to Church Street and
nearby Mission Dolores.

258. Old Québec Funicular
Québec City, Canada

Québec City was
founded by French
explorer Samuel de
Champlain in 1608. The
Old Québec Funicular
links the handsome
walled city's Upper and
Lower Towns.

VERMONTER / ETHAN ALLEN EXPRESS

New York and Vermont, United States

Forge into Vermont on the trail of the American patriot and
pioneer who founded the Green Mountain State.

Need to know

- *Point in time: 1738–1789 (life of Ethan Allen)*
- *Length: 611 miles (983km) / 241 miles (388km)*
- *Minimum time: 13 hours 45 minutes / 5 hours 30 minutes*
- *Key stops: Washington DC, New York City, Battleboro, Essex Junction–Burlington, St Albans / New York City, Albany, Castleton, Rutland*
- *Countries crossed: United States*

Ethan Allen: farmer, philosopher, politician, patriot, pioneer, hero. No wonder he has a train service named after him. Allen is known as the man who, in the 1760s, helped establish the Green Mountain Boys militia; their fight for land rights ultimately led to the foundation of the state of Vermont. Also, in 1775 Allen and his 'Boys' captured Fort Ticonderoga from the British, a vital stepping stone to American victory in the War of Independence.

Amtrak runs two train services into Allen's heartland. The 241-mile (388km) Ethan Allen Express runs from New York City to the Vermont city of Rutland along the Hudson Valley. En route it stops in historic Castleton, a picture-perfect New England town with a tree-flanked Main Street

and a handsome university (founded 1787). It's also where Ethan Allen and General Benedict Arnold met to plan their attack on Fort Ticonderoga. That striking star-shaped stronghold is a 45-minute drive north, at the southern narrows of Lake Champlain.

Amtrak's 611-mile (983km) Vermonter service starts in Washington DC, heads to New York City, then takes a more northeasterly route than the Ethan Allen Express. It cuts through Connecticut (where Allen was born) then Massachusetts before entering the rural pastures and forested mountains of Vermont. There are fine views of Mount Ascutney, rural villages and rivers spanned by traditional timber-trussed covered bridges, all of which look especially spectacular when the fall foliage is aflame.

The Vermonter's penultimate stop is Burlington, known for being the smallest American city that is also the largest in the state. Ethan Allen spent his last days here, in a small Cape Cod–style homestead he built just above the Winooski River. It's now a museum, offering a look at life as an 18th-century pioneer. Allen died in 1789 and his body now rests beneath a soaring, statue-topped column at Burlington's leafy Greenmount Cemetery.

REVOLUTION RAILWAYS
- - - - - - - - - - - - - - - - - - - -

260. Guanajuato Funicular
Mexico

Visit the UNESCO World Heritage–listed colonial city of Guanajuato to ride the short funicular up to the monument to El Pípila (1782–1863), Mexican War of Independence hero.

261. Boston and Maine Railroad
Massachusetts, United States

A section of this old railroad is now the Minuteman Bikeway, a cycle path roughly following the route of Paul Revere's famous revolutionary ride to Lexington in 1775.

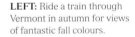

LEFT: Ride a train through Vermont in autumn for views of fantastic fall colours.

Take a 135-mile (217km) journey between two of the United States' most seminal cities. Philadelphia was the 'birthplace of the nation' and is thick with historic sites, not least Independence Hall where the Declaration of Independence (1776) and US Constitution (1787) were created. From Philly, the train runs southwest via the cantilever Commodore Barry Bridge, the Delaware and Susquehanna rivers and the seaport of Baltimore. After 2 hours the train arrives in Washington DC, the country's capital, founded in 1790. DC is bursting with museums and monuments, including the National Archives Building where original copies of the country's founding documents are on display.

Such a beautiful route, such divisive history. The 27-mile (44km) railway between the ancient walled city of Derry / Londonderry and the town of Coleraine is a knockout, following the River Foyle through emerald landscapes before tracing the wild Atlantic coast. It also dives into Ireland's longest rail tunnel. But this area once entertained a different drama. The Siege of Derry was the first big clash in Ireland's Williamite War (1688–91), fought between Catholic followers of King James VII of Scotland (James II of England) and Protestant supporters of the Dutch Prince William of Orange. Both Derry and Coleraine were strongholds of Protestantism, which ultimately defeated Catholic forces, shaping the following centuries of Irish history.

RIGHT: Pure Harry Potter! A steam train runs across the Glenfinnan Viaduct.

JACOBITE STEAM TRAIN

Scotland, United Kingdom

Chug along one of Britain's most spectacular railways in the company of Bonnie Prince Charlie and Harry Potter.

Need to know
- *Point in time: 1745 ('Forty-Five' Jacobite Rising)*
- *Length: 41 miles (66km)*
- *Minimum time: 2 hours 10 minutes*
- *Key stops: Fort William, Banavie, Glenfinnan, Lochailort, Arisaig, Morar, Mallaig*
- *Countries crossed: United Kingdom*

Scotland's Jacobite train is pure magic. The billowing steam! The shimmering lochs! The broomstick-riding wizards overhead! OK, maybe that's just in the *Harry Potter* movies (in which this train stars) but it's still a remarkable ride.

The Jacobite Steam Train runs on the Mallaig branch of the West Highland Line. The 123-mile (198km) section from the city of Glasgow to the Highlands town of Fort William was built 1889–94. No mean feat: it had to plough through the mountainous wilderness, not least the desolate peat bog of Rannoch Moor where the line must levitate on turf.

The next stage was to build from Fort William to the fishing communities on the west coast. Engineer Sir Robert

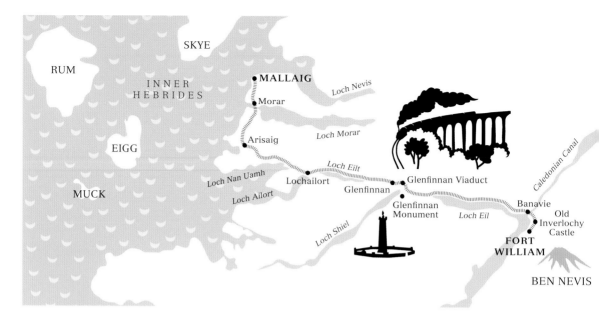

LIKE THAT?
TRY THIS

----

265. Glasgow–Stranraer
Scotland, United Kingdom

Barrel through Scotland's southwest into Burns Country. This 94-mile (152km) ride runs via Alloway, where poet Robert Burns was born in 1759; that house is now a museum.

McAlpine employed all his nous, and a lot of concrete, to conquer the mountainous terrain. The twenty-one-arch Glenfinnan Viaduct was his masterpiece. The 41-mile (66km) Fort William–Mallaig line finally opened in 1901.

This line doesn't only travel through jaw-dropping scenery it travels through time, back to the 17th and 18th centuries – Catholic King James VII (of Scotland) and II (of England) ruled from 1685 to 1688, when he was overthrown in favour of his Protestant daughter Mary and her husband, William of Orange. Supporters of exiled James became known as 'Jacobites'. The Jacobite Rising of 1715 failed to restore James's son to the throne, but in 1745, James's grandson, Charles Stuart – 'Bonnie Prince Charlie' – had a go. He landed at Glenfinnan, on Loch Shiel, with fifty men. Slowly, more came from the clans at Keppoch, Moror and Lochiel. Encouraged, he raised his father's standard on a loch-side hill. The Forty-Five Jacobite Rising had begun. This failed, too: in 1746, Charlie was defeated at the Battle of Culloden. The Jacobite era was over. But at Glenfinnan, a tower topped with a highlander commemorates the period.

Regular ScotRail trains run the same route between Fort William and the port of Mallaig, but the Jacobite Steam Train offers more Potteresque enchantment. It runs mid-May to early October, with old steam locomotives pulling 1960s Mark 1 first-class and standard carriages.

The railway sets off from Fort William, in the shadow of Ben Nevis (1,345m / 4,411ft), the United Kingdom's highest mountain. It passes the ruins of Old Inverlochy Castle. Then it hits the village of Banavie, crossing the Caledonian Canal near the eight locks of Neptune's Staircase.

After Banavie, the train hugs mountain-flanked Loch Eil – once home of Highland chieftain Donald Cameron, whose support was key to the 1745 Rising. Continuing into the wilds, the Jacobite prepares for its 'big screen moment': the crossing of Glenfinnan Viaduct. With a full head of steam, the train curves irresistibly over the 380m (1,247ft) long bridge as if it really were carrying Harry and co to school at Hogwarts. Down below, the Glenfinnan Monument gazes over the glens. There's a visitor centre here and, at Glenfinnan Station, a railway museum.

The train skirts islet-dotted Loch Eilt, Loch Ailort and Loch Nan Uamh. The Prince's Cairn on the shore here marks where Charlie, on the run after Culloden, escaped on a French ship, never to see Scotland again. At the village of Arisaig, the train reaches Britain's westernmost railway station. It then runs along the seashore via Loch Morar (Britain's deepest freshwater loch), white-sand beaches and rocky spurs. Finally, it pulls into little Mallaig, end of the line – though boats run over to Skye, if you want to go 'over the sea' like the Bonnie Prince.

EARLY TRAIN
- - - - - - - - - - - - - - - - - - - -

266. Alloa Waggonway
Scotland, United Kingdom

This now-disappeared old wagon-way, a precursor of the railway, was built around 1766, linking Alloa's Sauchie area to its harbour, on the Firth of Forth.

BELOW: The Glenfinnan Monument is a tribute to the clansmen who fought with Bonnie Prince Charlie.

MAIN NORTH LINE

New South Wales, Australia

Take the train from Sydney to the Hawkesbury River
region, where Australia's first settlers set up home.

Need to know
- *Point in time: 1789 (Hawkesbury River first explored)*
- *Length: 50 miles (80km)*
- *Minimum time: 1 hour 20 minutes*
- *Key stops: Sydney, Strathfield, Hornsby, Mount Kuring-gai, Berowra, Cowan, Hawkesbury River, Gosford*
- *Countries crossed: Australia*

For thousands of years, the Hawkesbury River area of New South Wales was populated by indigenous Australian Guringai peoples. They called it Deerubbun: 'wide, deep water'. But the local demographic changed dramatically in 1788, when the First Fleet of British ships arrived at Botany Bay to the south. The newcomers first explored the Hawkesbury in 1789. By 1794, settlement had begun and before long, as more convicts, soldiers and freeholders arrived, the fertile Hawkesbury was the breadbasket of the burgeoning colony of New South Wales. The Guringai were forced off their land, or worse.

Visiting today, the area feels little changed, despite being so close to Sydney, Australia's biggest city. Ferries still ply

the river from the village of Wisemans Ferry, where ex-convict Solomon Wiseman established the first boat service in 1827. However, train travellers riding the Main North Line from downtown Sydney use an alternative crossing. Between the old oyster-farming town of Brooklyn on the Hawkesbury's south shore and Cogra Point on the north, an eight-arch railway bridge spans the river. The original, opened in 1889, was built by the Union Bridge Company of New York. It was replaced by a new bridge in 1946, although the old piers are still visible.

The Main North Line leaves Sydney's Central Station. It passes the Olympic Park (home of the 2000 games), crosses the Parramatta River via the box-girder John Whitton Bridge and heads up to the suburb of Hornsby. From here the line edges Ku-ring-gai Chase National Park, a city-limits wilderness of sinuous creeks, rainforest and eucalypts, mangroves, rocky cliffs and Aboriginal rock art sites. Mount Kuring-gai, Berowra and Cowan train stations all provide access. Alternatively, continue to Brooklyn's Hawkesbury Station to disembark for boat trips. Or cross the Hawkesbury River Railway Bridge for the scenic ride through Brisbane Water National Park to Gosford, a town on the Hawkesbury's glorious northern arm.

LEFT: The Main North Line begins its journey amid the skyscrapers of downtown Sydney.

WEST MINAS RAILWAY

Minas Gerais, Brazil

Rumble through 17th-century Brazilian gold-rush
country aboard a vintage steam train.

Need to know
- *Point in time: 1693–95
  (Minas Gerais gold
  rush)*
- *Length: 8 miles (13km)*
- *Minimum time:
  35 minutes*
- *Key stops: São João
  del Rei, Tiradentes*
- *Countries crossed:
  Brazil*

The West Minas Railway started building train lines in 1879.
At its peak, it operated 482 miles (775km) of tracks across
Brazil's southeastern state of Minas Gerais. That network
is now reduced to an 8-mile (13km) narrow gauge stretch
between the city of São João del Rei and the pretty town
of Tiradentes. But it's still long enough to understand what
once made this the richest spot in Brazil.

Fortune-hunting Portuguese cowboys – known as
bandeirantes – first found gold amid the mountains of
Minas Gerais in 1693, sparking a rush that brought
thousands more hopefuls to the area. For a time the capital
of the state, Ouro Preto, was the most populous city in the
New World. As the train chugs along today, passengers can
see reminders of the 18th-century mine workings up on the
slopes. Also visible are rafts floating on the river: these
belong to modern-day *garimpeiros* (prospectors), who
use pumps to extract gold from the riverbed.

Tiradentes is a glorious place to begin the journey –
colonial charm incarnate, with cobbled streets and
whitewashed houses amid green hills. Appropriately, the
interior of its Igreja Matriz de Santo Antônio church is
festooned with hundreds of kilograms of gold. Tiradentes
still has its original 1881 station, where, on Fridays, Saturdays
and Sundays, the train awaits. It's pulled by a steam engine,
which locals call Maria-Fumaça (Smoking Mary).

From Tiradentes 'Mary' puffs along the Mortes River,
with the São José mountains rolling behind. Then the train
arrives at São João, where the old station, workshops and
roundhouse have been turned into a railway museum filled
with old wagons and loco paraphernalia. Venture further
afield to explore São João's lively historic centre, filled with
colonial mansions, tree-lined squares and more churches
gilded with Minas Gerais gold.

RIGHT: Vintage steam trains
leave from the pretty colonial
town of Tiradentes.

269
WOLLATON WAGONWAY

Nottinghamshire, United Kingdom

'Alonge the passage now laide with railes, and with suche or the lyke Carriages as are now in use for the purpose . . . ' This sentence appears in the 1604 lease given by Sir Percival Willoughby, lord of Wollaton Hall, to Huntingdon Beaumont, tenant of Strelley coal pits. It refers to the Wollaton Wagonway – the world's first overground railway. Using wooden rails, it was 2 miles (3km) long and plied by horse-pulled carriages. Nothing of it remains today but it's thought the route may have followed the current Old Coach Road linking the village of Strelley with the Nottingham suburb of Wollaton. Elizabethan Wollaton Hall does still stand and is now a museum. It was also used as Wayne Manor for the filming of *Dark Knight Rises,* in 2012.

270
MIDDLETON RAILWAY

Yorkshire, United Kingdom

Small in proportions but large in significance – that's the Middleton Railway. The line measures just 1 mile (1.6km), from the suburb of Hunslet into the city of Leeds. But in 1758 it became the first railway to secure its route via an Act of Parliament. At first horses pulled the wagons of coal, but from 1812 they were replaced by steam locomotives using a pioneering rack and pinion system. The area became a hub of engine design, and the line has operated in various capacities ever since, making it the world's oldest continuously working public railway. These days it carries tourists on weekends and some holidays, and is run by volunteers.

MERTHYR TRAMROAD

Wales, United Kingdom

Richard Trevithick was born in Cornwall in 1771 and grew up immersed in the mining industry. By the 1790s, he was experimenting with high-pressure steam engines and soon began applying his ideas to locomotion. In 1804, he took his wheel-mounted engine to the Merthyr Tramroad, South Wales, to prove it could haul 10 tonnes of iron. The 9.5-mile (15km) tramroad, built to serve the local ironworks, was one of the country's first metal-railed tracks. Usually horse-drawn, on 21 February 1804 the Merthyr wagons were pulled by Trevithick's contraption: the world's first steam locomotive on rails. The tramroad no longer exists but the Penydarren–Abercynon Trevithick Trail enables hikers to follow its route.

MIDLAND RAILWAY

Peak District, United Kingdom

The Peak District became the United Kingdom's first national park in 1951 – a major moment for the British countryside. Since 1604, a series of Parliamentary Enclosure Acts increasingly restricted access to previously common land and progress was put before nature. Indeed, in the 1860s Midland Railways hacked through idyllic bits of Derbyshire (now within the national park) with little care for scenery, 'blighting' Monsal Dale with the Headstone Viaduct. Ironically, the railway is now defunct but this 23m (74ft) high five-arched viaduct is revered as an engineering marvel. Nature-loving walkers can cross it on the Peak District's 8.5-mile (13km) Monsal Trail.

COPPER CANYON RAILWAY

Northwest Mexico

Take a gravity-defying railway ride through a network of ravishing ravines where Spanish explorers once struck it rich.

Need to know

- Point in time: 1600s (Spanish arrived in the Copper Canyon area)
- Length: 407 miles (655km)
- Minimum time: 15 hours
- Key stops: Los Mochis, El Fuerte, Témoris, Bahuichivo, Posada Barrancas, Divisadero, Creel, Cuauhtémoc, Chihuahua
- Countries crossed: Mexico

Spanish explorers first ventured into Mexico's Chihuahua region in the late 16th century, on the hunt for silver and gold. They found a formidable landscape: the Sierra Madre Occidental range ruptured by the Copper Canyon – not just one canyon but a vast, rugged network of them, at points over 1,800m (5,905ft) deep.

This network has no copper. The Spanish, who coined the name, thought the canyon's greenish hue was caused by the metal; in fact, it's down to the lichen. But the Spanish did find silver. In 1632 they started mining rich seams deep in the canyon's belly. Removing the ore wasn't easy – so they forced the local Rarámuri (Tarahumara) people to work the mines, and slogged the silver out by mule.

If only they'd had 'El Chepe' – the Copper Canyon Railway. Sadly for the Spanish miners, El Chepe wasn't opened until 1961. A line between the Gulf of California and the Chihuahuan interior was first mooted in the 1870s, not by riches-seeking miners but by American socialist Albert Kinsey Owen. He wanted to found a utopian colony at the coastal town of Topolobampo, and he wanted a railway to connect his utopia to the United States. Owen's colony failed, but the railway idea endured. Sections were built across the plains but it wasn't until the 1940s that workmen tackled the mountains. Almost 90 years later, the line finally opened in full.

Riding El Chepe today, it's clear to see why construction took so long. Along the 407-mile (655km) route there are eighty-seven tunnels and thirty-six bridges. Trains must take hairpin bends, slide past sheer rock faces and climb from sea level to 2,400m (7,874ft).

The Copper Canyon Railway runs two services, the thrice-weekly Clase Economica and the daily first-class Primera Express, which has reclining seats and a restaurant

ABOVE: El Chepe approaches Divisadero Station, at the edge of the Copper Canyon .

car. They both have timetables but these tend to be a little elastic: delays are not uncommon. The ride, however, is worth the wait.

Ridden west to east, El Chepe starts at the coastal city of Los Mochis and trundles over flat farmland to El Fuerte, a sleepy colonial town that grew rich on mining spoils. It still has a fine flower-filled plaza and colonnaded town hall. After El Fuerte, things get more interesting as the line starts to climb. And climb. It surmounts cacti-pricked foothills and rises into the sierra, an ancient, vertiginous landscape of sinuous creeks, pine forests and split and sundered rock.

At the town of Témoris, the train tackles the Santa Barbara Canyon. It hairpins twice, via the 180-degree tunnel of La Pera ('the pear') and the curvaceous Rio Septentrion bridge, resulting in three levels of track layered up the canyon wall. Then there's spectacular scenery all the way to Bahuichivo Station, a good place to break the ride. From here you can access Cerocahui, a valley-nestled pueblo with an old Jesuit mission church, and Urique Canyon, the deepest canyon in the system.

A little on from Bahuichivo, the train pauses at Divisadero Station for the greatest view of all. Teetering on the rim, the platform here looks out onto the Copper Canyon itself, as it meets the Tararecua and Urique Canyons in a magnificent mashing and melding of rock. There's also time to buy corn cakes and woven baskets from the station's Rarámuri traders.

Now the train begins its descent. It passes Creel, capital of the Sierra Tarahumara and home to a handicrafts museum and many Rarámuri people. It stops at the Mennonite community of Cuauhtémoc (famed for its cheese). Finally El Chepe halts in sprawling Chihuahua. It's not the loveliest city, but in the old colonial centre there's a smatter of mansions that owe their splendour to the silver in those nearby hills.

SUCRE–POTOSÍ BUSCARRIL

Central Bolivia

Is it a bus? Is it a train? Bolivia's Buscarril is a bit of both: a bus modified to run on rails. The service is a local lifeline, connecting tiny villages on its 8-hour journey through the spectacular Cordillera de los Frailes between Sucre and Potosí. Sucre, founded in 1538, is Bolivia's constitutional capital and its most attractive city, a UNESCO World Heritage–listed collection of whitewashed houses and leafy plazas. Potosí is also UNESCO World Heritage–recognised for its ancient industry. The city was founded in 1545, when large deposits of silver were found in its Cerro Rico (Rich Hill). It became the world's largest industrial complex, and remnants of 16th-century mining can still be seen.

LEFT: The Spanish explored the dramatic Copper Canyon from around the 17th century.

CERVANTES TRAIN

Central Spain

Take a short rail ride from elegant Madrid to
trace the life of Spain's greatest writer.

Need to know
- *Point in time: 1547–
  1616 (life of Miguel
  de Cervantes)*
- *Length: 19 miles
  (30km)*
- *Minimum time:
  30 minutes*
- *Key stops: Madrid,
  Alcalá de Henares*
- *Countries crossed:
  Spain*

BELOW: The great writer
Miguel de Cervantes is buried
in a convent in Madrid.

'He who reads much and walks much, goes far and knows
much.' So said Miguel de Cervantes in his masterpiece,
Don Quixote (written 1605–15). Clearly, Spain's greatest
author didn't have access to trains in the 17th century.
But as it seems he appreciated distance travel, we might
assume he'd have approved.

The Cervantes Train, a tourist excursion from Madrid
to the town of Alcalá de Henares, is certainly designed to
impart much. It follows the life and death of the 'Father of
the Modern Novel', beginning in Madrid, Spain's elegant,
effervescent capital, where Cervantes died in 1615. He was
buried at the city's Convent of the Barefoot Trinitarians, but
when the convent was rebuilt in the late 17th century his

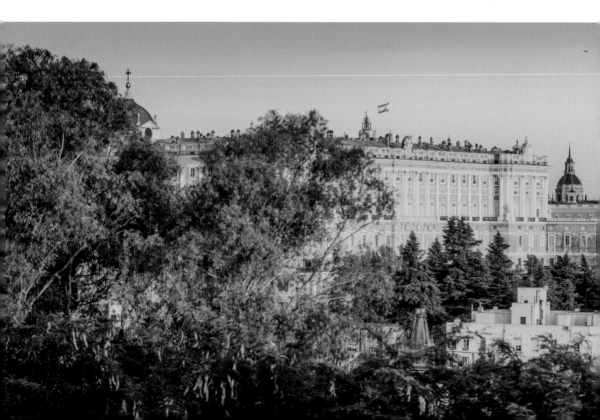

tomb was moved and lost. Cervantes' remains were only rediscovered – with the help of ground-penetrating radar and DNA analysis – in 2015. They've now been reburied in the convent's Church of San Ildefonso. There's also a large monument to the great man, featuring bronzes of Don Quixote and his sidekick, squire Sancho Panza, in Madrid's Plaza de España.

Passengers for the Cervantes Train gather at Madrid's magnificent Atocha Station with a cast of fancy-dressed characters: Don Quixote, Sancho Panza, a blind bard and Cervantes himself. These actors weave tales and tell jokes on the 30-minute ride east out of the city over sun-scorched farmland to Alcalá de Henares. This is where Cervantes was born, and its UNESCO World Heritage–listed medieval centre offers a glimpse back to Spain's literary golden age. Must-sees include one of Europe's longest-standing universities (founded 1293), striking Santos Niños Cathedral and the white storks that nest in the town's spires and bell towers. At Alcalá's heart is the Plaza de Cervantes and the pedestrianised main street, Calle Mayor. Here, a Cervantes museum now occupies the very house in which Miguel was born.

ARTISTIC AND LITERARY LINES

276. Mantua–Verona
Northern Italy

Make a 23-mile (37km) hop between locations in Shakespeare's *Romeo and Juliet* (written 1595): lakeside Mantua and balcony-boasting Verona.

277. Coast Line
Denmark

It's just 29 miles (46km) by rail from capital Copenhagen to the town of Helsingør (Elsinore), setting of Shakespeare's *Hamlet* (published 1603).

278. Borders Railway
Scotland, United Kingdom

Visit the memorial to Sir Walter Scott (1771–1832) in Edinburgh's Princes Street Gardens, then ride from nearby Waverley Station to Tweedbank, the closest stop to Abbotsford House, Scott's former home.

279. Amsterdam–Leiden–Delft
Netherlands

Tour the cities of the 17th-century Dutch Golden Age by rail, including canal-laced Amsterdam and Delft, home of *Girl with a Pearl Earring* painter Jan Vermeer.

WINNIPEG–CHURCHILL

Manitoba and Saskatchewan, Canada

Plunge into subarctic wilderness aboard the world's slowest railway to explore the lair of fur-trappers and polar bears.

Need to know
- *Point in time: 1670 (Hudson's Bay Company established)*
- *Length: 1,063 miles (1,710km)*
- *Minimum time: 44 hours*
- *Key stops: Winnipeg, Portage la Prairie, Togo, Hudson Bay, The Pas, Thompson, Gillam, Churchill*
- *Countries crossed: Canada*

BELOW: The Northern Lights may be seen shimmering above the far-north town of Churchill.

There's no road to the Hudson Bay town of Churchill. The only way to get there overland is by train: a journey on arguably the world's slowest railway, to Canada's northernmost main-line station.

The first explorers came here by boat. English navigator Henry Hudson, who was looking for the fabled Northwest Passage to China, discovered enormous Hudson Bay in 1610. In 1668 the sailing ketch *Nonsuch* became the first trading vessel to enter the bay's waters. Its crew spent a season trading with the local First Nations peoples and returned to England with a cargo of furs. This successful mission led, in 1670, to a royal charter being issued to 'The Governor and Company of Adventurers of England Trading into Hudson's Bay', or the Hudson's Bay Company (HBC). More trading posts were built around the great bay – including at Churchill in 1717 – which were used by the HBC until the early 20th century.

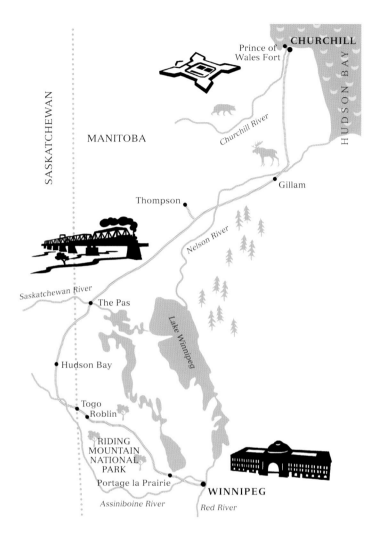

SASKATCHEWAN

MANITOBA

Prince of
Wales Fort

CHURCHILL

H U D S O N   B A Y

Churchill River

Gillam

Thompson

Nelson River

Saskatchewan River

The Pas

Lake Winnipeg

Hudson Bay

Togo
Roblin

RIDING
MOUNTAIN
NATIONAL
PARK

Portage la Prairie

WINNIPEG

Assiniboine River

Red River

The railway arrived a little too late for HBC trading posts. Charters for a line to Hudson Bay were granted in 1880, but money problems, route changes, the First World War and a whole lot of muskeg (mossy bog) hindered progress. The Winnipeg–Churchill railway finally opened in full in 1929.

The tortoise pace of construction mirrors the speed of the passenger trains running this route today – at times no faster than a brisk walk. The muskeg's continual cycle of freezing and thawing causes tracks to buckle, so travelling too fast would derail the train. This is evidenced by the occasional sight of a freight wagon lying capsized beside the track. The upside is: passengers have plenty of time to take in over 1,000 miles of Canadian wilderness.

Ridden northwards, the thrice-weekly Winnipeg–Churchill service starts in the Manitoban capital of Winnipeg. This thriving city, at the confluence of the Red and Assiniboine rivers, is gateway to both the Canadian west and the subarctic north. Its Forks district, a lively riverside hub of restaurants and bars, is a good place to grab dinner before boarding the train at noon the next day.

From Winnipeg's Beaux Arts Union Station, the train clicks through various ecozones: prairie wheat fields and one-street towns; deciduous woodland pocked by farmsteads; the vastness of the coniferous boreal forest. Somewhere amid all these trees, the train stops at the town of The Pas, inhabited by the Cree peoples for around 9,000 years and first visited by Europeans in the 1690s. The railway reached The Pas in 1909 and would go no further north until the Canadian government committed to financing the route to Hudson Bay. Construction of the bridge over the Saskatchewan River here in 1910–11 was the first step.

Further on, the train hits the town of Gillam, named after Zachary Gillam, captain of the *Nonsuch*. Just beyond, the railway crosses the long bridge over the Nelson River. Now the spruce becomes ever thinner before petering out into the Barren Grounds, a treeless eternity of mosses and lichens, riddled with lakes and streams and roamed by caribou.

Finally, after almost 45 hours, the train crawls into Churchill. Canada's only Arctic deep-water port, Churchill is home to just 800 people. However, its healthy numbers of beluga whales (July–August), polar bears (October–November) and shows of Northern Lights (September–March) ensure influxes of tourists.

It's also possible to see reminders of HBC's fur-trading days here. On a lonely peninsula across the Churchill River is the Prince of Wales Fort. Built between 1732 and 1771, this huge star-shaped stronghold has 11m (36ft) thick walls and once boasted forty cannon. It was captured and damaged by French troops in 1782. Soon after, it was abandoned to the elements. However, recognised as an important historic site, reconstruction of the fort began in the 1930s – thanks to equipment and manpower brought by the railway.

CASS SCENIC RAILROAD

West Virginia, United States

The Cass Scenic Railroad runs through West Virginia's Pocahontas County, named for Pocahontas (1596–1617), a Native American chief's daughter famed for trying to keep the peace between the first European settlers at nearby Jamestown and her own people. The railroad runs up Bald Knob, in the Alleghenies, the range agreed as the western boundary of settler lands – though the settlers soon reneged on that agreement. The line was built in 1901 to lug timber; Shay steam locomotives, designed with direct gearing to each wheel, were employed to climb the steep, twisty gradients. These locos now haul tourists up the 11-mile (18km) route, pistons clanging and engine whistling all the way.

LEFT: Henry Hudson discovered what's now named Hudson Bay in 1610.

285
MONT BLANC TRAMWAY

Alps, France

On 8 August 1786, Jacques Balmat
and Michel Paccard became the
first mountaineers to successfully
summit Mont Blanc. Doubtless
they would have appreciated the
Mont Blanc Tramway, which now
lessens the effort. Opened in 1907,
this 8-mile (12km) rack railway is
popular with climbers tackling the
fearsome 4,810m (15,780ft) peak.
They ride from the village of
Saint-Gervais past the Bionnassay
Glacier, and disembark at the
2,372m (7,782ft) high Nid D'Aigle
(Eagles Nest). From here they join
the main route up, overnighting at
a mountain hut to make a summit
bid the next morning. Of course,
non-climbers can ride the Mont
Blanc Tramway simply to enjoy the
spectacular views.

286
MOUNT WASHINGTON COG RAILWAY

New Hampshire, United States

The first recorded ascent of 1,917m
(6,288ft) Mount Washington was
made by settler Darby Field in
1642. The local Abenaki people
believed that the mountain was
the home of the gods, so wouldn't
climb it. Field's ascent was an
attempt to prove that the gods held
little sway over the land. Man
mastered the mountain again in
1869, when the world's first
(and, even today, the second-
steepest) cog railway opened on
Washington's slopes. Hauled by
either biodiesel or vintage steam
locomotives, it takes 65 minutes
to grind up the 3-mile (5km) track.
The views from the top are terrific,
over New Hampshire's valleys,
north to Canada and east to the
Atlantic Ocean.

BIG SOUTH FORK SCENIC RAILWAY

Kentucky, United States

The 16-mile (26km) Big South Fork Scenic Railway owes its existence to 20th-century loggers and a 17th-century woodsman. The tracks were first laid to serve the mining and timber industries around the town of Stearns; the diesel-hauled tourist train that now runs the route stops at the former Blue Heron Mining Community for insights into this era. The train also runs amid the lush, stream-tinkled mountains of the Daniel Boone National Forest, named for buckskin-wearing frontiersman Daniel Boone (1734–1820), who helped open the Kentucky wilds to new settlers. Thanks to some sensationalised tales, he became the first all-American folk hero.

END OF THE WORLD TRAIN

Tierra del Fuego, Argentina

Portuguese explorer Ferdinand Magellan first sailed around the island-dotted tip of South America in 1520, and named it Tierra del Fuego (Land of Fire). It took until 1902 for a railway to arrive in this end-of-the-world place. A narrow gauge logging line was built from the penal colony at Ushuaia (the planet's southernmost city) to Mount Susana. The prison closed in 1947; today it's tourists who ride its steam-pulled trains along 4.5 miles (7km) of the old convict line. It starts near Ushuaia and runs up the Pipo River Valley, into Tierra del Fuego National Park. En route it passes Macarena Waterfall and the 'tree cemetery', cleared by convicts 70 years ago.

GRAND TOUR

United Kingdom, France and Italy

Expand your mind on a rail ride between the cultural hubs
of Europe, in the carriage-tracks of the 18th-century elite.

Need to know
- *Point in time: 1720–1790 (heyday of the Grand Tour)*
- *Length: Around 1,100 miles (1,800km)*
- *Minimum time: From 17 hours to several years*
- *Key stops: Dover, Calais, Paris, Lyon, Turin, Venice, Florence, Rome*
- *Countries crossed: United Kingdom, France, Italy*

For coming-of-age aristocrats in 18th-century Britain, the
Grand Tour was a rite of passage. It went without saying
that fellows of fine breeding, with deep pockets and social
ambition, needed first-hand experience of foreign culture
before making their marks on the world. Legions of them
set off with an interest in art, a grounding in Greek and
Latin, and a 'bear-leader' – an older chaperone to try to keep
them out of trouble.

Most Grand Tourists were away for months, if not years.
They headed for the matchless antiquities and Renaissance
splendours of Italy – by way of Paris, naturally, for lessons in
sophistication (and sex). The young men – it was largely men

– began with a sea passage from Dover's White Cliffs to the French port of Calais, which could take up to 36 hours. From Calais it was a 180-mile (290km) trip south to the French capital. Today, the Eurostar connects London and Paris in just over 2 hours.

Once in Paris, the Tourist would make day trips to the magnificent Palace of Versailles (now just 13 minutes from the centre by train). He'd stroll along the River Seine to absorb some Parisian chic. And he'd admire the grandeur of the Louvre Palace, if not its vast modern-day repository of art (it only became a public museum in 1793).

If the Tourist were not in possession of a private carriage, he could take the horse-drawn *diligence* (public stagecoach) from Paris to the city of Lyon, then continue overland across the Alps via the Mont Cenis Pass. This was a steep, somewhat scary undertaking, requiring a sledge in winter. By 1810, too late for Grand Tourists, Napoleon built a road over the pass. Later still, from 1868 to 1871, the Mont Cenis Pass Railway operated here – the first mountain railway in the world. Today's train travellers can ride from Lyon into Italy right through Mont Cenis, via the 8.5-mile (14km) Fréjus Rail Tunnel.

LIKE THAT? TRY THESE

290. Saint-Raphaël–Ventimiglia
France and Italy

Ride along the glorious clifftops and turquoise-lapped bays of the French Riviera, the health-giving benefits of which were first touted in the late 18th century.

291. Genoa–Casella Railway
Liguria, Italy

This 15-mile (25km) line runs from the port of Genoa (an all-powerful republic in the 16th century) to the town of Casella, along the scenic Scrivia Valley.

292. Dresden–Prague
Germany and Czech Republic

Link two countries via a 119-mile (192km) railway that runs through the Elbe Gorge, a region that inspired Romantic artists during the 18th and 19th centuries.

293. Mont Blanc Express
France and Switzerland

This breathtaking ride from Saint-Gervais / Le Fayet, through the Chamonix valley to Martigny gives views of Mont Blanc, which was first climbed in 1786.

LEFT: Take a Grand Tour by train through the Alpine splendour of Mont Cenis.

On this route the next stop would be the same for past and present: the mountain-backed city of Turin. It was quite the cultural hub in the 18th century and, in 1861, briefly became the first capital of a newly unified Italy. Turin is still home to elegant boulevards, baroque buildings and (allegedly) the burial cloth of Christ, which has been kept in Turin Cathedral's Chapel of the Holy Shroud since 1694.

However, most bygone Tourists wouldn't have lingered in Turin. They'd have beelined for Venice (now around 4 hours from Turin by train). Fairy-tale, canal-laced Venice, so powerful in the Middle Ages, was in decline by the 18th century. But a little artful dilapidation is what makes it so romantic, to this day. Besides, a lot of Tourists came here for the ladies – Venice was known as a 'city of sin'.

Next comes Florence (2 hours by train), capital of the Renaissance, a gorgeousness of domes, palazzos and piazzas beside the River Arno. Then, as now, the Uffizi was top of the list. Established in 1581, it remains Italy's finest art gallery, home to Botticellis, da Vincis, Caravaggios, Michelangelos – everything art-lovers could wish to see.

Finally, the Tourist reached Rome (90 minutes by train), the city of all cities for young minds schooled on Latin and Julius Caesar. Here stand the Colosseum, the Pantheon, the Forum; nowhere has more classical sculpture or ancient sites. Indeed, the heyday of the Grand Tour coincided with extensive archaeological excavations.

The French Revolution (1789) and Napoleonic Wars (1803–15) put the kibosh on the Grand Tour. But the precedent had been set: travel for pleasure. Before long, thanks to new technology, a new wave of tourists (not just the moneyed elite) would be holidaying on the continent. They would be Grand Touring by train.

RIGHT: In the 18th century, Venice had a reputation for being a 'city of sin'.

CHEMINS DE FER DE LA CORSE

Corsica, France

Make a marvellous advance across the Mediterranean
island of Corsica, birthplace of Napoleon.

Need to know
- *Point in time: 1769
  (birth of Napoleon
  Bonaparte)*
- *Length: 144 miles
  (232km)*
- *Minimum time:
  3 hours 30 minutes*
- *Key stops: Ajaccio,
  Corte, Ponte Leccia,
  Casamozza, Bastia,
  Calvi*
- *Countries crossed:
  France*

MORE FRENCH
RAIL RIDES
----

295. Paris–Versailles
France

Jump on a suburban
train from the French
capital to the glorious
Palace of Versailles,
which became the
country's seat of power
in 1682 under Louis XIV.

Fly into the port town of Ajaccio on Corsica's west coast,
and you'll land at Napoleon Bonaparte Airport. You might
walk down the main thoroughfare of Cours Napoleon,
maybe stop at Le Grand Café Napoleon for coffee before
visiting Jardins de Casone, with its monumental Napoleon
statue. You may even pop into La Maison Bonaparte (now
a museum), where Napoleon was born in 1769. However,
while 'Boney' is one of the preeminent figures of French
history (Emperor of France 1804–15) and Corsica's most
famous son, he's probably the least interesting thing about
this spectacular Mediterranean island.

Corsica's topography is more impressive than any of
Napoleon's military successes. It's a dramatic rumple of
high, rocky mountains and dense *maquis* (scrub) that proved
quite a challenge to early railway engineers. The Chemins
de Fer de la Corse, the island's 144 miles (232km) of metre-
gauge railway, was begun in 1879. By 1894 the towns of
Ajaccio, Calvi and Bastia were connected by rail, three lines
spidering out from the hub town of Ponte Leccia.

This was no mean feat, especially the section through
Corsica's central spine, between the crag-side town of
Corte and the tiny village of Bocognano. Many tunnels and
bridges had to be built, including the 2.4-mile-long (3.9km)
Vizzavona Tunnel and the 94m (300ft) high Vecchio viaduct,
designed by Gustave Eiffel. This all makes for a scenic ride.

It takes around 3.5 hours to travel the Ajaccio–Bastia line.
First the railway leaves the Mediterranean coast, climbing
inland along the Gravona Valley to Bocognano (640m / 2,100ft
above sea level). Then it faces dramatic ascents and a series
of reverse curves amid the island's Corsica Natural Park,
a highland paradise cut with gorges and fragrant with herbs.
It continues over the viaduct at Vecchio and descends to
Corte, then Ponte Leccia. From here, it's a relatively easy run
over farmland to the historic port of Bastia on the east coast.

MEDITERRANEAN SEA

BASTIA

L'Île-Rousse

CALVI

Casamozza

Ponte Leccia

Corte

CORSICA
NATIONAL PARK

Vecchio Viaduct

Vizzavona

Bocognano

AJACCIO

BELOW: The mountainous terrain around Corte was a challenge to railway builders.

NAIROBI–MOMBASA

Southern Kenya

Travel from Kenya's capital, across wildlife-roamed savannah,
to an ancient trading port on the Indian Ocean.

Need to know
- *Point in time: 1593–96 (Mombasa's Fort Jesus built)*
- *Length: 329 miles (530km)*
- *Minimum time: 18 hours*
- *Key stops: Nairobi, Konza, Makindu, Kibwezi, Voi, Mombasa*
- *Countries crossed: Kenya*

Nairobi owes its existence to trains. The city was an unprepossessing swamp on the edge of the Rift Valley before the engineers of the Uganda Railway built a supply depot here in 1889, to serve their route to the port of Mombasa. Now Nairobi is the Kenyan capital, one of the biggest cities in Africa, with a huge diversity of inhabitants – not least the rhino, lion and more living in its national park.

Trains still run from Nairobi to Mombasa, a slow, often-delayed journey of 329 miles (530km). Indeed, it's less a journey, more an experience, with old-fashioned first-class sleeper compartments and a linen-tabled restaurant car serving three-course dinners, English breakfasts and cheap local Tusker beers.

Ridden west to east, the railway runs downhill from Nairobi, 1,795m (5,889ft) above sea level, to the Indian Ocean. En route it traverses big African landscapes: blood-orange earth fuzzed with acacia and scrub; villages of mud-and-thatch huts; yellow savannah segueing to distant hills. The train cuts right through Tsavo East National Park, where animals might well be seen from the window – perhaps sprinting ostrich or grazing giraffe.

Mombasa's heritage extends much further back than Nairobi's. It's one of East Africa's oldest settlements. Though stories of visits by ancient Egyptians may be apocryphal, Mombasa was definitely a key trade hub for gold and spices when Portuguese explorer Vasco da Gama arrived in 1498, the first European known to have stopped by. In 1593, the Portuguese attempted to cement their hold on Mombasa by building Fort Jesus, a walled citadel guarding the Old Port. The fort ended up changing hands nine times between 1631 and 1875, with everyone from Omanis to Brits staking a claim. Amazingly, given its tumultuous past, the fort still stands. You can explore its cisterns, turrets and peeling ramparts, before flopping onto one of Mombasa's dazzling stretches of sand.

LINES TO SHRINES
----

297. Bom Jesus do Monte Funicular
Braga, Portugal

Ignore the baroque zigzag staircase up to the Bom Jesus shrine (begun in 1722) and instead make a pilgrimage by funicular in 4 minutes.

298. Madrid– El Escorial
Spain

Take a 50-minute ride from the Spanish capital to the town of El Escorial. It's home to a royal complex, completed in 1584, in which most Spanish kings are buried.

299. Sassi–Superga Tramway
Turin, Italy

Ascend for 2 miles (3km) from the city suburb of Sassi up Superga Hill, atop which the baroque-classical-style Basilica of Superga was completed in 1731.

FAR LEFT: The train sweeps across the savannah, where wild animals might be spotted.

LEFT: Mombasa's Fort Jesus was built in 1593.

300
THURINGIAN RAILWAY

Central Germany

The 130-mile (210km) Thuringian
Railway runs from the city of Halle
to the town of Bebra. It navigates
the vineyard-lined Saale Valley,
meanders with the Ilm River
through undulating 'Thuringian
Tuscany', passes hilltop castles and
scythes the Thuringian Forest.
It also stops at the historic town
of Eisenach where German
theologian and Protestant
Reformation leader Martin Luther
hid in Wartburg Castle in 1521,
translating the New Testament
into German. In 1777, writer
Johann Wolfgang von Goethe
translated the whole Bible in the
same castle. Wartburg is now
open for tours. Eisenach is also
the birthplace of composer Johann
Sebastian Bach (1685–1750) –
there's a Bach museum hosting
frequent recitals of his tunes.

301
LITTLE YELLOW TRAIN

Pyrenees, France

Impressive architecture abounds
along the route of the Little Yellow
Train. This narrow gauge electric
railway between the city of
Villefranche-de-Conflent and the
station of Latour-de-Carol opened
in 1909. It's a triumph of bridges
and viaducts that serves France's
highest railway station, 1,592m
(5,226ft) high Bolquère Eyne.
But it also passes astonishing sites,
including two fortresses built by
Sébastien Le Prestre de Vauban
(1633–1707). For at least a century,
Vauban was *the* name in fort
design. Villefranche itself is
encased within Vauban walls.
Further along the line, at the head
of the Aude and Tet valleys, is
Vauban's Mont-Louis Citadel
(completed 1682); it's still occupied
by the military today, although
open for anyone to look around.

302
ST PETERSBURG–
TSARSKOYE SELO

Northwestern Russia

Opened in 1837, the 17-mile
(27km) line between St Petersburg
and the royal estate of Tsarskoye
Selo (now Pushkin) was Russia's
first passenger railway, providing
a link between some of the finest
buildings in Russia. The original
railway closed in 1899 but
suburban trains run from
St Petersburg's Vitebsk Station to
Pushkin. St Petersburg is full of
glories – the Hermitage Museum,
Peter and Paul Fortress – but also
the small cabin in which Tsar Peter
the Great lived when he founded
the city in 1703. Tsarskoye Selo is
home to a flamboyant baroque
palace and park, built for Peter's
wife Catherine from 1708.

303
SILVER METEOR

Eastern United States

Amtrak's Silver Meteor route runs
from New York to Miami. But its
most charming stops are the
southern belles of Charleston and
Savannah. Charleston, South
Carolina, was founded in 1670;
its oldest stone building, the Pink
House, dates from around 1700.
The entire historic centre is a treat
of narrow houses with bright
stucco and wooden shutters.
It's also home to the Charleston
Museum, opened in 1773 and
considered America's first
museum. Around 100 miles (160km)
south is Savannah, Georgia, which
is lovelier still. Founded in 1733 and
thankfully saved from Civil War
destruction, Savannah is a dazzle
of handsome squares, Federal and
antebellum-style houses, and oak
trees draped in Spanish moss.

ST KITTS SCENIC RAILWAY

St Kitts and Nevis

Take a short and very sweet ride through the
Caribbean island's sugar-growing past.

Need to know
- *Point in time: 1640s
  (sugar cane introduced
  to St Kitts)*
- *Length: 30 miles
  (48km)*
- *Minimum time:
  3 hours*
- *Key stops: Needsmust,
  Dieppe Bay, St Paul's,
  La Vallee, Brimstone
  Hill Fortress, Old Road
  Town, Basseterre*
- *Countries crossed:
  St Kitts and Nevis*

St Kitts' narrow gauge tourist train calls itself the 'Last
Railway in the West Indies'. And it serves as a reminder
of a time when the island's primary industry was not
tourism but sugar.

St Kitts first entered the written history books in 1493,
when Christopher Columbus sailed past but didn't land.
He named it St Kitts, either after himself or St Christopher,
patron saint of travellers. However, the island's resident
Arawak and Kalinago peoples knew their home as
Liamuiga: 'fertile land'. It was cloaked in forest, had an
abundance of fresh water and, thanks to a spine of
volcanoes, was blessed with rich volcanic soil.

This fecundity didn't go unnoticed for long. In 1624,
Englishman Thomas Warner founded the Caribbean's first
non-Spanish European colony here. A handful of French

settlers followed. In 1626, a massacre of the Arawak and Kalinago population – at what's now known as Bloody Point – gave these newcomers the island to themselves. They enlarged their plantations, brought over African slaves and, from the 1640s, started growing sugar cane.

Sugar was at that time 'white gold', one of the world's most desired commodities. By 1775, St Kitts had 200 sugar estates, and was vital to the British Empire. Some historians even argue that Britain lost the American War of Independence in 1776 because so many of its soldiers were too busy protecting Caribbean interests.

But times change. International competition hit St Kitts hard and by the early 20th century things weren't looking so sweet. The island's last-ditch attempt to remain a sugar player was to consolidate small plantations into a single more efficient industry. From 1912, construction started on a round-island narrow gauge railway that would transport the cane to a central factory near capital Basseterre. It worked – for a while. St Kitts produced sugar for far longer

ABOVE: In the 17th and 18th century, St Kitts was a key producer of sugar, or 'white gold'.

CARIBBEAN RAIL REMAINS

305. Barbados Railway
Barbados

The defunct train line that once carried sugar cane across Barbados, from Bridgetown to Belleplaine, is now used as a walking trail. Guided hikes are run by Barbados National Trust.

306. Antigua Sugarcane Railways
Antigua and Barbuda

Antigua once had a 50-mile (80km) network of narrow gauge lines, ferrying sugar cane around the island. It ran from 1903 to 1971.

307. Chemin de Fer Touristique du Pays de la Canne
Guadeloupe

A 4-mile (7km) tourist railway runs on sugar-train lines between the old plantation at Beauport and the northern port of Petit-Canal on the French Caribbean island.

than neighbouring islands. But losses were mounting, and on 31 July 2005 the last sugar train switched off its engine. Now the commodity shifted by the St Kitts Scenic Railway is tourism.

St Kitts, one of the Leeward Islands, is a more offbeat travel choice than nearby Antigua. It has beach resorts but it also has a rugged, forested interior, little touched by development. And there are sugar reminders everywhere, from ruined chimneys in the foothills to great plantation houses that are now characterful hotels.

The original railway tracks made a 30-mile (48km) circumnavigation of St Kitts. However, the current Scenic Railway tour comprises an 18-mile (29km) train ride along the island's Atlantic coast, from Needsmust Station to La Vallee Station. From the latter, passengers complete the remainder of the original railway route loop by bus.

The train is an unusual white double-decker, with enclosed, air-conditioned parlours at the bottom and open-air viewing platforms up top. On board, waiters serve rum punch, a conductor delivers historic commentary and the St Kitts Railway Choir belts out Caribbean songs and hymns.

The journey is unhurried, designed for taking in the view. On one side the ocean glitters, crashing into cliffs and swelling around formations such as Black Rocks, the remains of an ancient lava flow. On the other side, the interior rises into emerald highlands, with the 1,156m (3,792ft) peak of Mount Liamuiga highest of all. The train crosses ravines via box-girder bridges, rolls past palm trees and little villages, and looks out at the crumbling windmills of old cane plantations. It also passes Dieppe Bay, site of St Kitts' first French settlement in 1625.

The bus ride along St Kitts' Caribbean coast then takes in the well-preserved ramparts of Brimstone Hill Fortress, built by the British from 1690 to protect their cherished sugar isle. And it passes Old Road Town, site of Thomas Warner's original colony, where St Kitts' sugar story first began.

COAST LINE

Sri Lanka

Trace Sri Lanka's southwest shore to explore
rich colonial history – and recent tragedy.

Need to know
- *Point in time: 1663 (Galle Fort built)*
- *Length: 72 miles (116km)*
- *Minimum time: 2 hours*
- *Key stops: Colombo, Mount Lavinia, Kalutara, Bentota, Telwatta, Galle*
- *Countries crossed: Sri Lanka*

BELOW: Sri Lanka's Coast Line hugs the shore from Colombo to Galle.

Completed in 1894, Sri Lanka's Coast Line between capital Colombo and the southern city of Galle does exactly what it says on the tin. For virtually all of its 72 miles (116km) the railway hugs the Indian Ocean, its tracks seemingly within touching distance of the palm trees and sparkling blue waters. It's a scenic ride, though one tinged with tragedy. On 26 December 2004 a southbound train, packed with more than 1,500 people, was swamped by tsunami waves caused by the now-infamous Boxing Day earthquake off Indonesia. It remains the biggest rail disaster in history.

The line has since been upgraded, made smoother and safer, and is a glorious way to travel from Sri Lanka's bustling capital to one of its most charming colonial centres. En route, the windows open onto swathes of white sand, wriggling river estuaries and a hinterland of tropical green. Small wooden boats bob out to sea or haul up on shore; their catch can be seen drying on railway-side stalls.

The train passes Kompannavidiya Station, an elegant Victorian construction of wood, iron and stone. It passes Kalutara, a former spice-trading hub, now famed for its sacred Buddhist Bodhi tree and delicious mangosteens. It passes the low-key beach resorts around Bentota. And it passes Telwatta Station, near the site of the tsunami disaster, where a bronze memorial stands on the beach.

The Coast Line technically terminates at the commercial city of Matara, but its much better to disembark at Galle. The Dutch wrested Galle from Portuguese settlers in 1640. By 1663 they had girdled all of Galle's sea-facing headland within meaty walls, laid out neat streets, and built a sewer system and other mod cons. Galle Fort is little changed to this day, and an amble amid its low-rise Dutch houses, colonial churches and winding alleys is a peaceful step back in time to the 17th century.

BELOW: The train leaves from Colombo, Sri Lanka's bustling capital.

309
OVERSEAS RAILROAD

Florida, United States

In the late 19th century, American oil tycoon Henry Flagler saw tourism potential in Florida. First he built St Augustine's Ponce de Leon Hotel, an extravagant resort named after the Spanish explorer Juan Ponce de León who discovered Florida in 1513. But Flagler had bigger plans. Like León, Flagler looked to cross the sea. In 1905, work began on his Overseas Railroad, a 128-mile (204km) line from Florida's southern tip to the island of Key West – 91 miles (136km) was built atop the chain of islands while the rest required long embankments and bridges. The railroad opened in 1912 but was part-destroyed by a storm in 1935. However, the road to Key West still utilises parts of Flagler's audacious enterprise.

LIKE THAT? TRY THIS

310. Downeaster
Maine–Massachusetts, United States
Navigate down the coast from Brunswick to Boston on a train named after the sailing ships built in this area. The train stops at the shipbuilding settlement of Freeport, originally founded in 1789.

311
KUSTTRAM

Northern Belgium

The entire seashore of Belgium is traced by the world's longest tram ride. The Kusttram (Coast Tram) runs for 42 miles (68km) between the towns of Knokke-Heist, on Belgium's border with the Netherlands, and De Panne, on the border with France. It trundles along the Belgian Riviera, via fine beaches and restaurants serving Flemish shrimps and Ostend oysters. Ostend, the biggest city on the Kusttram is today a genteel seaside spot. But from 1601 to 1604 it was the site of one of the world's longest, goriest sieges, when the occupying Dutch tried (and failed) to hold off the invading Spanish; 100,000 people lost their lives.

TRANS-MONGOLIAN RAILWAY

Russia, Mongolia and China

Trace the tea trade route across Siberia and over the
Great Wall to reach the Chinese capital.

Need to know
- *Point in time: 1689
  (Treaty of Nerchinsk
  signed)*
- *Length: 4,735 miles
  (7,621km)*
- *Minimum time:
  6 nights*
- *Key stops: Moscow,
  Yekaterinburg, Irkutsk,
  Ulan-Ude,
  Ulaanbaatar, Erlan,
  Beijing*
- *Countries crossed:
  Russia, Mongolia,
  China*

It takes 6 days to ride the train non-stop from Moscow
to Beijing. It's one of the world's longest rail journeys.
But that's a mere eye-blink compared with the 16 months it
took tea-toting camel caravans to make the same crossing
400 years ago.

There are nearly 5,000 miles (8,000km) between the
Russian and Chinese capitals. Many of those miles are
subsumed by the raw immensity of Siberia. In the late
Middle Ages, when Genghis Khan's Mongol hordes ruled
the region, few dared venture to this fearsome wilderness.
But in the 1500s, Tsar Ivan the Terrible gained dominance
over the Mongols. Cossack soldiers began establishing
settlements in Siberia and Russian trappers and traders
made forays into the little-known east. This meant trade
with China, which meant trade in tea.

Russian high society developed a taste for tea in the mid-17th century. When the Treaty of Nerchinsk was signed in 1689, agreeing the boundary between Russia and China, traders could pass peaceably between the two. Chests of the precious cargo would be purchased in Kalgan (now Zhangjiakou), near Beijing. From here, camel caravans crossed Mongolia's Gobi Desert to reach Kyakhta, on the Russian border, before striking northwest across Siberia, bound for the Russian royal court. The tea route was officially born.

Today the Trans-Mongolian Railway traces largely the same course as those hardy traders. It's a branch of the Trans-Siberian, the train line that has connected Moscow with the port of Vladivostok since 1916. The Trans-Mongolian, which veers south at the city of Ulan-Ude, was completed in 1956.

There's just one direct Trans-Mongolian train a week, which leaves Moscow every Tuesday night, returning from Beijing every Wednesday. The carriages are a mix of two- and four-berth compartments. A dining car serves up location-specific dishes: *borsh* (beetroot soup), meat, potatoes and vodka in Russia; rice and mutton in Mongolia; spicier stir fries in China.

Like the Trans-Siberian, the Trans-Mongolian visits the big cities of the Russian west, including Perm, gateway to the Ural Mountains, and Yekaterinburg, where the Russian royal family was executed in 1918. It slices through classic

LEFT: The Trans-Mongolian takes 6 days to travel from Moscow to Beijing.

Siberian terrain, providing an endless unfurling of empty tundra, distant peaks and billions of birch trees. And it skirts the edge of Lake Baikal, the world's deepest lake, home to unique wildlife and Buryat culture.

Unlike the Trans-Siberian, the Trans-Mongolian plunges south across the steppes of Mongolia, where occasional *ger* (yurt) camps interrupt the grasslands. It stops at Mongolian capital Ulaanbaatar, with its varied skyline of Soviet blocks, skyscrapers, tents and temples. It cuts into the mountains of northern China before crossing the line of the Great Wall. And it passes the ancient city of Zhangjiakou before reaching the smog and splendour of Beijing.

The view from the window is hypnotic: a relentless nothingness, bleak and beautiful in equal measure. It's especially atmospheric to ride the Trans-Mongolian in winter, when the outdoor temperature plummets but the train's heating is turned up, and the snow-cloaked wilds are the Siberia of your imagination.

However, perhaps the greatest joys lie inside the train. Enjoy making friends with your carriage-mates, be they Russian students, Buddhist monks, Chinese businessmen or fellow train-lovers. Spend hours playing cards and raising toasts of vodka. Hop out to buy hot sausages from station vendors. Be rocked to sleep by the train's rhythmic jiggle.

Each carriage has its own *samovar* (hot-water urn) from which you can keep filling your mug. After all, there's nothing like a steaming brew to keep the cold at bay and the conversation flowing. This journey, originally paved by tea, is fuelled by it still.

RIGHT: The Douro Line enters the city of Porto via the majestic Luis Bridge.

313
DOURO LINE

Northern Portugal

Raise a glass to the Douro Line! The railway through the rugged Douro Valley is 101 miles (163km) of marvellously meandering and beautifully boozy riverside track. It links the village of Pocinho (with its rock art and waterfall) to the city of Porto, at the Douro's mouth. En route there are more than twenty tunnels, thirty bridges and thirty-four stations, not to mention endless terraced slopes of vines. In 1756 this region became one of the world's first demarcated wine appellations, guaranteeing the provenance and quality of its wines. Hop off at the charming port-producing town of Pinhão for a tasting or indulge at the many port houses in Porto's sister city across the river, Vila Nova da Gaia.

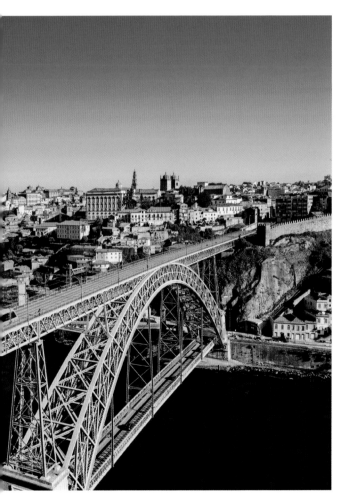

314
JOSE CUERVO EXPRESS

Jalisco, Central Mexico

Take a classy ride across the quintessentially Mexican state of Jalisco to the town that gave us the most quintessentially Mexican drink: Tequila! The luxurious Jose Cuervo Express is named for the family-owned company that's been distilling tequila since 1795. The train runs northwest for around 37 miles (60km) from the colonial city of Guadalajara to Tequila (founded 1666). Tequila is a colourful little town but the main draws are the surrounding fields of pointy blue agave plants from which the spirit is made. The express includes a tour of the Jose Cuervo Factory and, of course, a tasting or two.

AROUND THE WORLD

Worldwide

Make like a 16th-century navigator and travel
right around the globe by train.

Need to know

- *Point in time: 1519–22
  (first circumnavigation
  of the globe)*
- *Length: Around
  23,000 miles
  (37,015km)*
- *Minimum time:
  51 days*
- *Key stops: London,
  New York, San
  Francisco, Shanghai,
  Beijing, Ulaanbaatar,
  Moscow, Venice, Paris*
- *Countries crossed:
  United Kingdom,
  United States, China,
  Mongolia, Russia,
  Italy, France*

LIKE THAT?
TRY THIS
- - - - - - - - - - - - - - - - - - -

316. Shinjuku Station
Tokyo, Japan

Take a train from the
world's busiest station,
built on the site of a
hub on the imperial
highway to Edo Castle,
created in 1698.

RIGHT: San Francisco is just
one of the iconic stops on this
round-the-world ride.

In September 1519, an armada of five ships set off from the
port of Sanlúcar de Barrameda in southern Spain. Led by
Portuguese navigator Ferdinand Magellan, its mission was
to find a route around the Americas to Asia, via the Pacific
Ocean. In September 1522, one of the five ships – now
commanded by Juan Sebastián Elcano (Magellan having died
in the Philippines) – made it back. It had taken three years to
make the first circumnavigation of the globe.

Today you could circumnavigate in around 51 hours using
commercial flights. Or you could take 51 days doing the
journey by rail, at a relaxed sightseeing pace, with a few
plane hops in-between. The travel company Great Rail
Journeys offers an Around the World trip for around £25,000,
incorporating some of the planet's most luxurious and iconic
trains. It does a complete circuit of the northern hemisphere
– the opposite of Magellan's more southerly route, which
skirted South America, eastern Asia and Africa.

From London, the Around the World trip flies to New York
and uses Amtrak train services to cross the United States,
with some heritage line detours (the Grand Canyon Railway,
for example) thrown in.

The trip crosses the Pacific by plane in around 14 hours
(it took Magellan around four months), landing in Shanghai
and picking up Chinese railways to visit Xi'an's Terracotta
Warriors and Beijing's Forbidden City. Then it's all aboard
the opulent Tsar's Gold private train to cross the Mongolian
steppe and ride on to icy Siberia, via Lake Baikal, the Ural
Mountains and historic Yekaterinburg, ending in Moscow.

After a short flight to Venice, the trip picks up the belle
époque carriages of the Venice Simplon-Orient-Express for
the journey to Paris. Then it's through the Channel Tunnel
to emerge at Folkestone, where the steam-pulled Belmond
British Pullman awaits for the last leg back to London,
circuit complete.

PANAMA CANAL RAILWAY

Panama

Make a transcontinental train journey between the
Atlantic and the Pacific in just 1 hour.

Need to know
- *Point in time: 1513
  (Vasco Núñez de
  Balboa crossed the
  Isthmus of Panama)*
- *Length: 48 miles
  (77km)*
- *Minimum time: 1 hour*
- *Key stops: Balboa
  (Panama City), Cólon*
- *Countries crossed:
  Panama*

In 1513, Spanish conquistador Vasco Núñez de Balboa
became the first European to lay eyes on the Pacific Ocean.
It took him around a month of hacking through dense bush
and clambering over mountains to cross the Isthmus of
Panama. Reaching this new shore, he waded into the water,
named it the 'South Sea' and claimed it for the Spanish
crown. Now you can do the journey by rail, which effectively
connects the Atlantic to the Pacific in just 1 hour.

That two mighty oceans are separated by such a skinny
sinew of land has been a boon ever since. The Spaniards
soon created a pathway across the isthmus, which they called
the Camino Real (Royal Road). They used it to transport Inca
gold overland from the Pacific, so it could be sailed across the
Caribbean Sea and into the Atlantic back to Spain.

A few centuries on it made perfect sense to build
a railway across the isthmus, although swampy, mosquito-
buzzed and alligator-infested jungle presented quite
a challenge. Construction on the Panama Railroad began in
1850; in 1855 the last spike was hammered in. The world's
first-ever transcontinental railway was complete, running
from the purpose-built railhead of Colón on the Atlantic, to
Panama City on the Pacific. The Spanish would have loved it:
during its first 12 years of operation the railway transported
over US$750 million worth of gold.

It was good, but not good enough. From 1881 to 1914,
a canal was built across the isthmus. Its design, using
a system of locks and an artificial lake, meant flooding the
Chagres River valley – the route of the railway. So the railway
was moved, and now flanks the Panama Canal, offering
close-up views of this engineering marvel. Trains float across
Gatun Lake via narrow causeways, inch alongside the
man-made valley of Gaillard Cut, pass the immense locks
(which raise ships by 26m / 85ft) and glide through glorious,
bird-filled rainforest.

RIGHT: The Panama Canal
Railway seems to float across
Gatun Lake.

318
STOOMTRAM

Noord-Holland, Netherlands

During the Dutch Golden Age of the 17th century, the Netherlands boomed in everything from arts to commerce. Ports on the Zuider Zee (South Sea) – actually a shallow bay on the North Sea – did a roaring trade in spices from the East and beautified their streets on the riches. The gradual silting up of the Zuider Zee was a blow, but these 'dead cities' now boom with tourists instead. The multi-transport Stoomtram trip links three handsome harbours. First a steam tram connects the elegant port of Hoorn with the region's oldest city, Medemblik. Then an old-fashioned steam ship sails around the coast to Enkhuizen, a picturesque jumble of old streets and canals. From Enkhuizen, a regular diesel train runs back to Hoorn.

CHAPTER FIVE

19TH CENTURY

Hop aboard in the 1800s,
when science and invention
flourished and railways began
to transform the world.

METROPOLITAN LINE

London and Home Counties, United Kingdom

Ride the world's oldest underground, from the skyscrapers of the City to the fresh-aired commuter countryside.

Need to know
- *Point in time: 1863 (first underground railway opened in London)*
- *Length: 42 miles (67km)*
- *Minimum time: 1 hour 10 minutes*
- *Key stops: Aldgate, Farringdon, Baker Street, Harrow-on-the-Hill, Chorleywood, Amersham*
- *Countries crossed: United Kingdom*

LIKE THAT? TRY THIS

- - - - - - - - - - - - - - - - - - -

320. Tube Challenge
London, United Kingdom

The first stretch of London's 'Tube' opened in 1863. Now it has 270 stations. Current world record for visiting them all? Fifteen hours, 45 minutes, 38 seconds!

In the 19th century, London was the biggest city in the world, a seething mass of pollution, immigration, innovation, affluence and abject poverty. In the 1801 census, Greater London (comprising all London boroughs) logged 1,096,784 souls. By 1860 that number had tripled to 3,188,485. By 1901 it was 6,226,494. The city's increasingly crowded streets struggled. From the 1830s, railways arrived and lines running into stations such as Euston (opened 1837), Paddington (1838) and King's Cross (1850) delivered people to and from London. But this simply increased the horse-drawn traffic congestion within the city. Then a solution was posed: trains underground.

Construction of the first line began in 1860. Engineers mostly used a cut-and-cover method, digging up roads to avoid demolishing buildings. Tracks were laid in shallow trenches, a roof was built and then the road was restored.

London's – indeed, the world's – first underground railway opened on 10 January 1863. Wooden carriages hauled by steam engines ran the 3.75-mile (6km) route between Paddington and Farringdon Street (in the City business district); en route it called at the gas-lit subterranean stations of Edgware Road, Baker Street, Portland Road (now Great Portland Street), Gower Street (now Euston Square) and King's Cross. On that opening day, more than 30,000 people rode the Metropolitan Underground Railway; over the first year, it carried 9.5 million passengers. The Met was an immediate success.

The Metropolitan Railway grew quickly, in all directions. Most notably, there was rapid expansion to the northwest from Baker Street, underground and overground. By 1897 the Metropolitan Railway line reached far into Buckinghamshire, 50 miles (80km) from central London.

This sortie into the counties surrounding London was more than a transport link – it invented the idea of the commuter suburb. From 1919, the Metropolitan Railway built several housing estates along its network and advertised this 'Metro-land' as a place to find countryside charm within reach of the city. Mock Tudor houses in neat configurations cropped up in villages such as Chorleywood. Here, said the brochures, 'each lover of Metro-land may well have his own favourite wood beech and coppice' and benefit from 'the good air of the Chilterns'. It was a far cry from the unsanitary slums of Victorian London. Thanks to the underground and suburban railways, Londoners no longer had to live near their workplaces in squalid conditions.

The Metropolitan Railway was amalgamated with London's other underground railways in 1933; various Tube lines now use former Met tracks. However, it's the 42-mile (67km), purple-branded Metropolitan Line that traces the route from the City into 'Metro-land'. It starts in the City's financial district at Aldgate, site of the easternmost gateway through the Roman-era London Wall. From here the Met Line runs west through north-central London (Baker Street, Great Portland Street and Marylebone) via Barbican, Farringdon and King's Cross. At Finchley Road, in the borough of Camden, the rail line surfaces, running overground the rest of the way.

The line heads northwest via Wembley Park. This used to be a nothingness of soggy fields but, spotting a business opportunity, Metropolitan Railway Chairman Edward

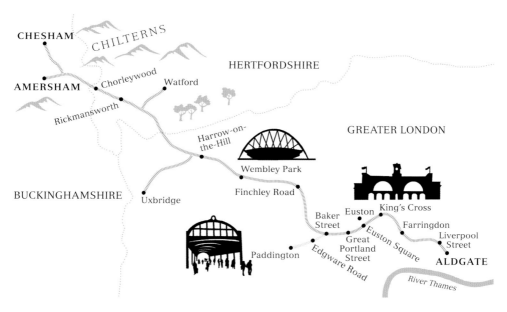

Watkin built an amusement complex of lakes, gardens and football pitches here, to open in time for the arrival of the railway in 1893. Wembley Park is now the site of Wembley Stadium, England's national football arena.

Continuing northwest, the Metropolitan Line splits in the borough of Harrow, a southerly branch heading to the town of Uxbridge, the more northerly forging right out of Greater London into Hertfordshire and Buckinghamshire. Here, the Met gives access to the chalk escarpment of the Chilterns, an Area of Outstanding Natural Beauty. Just over an hour from central London, you can disembark at Amersham or Chesham stations to inhale that promised 'good air'.

BELOW: The Metropolitan Line runs from central London into the Chilterns.

323
LONDON AND BIRMINGHAM RAILWAY

England, United Kingdom

Engineer extraordinaire Robert 'Rocket' Stephenson designed the London and Birmingham Railway (L&BR), the first intercity line into the United Kingdom's capital. Opened in September 1838, the L&BR ran for 112 miles (180km) from Birmingham's Curzon Street Station, via Coventry and Rugby, to London Euston. Before the arrival of rail, Euston was city-edge farmland but architect Philip Hardwick built a grand terminus here complete with the Euston Arch, a 21m (70ft) tall gritstone Doric gateway, the largest ever built. Sadly, the whole station (along with the arch) was demolished in the 1960s. The Euston Arch Trust is campaigning to get it resurrected.

324
SWANSEA AND MUMBLES RAILWAY

Wales, United Kingdom

In 1807, the Swansea and Mumbles line transported the world's first fare-paying railway passengers. It opened in 1806 to lug mined goods between the fishing village of Oystermouth and the canal at Swansea, Wales's second-largest city. However, the railway owners saw an opportunity and soon people were riding the iron rails in horse-drawn carriages, enjoying sweeping views of Swansea Bay. Horses were fully replaced by steam locomotives by 1896; by 1898 the line was extended further south to Mumbles Head. The train stopped running in 1960 and was replaced by a 5-mile (8km) promenade, which ends at Mumbles' Victorian pier.

MILLENNIUM UNDERGROUND RAILWAY (M1)

Budapest, Hungary

Ride beneath the Hungarian capital on one of the world's
first, and most handsome, underground railways.

Need to know
- *Point in time: 1896 (Millennium Underground Railway opened)*
- *Length: 2.7 miles (4.4km)*
- *Minimum time: 11 minutes*
- *Key stops: Vörösmarty Square, Opera, Vörösmarty Street, Széchenyi Baths, Mexikói Street*
- *Countries crossed: Hungary*

BELOW: For the historic
Café Gerbeaud alight at
Vörösmarty Square.

Budapest's first metro line was the world's second. Only the
London Underground predates the Hungarian capital's M1,
which runs beneath grand Andrássy Avenue. It's officially
called the Millennium Underground Railway because it was
built to coincide with the thousandth anniversary of the
Magyars' arrival in Hungary. Construction began in 1894
and it opened in 1896, just in time to ferry patriotic revellers
to the massive Magyar celebrations in City Park. One of the
first passengers was Austro-Hungarian Emperor Franz
Joseph I, who travelled aboard a special royal subway car.

The M1 still runs, now serving eleven stops along the
city's glamorous thoroughfare. Ridden southwest to
northeast, it begins at Vörösmarty Square, where the
subway entrance sits amid the pavement tables of Café
Gerbeaud. This traditional white-stucco, chandelier-
sparkled coffee house has been serving customers in its
current location since 1870.

SITES, STEAM AND STATIONS

326. Semmering Railway
Eastern Alps, Austria

The 26-mile (42km) Semmering Railway, linking Gloggnitz and Mürzzuschlag, was completed in 1854. It has sixteen viaducts, fourteen tunnels and over 100 stone bridges.

327. Wolsztyn–Leszno
Western Poland

Steam trains started operating from the town of Wolsztyn in 1896 – and they still do, making this the world's last scheduled steam passenger service.

328. Paris–Marseille Railway
France

The 536-mile (862km) Paris–Marseille Railway got more glamorous in 1900 when Paris's Gare de Lyon terminus opened a new belle époque buffet, Le Train Bleu, still serving today.

329. Crystal Palace High Level
London, United Kingdom

After the 1851 Great Exhibition, the 'Crystal Palace' was moved to Sydenham and two railway stations were opened. The Low Level station is still in operation; the High Level is, for now, an elegant lost relic.

The second stop is Deák Ferenc Square, where an Underground Museum occupies an original M1 platform. Franz Joseph's royal carriage is on display. Bajcsy-Zsilinszky Street is the stop for the Neoclassical St Stephen's Basilica, said to contain the right hand of the 11th-century saint-king of Hungary. Opera is, unsurprisingly, the stop for Budapest's magnificent State Opera House, opened just before the Metro.

After Oktogon, the M1 calls at Vörösmarty Street Station, home to the House of Terror, a chilling museum dedicated to victims of the fascist and communist regimes in 20th-century Hungary. Lighter relief is available a few stops on at Széchenyi Baths. This is the entrance to the City Park, home to a zoo, botanical gardens, Vajdahunyad Castle (built for the 1896 celebrations) and a sunshine-yellow, neo-baroque bathhouse, where you can loll in the thermal outdoor pool.

BALTIMORE AND
OHIO RAILROAD

Maryland, United States

The Baltimore and Ohio Railroad
Museum, in the city of Baltimore,
is the birthplace of America's
railways. On this site, on 4 July
1828, Charles Carroll (last living
signatory of the Declaration of
Independence) did the initial
ground-breaking for the Baltimore
and Ohio Railroad (B&O).
Engineers then began building
the B&O, the country's first
commercial railway. In January
1830 the B&O launched a 1.5-mile
(2.4km) line, then a 13-mile (21km)
line to Ellicott's Mills (now a
national historic district). By
the 1970s, the B&O controlled
10,000 miles (16,000km) of railway.
The company no longer exists but
the museum's Mile One Express
runs along that original
momentous section of track.

SAINT-ÉTIENNE TO
ANDRÉZIEUX RAILWAY

Massif Central, France

France's fabulous railway network
started with an inauspicious
11-mile (18km) track in the Loire
Valley. In 1827, the country's –
indeed, continental Europe's – first
rail line opened, designed to link
the mines of Saint-Étienne to the
River Loire at Andrézieux.
Wagons were drawn by horse,
and originally full of coal.
In 1832, the first passengers and
the first steam locomotives
arrived. Now France is a-whizz
with speedy TGV trains, and few
people travel to Andrézieux's
tumbleweed station anymore.
However, rail aficionados should
give Saint-Étienne's Museum
of Urban Transport a look.

RIGHT: Brunel's vision
was to provide a rail link to
Dublin, along Ireland's coast.

DUBLIN–ROSSLARE

Eastern Ireland

Ride one of Isambard Kingdom Brunel's railway
masterpieces alongside the Irish Sea.

Need to know
- *Point in time: 1806–
  1859 (life of Isambard
  Kingdom Brunel)*
- *Length: 100 miles
  (161km)*
- *Minimum time:
  2 hours 45 minutes*
- *Key stops: Dublin,
  Dún Laoghaire, Bray,
  Wicklow, Arklow,
  Enniscorthy, Wexford,
  Rosslare*
- *Countries crossed:
  Ireland*

The Dublin–Rosslare line incorporates Ireland's first railway:
the short section from capital Dublin to the port of Dún
Laoghaire opened in 1834. It also incorporates the
handiwork of pre-eminent British engineer Isambard
Kingdom Brunel. Brunel was a one-man Industrial
Revolution whose many and varied endeavours transformed
transportation in the 19th century. He had a hand in all sorts
of escapades, from Bristol's Clifton Suspension Bridge to
the pioneering iron steamship, SS *Great Britain*. In 1846,
Brunel was planning a railway into Wales to serve a new
sea route from Fishguard to the Irish harbour of Rosslare.
He saw building a connection from Rosslare to Dublin as
an obvious next step, to connect to the Irish capital.

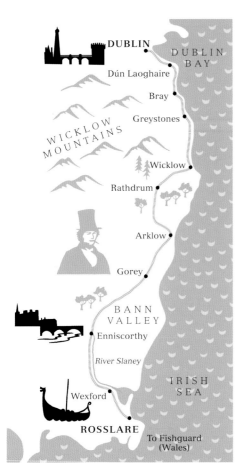

The most challenging – and spectacular – stretch of the Dublin–Rosslare railway was between the towns of Bray and Wicklow (opened 1855). Brunel chose to brave the coastal route rather than an easier, less scenic option inland. Subsequently, the line became known as 'Brunel's Folly'. Three tunnels were bored through the ancient rock of Bray Head; more have been dug since, in the railway's ongoing fight with nature.

But what a wonderful ride. From Dublin, trains trace Dublin Bay and skirt the coast down to Bray. From there follows the dramatic single-track, cliff-balancing section. After Wicklow, the train veers into the forested foothills of the Wicklow Mountains and back to the coast at the town of Arklow. Then it's inland again, along the Bann Valley to the heritage town of Enniscorthy. Here, during the 1916 Easter Rising, Irish Republicans seized control of the railway to prevent British troops from accessing Dublin. Next, the train stops at the Viking-founded town of Wexford before reaching Rosslare, where ferries leave for Fishguard, just as Brunel planned.

BRUNEL BRILLIANCE

333. Plymouth–Saltash
Southwest England, United Kingdom

Ride from Devon to Cornwall, crossing the River Tamar via Isambard Kingdom Brunel's wrought-iron Royal Albert Bridge, opened in 1859.

334. Thames Tunnel
London, United Kingdom

Brunel's Thames Tunnel (opened 1843) was designed for pedestrians and later converted for railways. Now the Brunel Museum in Rotherhithe occupies its old entranceway.

335. Taplow–Maidenhead
Berkshire, United Kingdom

When it was completed in 1838, Brunel's Maidenhead Bridge over the River Thames was the world's flattest and widest brick-arch bridge.

336. London Paddington–Bristol Temple Meads
United Kingdom

Brunel designed the two termini of the Great Western Railway. He also built the 1.83-mile (2.95km) Box Tunnel en route, the world's longest rail tunnel when it opened in 1841.

CAPE TO CAIRO RAILWAY

Africa

Piece together a train journey through the African continent
to live the dream of British Empire–builder Cecil Rhodes.

Need to know

- *Point in time: 1853–
  1902 (lifetime of
  Cecil Rhodes)*
- *Length: Around
  6,525 miles (10,500km)*
- *Minimum time:
  currently indefinable*
- *Key stops: Cairo,
  Aswan, Khartoum,
  Nairobi, Dar es
  Salaam, Lusaka,
  Livingstone,
  Bulawayo,
  Johannesburg,
  Cape Town*
- *Countries crossed:
  Egypt, Sudan, South
  Sudan, Ethiopia,
  Kenya, Tanzania,
  Zambia, Zimbabwe,
  South Africa*

MINING MARVELS

- - - - - - - - - - - - - - - - - - -

338. Great Laxey Mine Railway
Isle of Man

Visit the village of Laxey
for a ride on the railway
(opened 1870) that once
carried lead and zinc ore
from deep inside the
Great Laxey Mine.

At the end of the 19th century, entrepreneur and empire-builder Cecil Rhodes had a very grand plan: he wanted to link all of Britain's interests in Africa by train. The Cape to Cairo Railway would be a majestic line running the length of the continent, from the Mediterranean Sea to the Southern Ocean. Rhodes believed that it would be a unifying spine, connecting colonies and helping to 'paint the map red', spreading the cartographical colour of British imperialism across the globe.

Rhodes, the son of a Hertfordshire vicar, first moved to the British-ruled Cape Colony (now South Africa) in 1870 to farm cotton. He moved on to diamonds, co-founding De Beers Mining Company in 1880, then politics, becoming prime minister of the Cape Colony from 1890 to 1896.

Rhodes' main aim was expansion northward. He wanted to further his own mining interests, to increase British dominion and to ensure that the Cape Colony didn't become cut off from the rest of the continent by the Portuguese, Belgians and Germans grabbing land above. Rhodes thought little of the rights of 'the natives', as he called them; some historians call him the 'architect of apartheid', the racially discriminatory system of the later 20th century. Rhodes certainly succeeded in creating a vast empire, and his actions forever changed the make-up of southern Africa.

By the turn of the 20th century, the British Empire controlled an almost continuous top-to-toe corridor of territories. This ran from Egypt, through Anglo-Egyptian Sudan (now Sudan and South Sudan) and Uganda to British East Africa (now Kenya). Here, there was a hiatus: Germany controlled Tanganyika (Tanzania) and the Belgians dominated Congo. But south of that lay newly British Empire–incorporated Northern and Southern Rhodesia (Zambia and Zimbabwe) then Bechuanaland (Botswana), Swaziland, Basutoland (Lesotho) and South Africa.

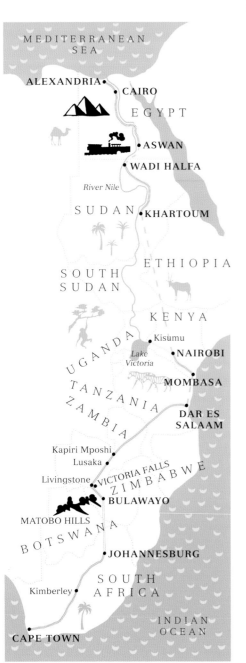

A Cape to Cairo Railway would, according to Rhodes, provide unity, assist governance, facilitate settlement and trade, and enable the military to mobilise quickly if necessary. Such a link was not built in Rhodes' lifetime, and still does not exist today. But with time and patience it's possible to cover much of the continent along a similar route.

Trains run right through Egypt, from the Mediterranean port of Alexandria along the Nile to Aswan, via the glorious monuments of the Ancient Egyptians. From Aswan, a weekly steamer sails along the Nile to the city of Wadi Halfa in Sudan. Here a train line, begun by the British in 1897, connects onwards across the desert to the Sudanese capital, Khartoum.

Things get sketchy after that. South Sudan (currently on the UK Foreign and Commonwealth Office no-go list), western Ethiopia, Uganda and northern Kenya have no connecting, functioning railways. In 1892 the British built a line – dubbed the 'Lunatic Express' – across Kenya, to

LEFT: The bridge over the Zambezi, near Victoria Falls no longer carries regular trains.

connect Kisumu, on Lake Victoria, to the Indian Ocean port of Mombasa. However, currently only the section from Nairobi to the coast is operational (see p. 244).

From Mombasa there's another gap. No trains link Kenya and Tanzania. However, once in Tanzania it's possible to take trains from Dar es Salaam all the way to Livingstone in Zambia. Passengers must walk over the border into Zimbabwe – the bridge over the Zambezi, near Victoria Falls, no longer carries regular trains except a short tourist steam loco.

In Zimbabwe, services run to the leafy city of Bulawayo (Cecil Rhodes is buried just to the south, amid the bulbous Matobo Hills). Currently, there are no functioning onward trains. Services used to connect into Botswana and South Africa but at the moment the best option is the Bulawayo–Johannesburg bus. In Johannesburg, the train picks up again, with a direct service running right to Cape Town. All in all, it's a slow, disjointed but epic adventure.

MINING MARVELS

339. Rio Tinto Railway
Andalucía, Spain

This narrow gauge railway, built in 1875, served the vast mine complex of Rio Tinto. A tourist train covers a 7.5-mile (12km) section, exploring the lunar-like mining landscape.

340. Denniston Mine, South Island
New Zealand

Denniston coal mine began operation in 1879; now you can take a ride on the old mine tracks into its inky depths.

341
THE CRESCENT

United States

Amtrak's Crescent service runs for 1,377 miles (2,216km) from the 'Big Apple' to the 'Big Easy', slowly sinking into America's Deep South via the Blue Ridge Mountains and plenty of Civil War history. Indeed, the New York–New Orleans train passes Manassas (Virginia), site of the 1861 Battle of Bull Run, the war's first major conflict. It visits Lynchburg (Virginia) where, in nearby Appomattox Courthouse, Confederate General Robert E. Lee surrendered to Union General Ulysses S. Grant in 1865, ending the war. It stops at Atlanta (Georgia), burnt to ashes by Unionists in 1864. And it wends via old antebellum plantations that whisper of pre-war days.

342
ARICA–LA PAZ RAILWAY

Chile and Bolivia

The 273-mile (440km) line between Bolivian capital La Paz and the Chilean port of Arica is a remuneration railway. Following the War of the Pacific (1879–83), which saw Bolivia and Peru lose territory to Chile, Bolivia was left landlocked. The Arica–La Paz Railway, completed in 1913, was built by the Chilean government as compensation, to give Bolivia access to the Pacific. It was no easy undertaking – this is one of the highest railways in the world, rising from sea level to over 4,200m (13,800ft). Sadly, it closed to passenger trains in 1996 but recently work has been carried out to restore the line and services may resume someday.

343
ALLEGRO

Finland and Russia

The high-speed Allegro service, which can travel at 137 miles per hour (220kph), links the cities of Helsinki and St Petersburg in just 3.5 hours. But then, Finland and Russia have long had close links. Following Russia's defeat of the Swedes in the Finnish War (1808–09), it took control of the region, creating the autonomous Grand Duchy of Finland. It was Russian Emperor Alexander I who moved the Finnish capital from Turku to Helsinki in 1812. Finland gained independence in 1917, and today even the border-crossing formalities – carried out on board at either Vyborg (Russia) or Vainikkala (Finland) – don't slow the Allegro down.

344
CANNONS RAILWAY

France and Germany

When Germany annexed Alsace-Lorraine from France in 1871 following the Franco-Prussian War, it sought to secure its new territory by building a railway. The 500-mile (805km) Kanonenbahn (Cannons Railway) linked the Lorraine city of Metz, on the banks of the Moselle, to German capital Berlin. Comprising both new and existing tracks, it was completed by 1882. The full line no longer exists but its flagship edifice, the Gare de Metz-Ville (opened 1908), still dazzles. The neo-Romanesque station has a 40m-high (131ft) clock tower, decorative arches, a palace-like arrivals hall and Holy Roman Emperor Charlemagne rendered in stained glass.

ERITREAN RAILWAY

Eritrea

Admire amazing African landscapes on a vintage
steam train trip along an Italian-built line.

Need to know
- *Point in time: 1887–1911 (Eritrean Railway built)*
- *Length: 73 miles (118km)*
- *Minimum time: 1 day*
- *Key stops: Massawa, Ghinda, Nefasit, Asmara*
- *Countries crossed: Eritrea*

BELOW: The restored
Eritrean Railway starts in the
Red Sea port of Massawa.

When the Italians grabbed Eritrea during the scramble for
African colonies in the late 19th century, they were quick
to start work on a railway. They wanted a line that would
connect the Red Sea port of Massawa to Asmara, their
capital in the highlands. Such a railway would be handy
for moving troops, as well as transporting goods from
mines to the coast.

It was not an easy build. Over its 73-mile (118km) route,
the line had to climb to the 2,394m (7,854ft) high Asmara
plateau. This meant slow progress and some impressive
engineering. For instance, the short section between the
town of Nefasit and Asmara required thirty-nine tunnels
and sixty-five viaducts and bridges. Asmara was reached
in 1911, from where the Italians continued westwards,
connecting the town of Bishia in 1932.

ABOVE: Ride through Eritrea's amazing landscapes on a vintage steam train.

However, the rest of the 20th century wasn't kind to the railway, with the Second World War and then the Eritrean War of Independence. However, in 1993, the government of Eritrea (newly independent from Ethiopia) decided to rebuild the Massawa–Asmara section.

It reopened in 2003, and journeys using restored Mallet steam engines plunged through the spectacular countryside. Magnificent locomotives puffed over stone-arch spans, crossed precipitous ravines and passed sheer cliffs, deep valleys, mountains laced with cloud and the odd camel.

The current status of the line isn't entirely clear, although it remains a bucket-list ride for ardent railway fans, and charter trains for tourists do periodically run. In any case Italian-influenced Asmara, with its attractive art deco architecture, its cafés serving perfect espressos, and its fascinating old railway workshop, is well worth a visit.

ORIENT EXPRESS

France—Turkey

Trace the route of the world's most glamorous train
service, crossing Europe from Paris to Istanbul.

Need to know

- *Point in time: 1883
  (Orient Express
  launched)*
- *Length: 1,975 miles
  (3,180km)*
- *Minimum time: 4 days*
- *Key stops: Paris,
  Strasbourg, Munich,
  Vienna, Budapest,
  Bucharest, Istanbul*
- *Countries crossed:
  France, Germany,
  Austria, Hungary,
  Romania, Bulgaria,
  Turkey*

The Orient Express is the epitome of rail glamour. The
original A-lister. The benchmark against which all other
trains are measured. It's not just that this trans-Europe
service was so opulent. It's that the route evokes rail travel's
most romantic era, the roaring 1920s: coupe champagne
glasses, neat tuxedos and dazzling evening gowns. This was
when the high style of the Orient Express best fitted the
spirit of the times and commercial planes had yet to provide
a faster option. Aristocrats, diplomats and starlets were
swaddled in its sumptuousness, while war-scarred Europe
rolled past the window.

The first Orient Express service left Paris in 1883, bound
for Romania. At riverside Giurgiu, passengers disembarked
for a boat across the Danube to Bulgaria, where another

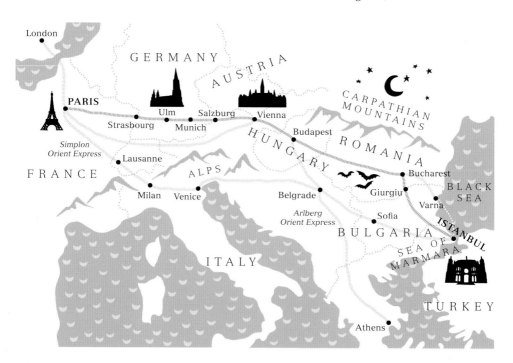

train whisked them to Varna to board the Black Sea ferry to Constantinople (Istanbul).

It was in 1889 that the first through-train ran from Paris to Istanbul, via Strasbourg, Munich, Vienna, Budapest and Bucharest. It took around 68 hours. The route changed, expanded and contracted over the years. For instance, a more southerly Simplon Orient Express (via Sofia and Venice) ran on and off from 1919 to 1977. The Arlberg Orient Express, which terminated in Athens, ran from 1930 to 1962 (excluding the Second World War). But the journey via Vienna and Bucharest is perhaps the most authentic.

If you look at the current timetable, you'll see that there's no longer a scheduled 'Orient Express'. The service finally ended when the EuroNight #469 Orient Express Strasbourg–Vienna train made its last run on 12 December 2009. That service, a seriously cut-back fragment of the original Paris–Istanbul route, was the last true descendant of the old Orient Express – the only service bearing the historic name that could trace its timetabling back to 1883. However, Europe has an extensive rail network, and it is possible to piece together separate trains that trace the Orient Express route – albeit without the be-gloved butlers and plush Wagons-Lits sleeping carriages.

MORE CLASSY CARRIAGES
- - - - - - - - - - - - - - - - - - - -

347. Metra Electric District
Illinois, United States

Take a short ride from downtown Chicago to the town of Pullman, which was founded by American industrialist George Pullman (1831–97), pioneer of the sleeping carriage.

BELOW: Istanbul's grand Sirkeci Station opened in 1888 as the eastern terminus of the Orient Express.

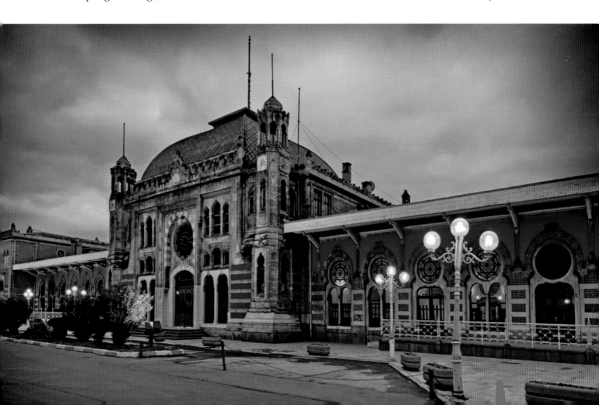

From Paris's Gare de l'Est station you can ride across the First World War battlefields of northern France to the Alsace city of Strasbourg, with its fine medieval centre and modern European parliament buildings. From Strasbourg, on the French border, take a train into Germany, passing Ulm's magnificent minster (with the world's tallest church steeple) before pulling into the Bavarian capital Munich. Stop here for oompah-and-*lederhosen* fun at the Hofbräuhaus beer hall. Then continue east into the Alps, via beautiful Salzburg (birthplace of Mozart), to Vienna. The Austrian capital is the height of elegance, all palaces, opera houses, Jugendstil (Art Nouveau) architecture and smoky old cafés serving delectable cakes.

It's a short train ride from here to Budapest. Straddling the Danube, the Hungarian capital is the place to soak in traditional bathhouses, climb to Buda Castle or board a clattering tram. Next, ride across Transylvania and the Carpathian mountains to reach Romanian capital Bucharest, where dictator Nicolae Ceauşescu's hulking Palace of Parliament is probably scarier than any vampire's castle.

From Bucharest it's possible to reach Istanbul, the edge of Europe. The old Orient Express would have swung around the Sea of Marmara and pulled up at Istanbul's central Sirkeci Station, a grand, Orientalist-style terminus opened in 1888. However, services into Istanbul are currently disrupted (a bus transfer is required), and Sirkeci itself closed to overground trains in 2013. The minaret-speared, continent-spanning city still makes a fantastic finale, though. Finish at the Pera Palace Hotel, opened in 1895 to host Orient Express passengers and refurbished in 2010. Book Room 411, where British crime writer Agatha Christie reputedly wrote her 1934 thriller *Murder on the Orient Express.*

BELOW: The Venice Simplon-Orient-Express aims to maintain the glamour of the original luxury railway.

VENICE SIMPLON-ORIENT-EXPRESS

United Kingdom—Italy

Sadly, the wonderful, original Paris–Istanbul Orient Express (launched 1883) no longer exists. But Belmond's uber-luxe Venice Simplon-Orient-Express does its best to keep the legendary journey alive. Belmond's classic 1-night trip from London to Venice starts with Bellini cocktails, served aboard the luxurious British Pullman train to Folkestone. Passengers then take a ferry across the English Channel before picking up the magnificently refurbished 1920s carriages of the Venice Simplon-Orient-Express itself. With delectable dinners, afternoon tea, silver service, exquisite sleeping cars and Alpine scenes rolling by, this is bygone rail glamour brought back to life.

EASTERN AND ORIENTAL EXPRESS

Singapore, Malaysia and Thailand

Travel between Singapore and Bangkok in cool colonial style, via a riot of tropical jungle.

Need to know
- *Point in time: 1819–1942 (Britain ruled Singapore)*
- *Length: 1,233 miles (1,920km)*
- *Minimum time: 3 days*
- *Key stops: Woodlands, Kuala Lumpur, Kuala Kangsar, Padang Besar, Hua Hin, Bangkok*
- *Countries crossed: Singapore, Malaysia, Thailand*

ALTERNATIVE MALAYSIA
- - - - - - - - - - - - - - - - - - -

350. East Coast Line
Singapore–Malaysia

The 445-mile (716km) 'Jungle Line' from Singapore to Kota Bharu is the alternative trans-Malaysia train, passing lush hills and plantations.

RIGHT: Before boarding the E&O train, passengers should visit the Raffles Hotel for a Singapore Sling cocktail.

In Singapore, the *only* place to be seen before boarding the Eastern and Oriental Express (E&O) is the Raffles Hotel. Opened in 1887, Raffles is a Colonial Revival–style local institution and birthplace of the Singapore Sling cocktail. It's also named for Sir Thomas Stamford Raffles, founder of modern Singapore.

In the early 19th century, Britain was expanding its influence over India and increasing trade with China. As such, there was a need to establish a safe port in the Far East. In 1819, Raffles – then lieutenant-governor of Bencoolen (Sumatra) – travelled to the southern tip of the Malay Peninsula. He made a quick survey of the outlying island of Singapore, recognised its potential and immediately concluded a treaty with the de facto sultan to secure Britain's rights to set up shop. When Raffles arrived, there were around 1,000 people living on the island. By 1869, some 100,000 had been drawn to the flourishing trading post. Today, Singapore's population is over 5.3 million.

Like the Raffles Hotel, the Eastern and Oriental Express feels like a throwback to pre-modern Singapore – a time when one lounged on rattan furniture and always dressed for dinner. Actually, the train's sleeping cars were built in the 1970s for use in New Zealand but have since been exoticised, with decor that combines colonial glamour with Asiatic motifs. The E&O also has silver-service dining cars, a piano bar and an open-sided observation deck that gives unhindered views and blasts of tropical air.

The E&O, launched in 1993, was the first train to run direct between Singapore and Thailand's capital, Bangkok. It used to depart from Singapore's crumbling, art deco Tanjong Pagar Station until the building closed in 2011. Now the train leaves from Woodlands Train Checkpoint just south of the causeway that links Singapore island to the Malaysian peninsula. This means that the first moments aboard involve gliding across the Johor Strait, skyscrapers receding behind.

The E&O's route follows the West Coast Line, the single-track railway that runs up the western side of Peninsular Malaysia to the Thai border. It was built between 1885 and 1932, and is currently undergoing modernisation. To begin, the line cuts through a profusion of oil palm and rubber plantations before reaching the bright lights of Kuala Lumpur, Malaysia's capital. Here it pulls into the 1911 Moorish Revival–style Kuala Lumpur Railway Station, a wedding-cake confection of arches and domed pavilions.

After a night ensconced in luxurious cabins, passengers wake to breakfast in bed (on a silver tray, of course). Soon the train arrives at the royal town of Kuala Kangsar, where there's a tour of the golden Ubudiah Mosque and the former sultans' palace, now a museum. It's not far from here to Thailand. Though no regular trains cross at the border town

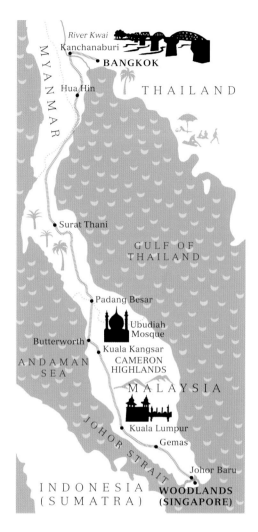

LIKE THAT? TRY THIS

----

351. Yangon–Mandalay Express
Myanmar

Travel the 388-mile (622km) British-built colonial railway (opened 1877) between two of Myanmar's biggest cities, a journey of around 15 hours.

of Padang Besar, the E&O is permitted to glide straight through. It picks up Thailand's Southern Line (opened 1903), spending the day and night chugging past mighty karst mountains, waterfall-splashed jungle and lively market towns.

Early on Day 3, the train detours down a branch line, past the town of Kanchanaburi, to the Bridge on the River Kwai. This is the notorious span, part of the Burma 'Death Railway', built by Allied prisoners during the Second World War. Passengers disembark for a boat trip beneath the bridge as the E&O is driven across – the ultimate photo op. Then it's back on board, to arrive in Bangkok by mid-afternoon.

Of course, the E&O isn't the only way to cover this route. Using regular trains, travelling Singapore–Kuala Lumpur–Butterworth–Padang Besar–Bangkok, the journey can be done in around 48 hours – for a fraction of the price. Just with fewer cocktails and less colonial charm.

ABOVE RIGHT: The train cuts along the steep cliffs of the Kwai River near the infamous bridge.

RIGHT: The Eastern and Oriental stops at Kuala Kangsar for a tour of the Ubudiah Mosque.

352
NORTH BORNEO RAILWAY

Borneo, Malaysia

North Borneo, now the Malaysian state of Sabah, became a British protectorate in 1882. And the steam-pulled carriages of the North Borneo Railway take passengers back to those colonial times, with their natural-wood interiors, polished brass fittings and traditional tiffin lunches. Trains run twice weekly, taking 4 hours to make the return trip from Tanjung Aru Station (near Sabah's capital, Kota Kinabalu) to the rice-growing town of Papar. En route it traverses a swathe of beautiful Borneo countryside, from coastal towns and teetering stilt villages to thick rainforests, coffee plantations and lush paddy fields.

PODI MENIKE

Sri Lanka

Tackle a spectacular series of tunnels and bridges to delve
into the Indian Ocean island's lush tea county.

Need to know
- *Point in time: 1824
  (first tea plant brought
  to Sri Lanka)*
- *Length: 181 miles
  (292km)*
- *Minimum time:
  10 hours*
- *Key stops: Colombo,
  Kandy, Hatton,
  Nanuoya, Haputale,
  Demodara, Badulla*
- *Countries crossed:
  Sri Lanka*

INDUSTRIAL ICONS

**354. Llangollen
Railway**
Wales, United Kingdom

Ride 10 miles (16km)
through the Dee Valley
on a mostly steam-
hauled heritage line, first
opened for commercial
service in 1865.

355. Inca–Manacor
Mallorca, Spain

Take a 22-mile (35km)
train ride from the town
of Inca to Manacor,
where the Majorica
company has been
making the world's finest
fake pearls since 1890.

Sri Lanka ranks fourth in the league table of tea-producing nations. Only China, India and Kenya grow more *Camellia sinensis* than the comparatively tiny teardrop isle. Indeed, Sri Lanka's central highlands are blanketed with plantations – great, green, glorious, shrubbery-swathed slopes. And yet the first tea plant didn't arrive here until 1824.

The British, who officially took control of Sri Lanka (then Ceylon) in 1815, brought a plant from China and placed it on display in the Royal Botanical Gardens in Peradeniya, near the city of Kandy. The country was a huge coffee producer at the time, so when Scottish coffee planter James Taylor decided to sow several acres of tea on the Loolecondera Estate in 1867, many thought he was rather odd. However, two years later coffee blight began decimating Sri Lanka's main cash crop. By 1870, coffee plantation owners had either left the island or switched to tea-growing instead. Today, more than a million Sri Lankans are employed in the tea industry and tea is still picked by hand to insure a high-quality brew.

Sri Lanka's plantations were the driving force behind its railways. From 1858, the British began constructing lines to transport coffee, then tea, from the interior to the capital, Colombo. The first line, running inland from Colombo to the town of Ambepussa, was completed in 1864; it was extended to Kandy by 1867. The full route to the city of Badulla, in the central hills, was finished in 1924.

While the high-altitude slopes were good for growing tea, they were not so kind for building railways. This 181-mile (292km) line required more than forty tunnels and many bridges to get into the country's undulating middle. It climbs from sea level to its highest point at Pattipola (1,898m / 6,227ft), then drops 1,250m (4,101ft) in just 40 miles (65km). The most vertiginous section is between the stations of Kadugannawa and Balana, where the train runs along the very edge of a 300m (1,000ft) drop.

One of the biggest challenges was the especially steep section at Demodara. This was overcome with the construction of the Demodara Loop: the rail line passes under itself via a 900m (3,000ft) long spiral, to emerge from a tunnel directly beneath Demodara Station. It's said that the engineers happened on this solution while watching the local *kangany* (supervisor) untie and retie the cloth of his turban-style hat.

The whole journey is a scenic unfurling of Sri Lankan countryside. From Colombo, the train passes city outskirts

BELOW: The Podi Menike cuts right through the highland tea plantations.

and bird-rich marshland. Then it heads uphill, running through an endless lushness of fragrant tea, the emerald of the leaves only outshone by the rainbow-bright saris of the women picking them.

At Peradeniya Junction a branch-line detours to Kandy. Not all Colombo–Badulla services take this branch; the Podi Menike train does, making it the best choice – because Kandy shouldn't be missed. Sri Lanka's second city is the island's cultural hub and home to the Temple of the Sacred Tooth Relic, said to contain one of Buddha's teeth.

The train also stops at Hatton, disembarkation station for Adam's Peak. Thousands of pilgrims make the climb to visit the (reputed) Buddha footprint on its summit. Others admire the peak from the train.

Tea pilgrims should stop at Nanuoya Station, railhead for Nuwara Eliya, Sri Lanka's highest town. Established as a cool-aired hill station by the British in 1846, it's a bizarre 'Little Britain' of mock-Tudor mansions, colonial hotels and gentleman's clubs amid the tropics. It's also one of Sri Lanka's most important tea-growing areas, where you can stay in a converted tea-planter bungalow and enjoy a perfect cuppa.

RIGHT: Be sure to take the branch line to Kandy, to visit the Buddhist Temple of the Tooth.

356
HAVANA–SANTIAGO

Cuba

The then-Spanish colony of Cuba
got its first railway in 1837, before
there were any railways in Spain.
The impetus was sugar. During the
19th century, Cuban sugar-cane
production boomed. Rail lines
spread across the length of the
island, with steam trains
transporting tonnes of 'white
gold'. Steam power persisted in
Cuba until the early 21st century.
Now diesel has taken over and the
rail network has shrunk but train
travel remains a good way to get
around and meet local people.
Try the 530-mile (854km) ride
between capital Havana and
salsa-swaying Santiago to link two
of Cuba's most atmospheric cities.

357
SUGAR CANE TRAIN

Hawaii, United States

Maui got its first railway in 1890.
Pioneer Mill, the island's first
commercial sugar plantation,
laid a short narrow gauge line
to transport its goods to market.
The line was closed in the 1950s
but didn't die. In 1969, the
Lahaina, Kaanapali and Pacific
Railroad – or 'Sugar Cane Train' –
began running vintage steam
locomotive rides along a 6-mile
(10km) section, from the mill at
Lahaina to Puukolii Station. At
Lahaina, visitors can see the mill's
old 69m (225ft) high smokestack,
renovated in 2010. There's also an
exhibit of antique equipment and
two 19th-century Baldwin
locomotives that once hauled
Pioneer's precious crop.

358
OURO PRETO–MARIANA

Minas Gerais, Eastern Brazil

The city of Ouro Preto was the nexus of the Brazilian Gold Rush, sitting at the heart of Minas Gerais's mining country. Hence, it became the first city in the region to be served by rail. Between 1883 and 1914, an 11-mile (18km) line was laid, with some effort, across the verdant mountains from Ouro Preto (now a UNESCO World Heritage site) to the colonial town of Mariana. The line fell out of use but was restored in the early 21st century. Now wide-windowed tourist trains run on Fridays, Saturdays and Sundays, offering views over swathes of forest and those precious gold-filled hills.

359
PRISON RAILWAY

French Guiana

France sent its first boatload of convicts to French Guiana in 1852. The South American outpost remained a French penal colony until 1951, and was a savage place to serve a sentence – in conditions made infamous by Henri Charrière's book *Papillon* (1969). Early convicts arrived at the city of St-Laurent-du-Maroni before being sent to *bagne* (prison camps) countrywide. To aid this, between 1890 and 1897 a railway was built from St-Laurent to a bagne in St-Jean, further upstream. No railway remains now but St-Laurent still has old colonial prison buildings as well as the remains of the railway's main depot, now an overgrown skeleton of steel.

THE OLD PATAGONIAN EXPRESS

Patagonia, Argentina

Take a short trip aboard 'La Trochita' via
Andean foothills and remote Welsh settler towns.

Need to know

- *Point in time: 1865 (Welsh arrived in Patagonia)*
- *Length: 103 miles (166km)*
- *Minimum time: 9 hours*
- *Key stops: Esquel, Nahuel Pan, La Cancha, Leleque, Bruno Thomae, El Maitén*
- *Countries crossed: Argentina*

'But, truly, the worst trains take one across the best landscapes.' That's how American writer Paul Theroux summed up his ride on the Old Patagonian Express in his book of that name. It was published in 1979 and introduced the world to this tough little narrow gauge steam loco – nicknamed 'La Trochita' – that has been wheezing across the remote wilds of southern Argentina since 1945.

When Theroux hopped aboard, La Trochita ran for 250 miles (402km) from the small outpost of Ingeniero Jacobacci (named after railway director Guido Jacobacci) to the town of Esquel. Esquel was founded by Welsh immigrants who arrived in Patagonia from 1865 to set up Welsh-speaking colonies. They expected to find something like the green valleys of home; instead they got the windswept pampas grassland, dramatic but bleak.

Bleak is just how things looked for La Trochita in the 1990s. Only public outcry saved it from cancellation; the railway was subsequently declared a National Historic Monument. However, there are no scheduled services. Irregular tourist trains run the 12-mile (19km) section between Esquel and Nahuel Pan. Infrequent chartered specials cover the 103 miles (166km) between Esquel and the town of El Maitén.

But even a short ride here is an atmospheric one. When La Trochita runs, it's still pulled by one of the original oil-fired steam locomotives, either a German Henschel or an American Baldwin. And, as Theroux noted, the train crosses the 'best landscapes': out of the window, the foothills of the Andes glide by.

ABOVE: Patagonia is a region of big-sky landscapes.

LEFT: 'La Trochita' continues to wheeze, albeit irregularly, from the town of Esquel.

DARJEELING HIMALAYAN RAILWAY

West Bengal, India

Take a gravity-defying 'toy' railway to a colonial hill
station for marvellous mountain views.

Need to know
- *Point in time: 1879–
  1881 (Darjeeling
  Himalayan
  Railway built)*
- *Length: 52 miles
  (84km)*
- *Minimum time:
  7 hours 15 minutes*
- *Key stops: New
  Jalpaiguri, Siliguri,
  Sukna, Tindharia,
  Kurseong, Ghum,
  Darjeeling*
- *Countries crossed:
  India*

ALTERNATIVE INDIA

- - - - - - - - - - - - - - - - - - - -

362. Kalka–Shimla Railway
Northwest India

In 1864 the British
declared that the hill
station of Shimla would
be India's summer
capital. In 1898, work
began on a daring
60-mile (96km) narrow
gauge line there.

RIGHT: The Darjeeling 'Toy
Train' is listed as a UNESCO
World Heritage site.

The hill station of Darjeeling was founded in the early
19th century as a health-reviving retreat for India's ruling
British Raj. Mansions, churches and social clubs sprang
up and tea bushes were cultivated. As Darjeeling's
popularity and trade grew, the cart road leading there
became increasingly congested. So in 1879 work started
on an ambitious 610mm (2ft) narrow gauge railway from
the lowly plains, an ascent of around 2,000m (6,700ft).

The Darjeeling Himalayan Railway – also known as the
'Toy Train' – opened in 1881, a gradient-defying triumph of
engineering that's now a UNESCO World Heritage site. The
full ride starts at New Jalpaiguri Station, near the bustling
city of Siliguri. At first the line follows the course of the old
road, skimming the flat plains, passing shops and houses.
From Sukna Station, the terrain changes and the train

grumbles slowly into the tree-frilled foothills. 'Slowly' being the operative word. Averaging around 7.5 miles per hour (12kph), the Darjeeling Himalayan Railway is not for those in a hurry.

The scenery, however, is spectacular. The line cuts through dense forest and lush tea plantations dotted with pickers. On a clear day some of the world's highest mountains are visible, including snow-capped Kanchenjunga. There are also extraordinary rail innovations including six zigzag reverses, numerous steep loops, Agony Point (the tightest bend on the line) and the Batasia Loop, where the railway spirals on top of itself through a tunnel and over a hill.

Diesel locomotives pull the New Jalpaiguri–Darjeeling train. Steam locos operate a shorter tourist joyride between Ghum (the line's highest station) and Darjeeling, giving the best Himalayan views.

BELOW: Take a steam loco to the hill station of Darjeeling, famous for its tea.

WHITE PASS AND YUKON RAILROAD

Canada and United States

Follow the hopeful prospectors of the Klondike
Gold Rush on a seemingly impossible railway.

Need to know
- *Point in time: 1897–98 (Klondike Gold Rush)*
- *Length: 67.5 miles (109km)*
- *Minimum time: 4 hours 45 minutes*
- *Key stops: Skagway, Heney, Glacier, Fraser, Bennett, Carcross*
- *Countries crossed: Canada, United States*

When three prospectors found gold in a tributary of the Klondike River in 1896, they triggered one of the world's greatest gold rushes. Between 1897 and 1898, more than 100,000 hopefuls set off for Canada's Yukon Province. Between 1898 and 1900, a narrow gauge railway was built to help them.

Despite the seemingly impossible terrain, the White Pass and Yukon Railroad (WP&YR) was blasted through Alaska's Coastal Mountains and into Canada in just over two years. The line features tunnels, trestles, grades of up to 3.9 percent and tight, cliff-teetering bends. It climbs almost 1,000m (3,300ft) in its first 20 miles (32km).

The railway originally ran between the port of Skagway and the city of Whitehorse. Since becoming a summer-only tourist service in 1988, the WP&YR's diesel-hauled trains now terminate at the mining outpost of Carcross. But this stretch includes the best bits.

Leaving Skagway, passing the old Gold Rush Cemetery, the train climbs along the Skagway River, with forests, falls and glaciers all around. It burrows through Tunnel Mountain, crosses Dead Horse Gulch and passes an abandoned steel bridge, once the tallest cantilever span in the world. Soon the line crests 873m (2,865ft) White Pass, the United States-Canada border. This is where Canadian mounties checked that prospectors had sufficient grubstake (supplies) before allowing them into British Columbia.

The WP&YR continues rising to Fraser, before descending to Bennett. Once a teeming tent city, this is where prospectors paused after hiking the Chilkoot Trail, the only way to the goldfields before the railway was built. A church (built 1899) still stands here. Finally, the train skirts Lake Bennett, enters the Yukon and stops in Carcross, where the railway's last spike was driven on 29 July 1900.

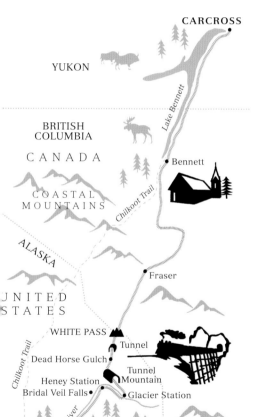

LEFT: The White Pass and Yukon Railway carried Klondike Gold Rush pioneers.

CALIFORNIA ZEPHYR

United States

Be blown away by the mountains, plains and deserts of the
American West as you ride with railway pioneers.

Need to know

- *Point in time: 1869 (Transcontinental Railroad completed)*
- *Length: 2,423 miles (3,900km)*
- *Minimum time: 51 hours 20 minutes*
- *Key stops: Chicago, Denver, Salt Lake City, Reno, Sacramento, Emeryville (San Francisco)*
- *Countries crossed: United States*

The California Zephyr isn't a train. It's a dream realised, a nation united, the West won. Before the arrival of railways, journeys across the enormity of the United States took 6 months on foot or horseback, if they were undertaken at all. Only the brave or desperate would contemplate such an arduous expedition from the civilised east into the deserts, mountains and 'Injun' country of the west.

The United States' first railways opened in the 1830s along the eastern seaboard. However, by the 1850s, with California granted statehood and seemingly full of gold, there was an increasing desire to link the country's Atlantic and Pacific coasts. The big problem? Mastering the mountains in between.

In 1862, then-president and railway fan Abraham Lincoln signed the Pacific Railway Act. This authorised land grants and government bonds, equal to an average of US$32,000

RIGHT: The California Zephyr pulls into Denver's Union Station on its route through the Rocky Mountains.

per mile of track laid, to two companies: the Central Pacific Railroad and the Union Pacific Railroad. The former began building eastwards from California, the latter built westwards from the Missouri River. Both faced extreme difficulties: tunnelling through solid granite; bridging precipitous ravines; working through blizzards; dealing with hostile Sioux, Cheyenne and Arapaho tribes who were unhappy about the railway ploughing through their lands.

However, on 10 May 1869 the two converging lines met at Promontory, Utah. A ceremonial golden spike was hammered into the ground and the United States was crossed by rail. This paved the way for all manner of cowboys, prospectors, oilmen and outlaws to expand into the western frontier. That perilous 6-month journey could now be made in just 2 weeks.

The current California Zephyr service, which provides a daily link between the cities of Chicago and San Francisco, takes just over 2 days to run parts of this historic route. It doesn't follow quite the same course, taking a more southerly line through Colorado to connect Omaha and Salt Lake City (the original line cut through Wyoming). But it showcases many impressive engineering endeavours. Not least the track section across the Donner Pass, the route's biggest obstacle.

The reputation of the 2,151m (7,056ft) high pass was chilling. In 1846–47, a group travelling by wagon got snowed in here over winter. Only half survived. Some resorted to cannibalism. However, in 1868, after the painstaking construction of four tunnels, miles of snow sheds (to protect against avalanches) and two huge retaining walls, Donner Pass was overcome, creating the first rail passage over the Sierra Nevada Mountains.

What made this route so challenging for early railway builders is what makes it such a joy for passengers today.

ALTERNATIVE AMERICA

368. Monongahela Incline
Pittsburgh, United States

Hop aboard the United States' oldest funicular, built 1869–70, which still rattles 194m (635ft) up Mount Washington, affording fine views.

369. Durango and Silverton Narrow Gauge Railroad
Colorado, United States

This 45-mile (72km) line, built to haul gold from the San Juan Mountains, has been in continuous operation since 1882, although its vintage steam locos now haul people instead.

The views out of the windows of the Zephyr's Sightseer
Lounge Cars are epic. There are mountains soaring to over
4,000m (13,000ft), capped with snow even in summer. There
are cascade-streaked ridges, forested slopes and primordial
gorges angry with white water. And there are unforgiving
deserts that seem to never end.

There are also fun stops. For instance, in Colorado you
could get off at Winter Park for skiing or at Granby to
explore Rocky Mountain National Park. In Nevada you could
hit the roulette tables of Reno, 'The Biggest Little City in the
World'. Rail buffs might fancy Sacramento, home to the
California State Railroad Museum, or Galesburg, Illinois,
which hosts the Railroads Days festival every June.

Ultimately, the best thing about the Zephyr (named
for Zephyrus, Greek god of the
west wind) is the journey itself.
And while the train runs in both
directions, there's something more
satisfying about riding it east–west
– into the sunset, the same way as
Zephyrus, the same way as those
original pioneers.

BELOW: Sit in the California
Zephyr's Sightseer Cars to
enjoy desert views that seem
to go on forever.

370
EMPIRE BUILDER

United States

In May 1804, American explorers Meriwether Lewis and William Clark set off from Missouri to survey the unknown west. They headed northwest, crossing the Great Plains and Rocky Mountains, hitting the Pacific at Fort Clatsop, south of modern-day Seattle. The Empire Builder train follows a similar course, running 2,206 miles (3,550km) between Chicago and Seattle. The train passes Fort Union (in North Dakota), where Lewis and Clark noted the confluence of the Missouri and Yellowstone rivers. It crosses the Rockies via Marias Pass (in Montana), a niche the duo desperately tried to find. And it follows Columbia Gorge (in Washington), which they traversed in October 1805.

371
BULAWAYO– VICTORIA FALLS

Western Zimbabwe

An overnight train, with carriages hailing from 1950s Britain, operates this 293-mile (472km) route across western Zimbabwe. It leaves the high plains city of Bulawayo late in the afternoon and, for much of the way, skirts Hwange National Park. Elephant, giraffe and antelope may be spotted. Then, nearing its terminus, vaporous mists billow into view. English explorer David Livingstone discovered Mosi-oa-Tunya ('The Smoke That Thunders') in 1855. He was dazzled, declaring: 'It had never been seen before by European eyes; but scenes so lovely must have been gazed upon by angels in their flight.' He named this 108m (355ft) high cascade for his queen – Victoria Falls.

Leaving the resort town of Banff, the Rocky Mountaineer (next page) inches out into spectacular, peak-flanked valleys, following tracks laid by railway pioneers in the late 19th century.

ROCKY MOUNTAINEER

British Columbia and Alberta, Canada

Master the Rocky Mountains via the old 'Kicking Horse'
route on the railway that opened up the Canadian west.

Need to know
- *Point in time: 1885
  (Canadian Pacific
  Railway completed)*
- *Length: 594 miles
  (955km)*
- *Minimum time: 2 days*
- *Key stops: Banff, Lake
  Louise, Craigellachie,
  Sicamous, Kamloops,
  Vancouver*
- *Countries crossed:
  Canada*

There was something symbolic about the Canadian Pacific
Railway's 'last spike' ceremony in 1885. Something that
nodded to how crisis-addled this historic train project had
been. For starters, the 'last spike' was not ceremonial gold
or silver – it was plain iron. A silver one had been made and
was supposed to be driven in by the governor-general of
Canada. However, bad weather meant that neither he nor
the spike made it. Instead, at 9.22 a.m. on 7 November 1885,
Canadian Pacific Railway (CPR) financier Donald Smith did
the honours at the siding of Craigellachie. He swung a maul,
landed a glancing blow and bent the spike. It was wrenched
out and replaced. Take two. This time Smith hammered it
home. The crowd burst into cheers.

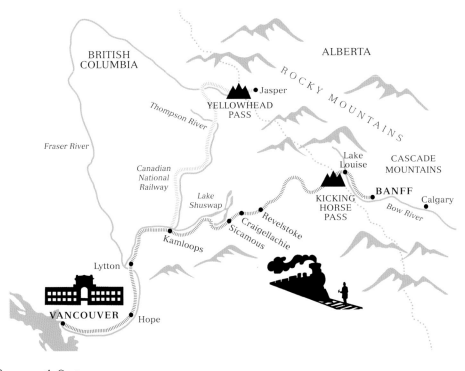

While the drab day and initial spike-sinking failure echoed the troubles of Canada's transcontinental railway, the ensuing 'Hurrah!' spoke volumes, too. Troubled or not, the CPR had united a country. A sign at Craigellachie now reads: 'A nebulous dream was a reality: an iron ribbon crossed Canada from sea to sea . . . a plain iron spike welded East to West.'

The CPR had built a southerly train line across Canada – southerly being most direct, if more challenging to build. From the city of Winnipeg (Manitoba) it ran via Calgary (Alberta), then over the Rocky Mountains and into British Columbia via Kicking Horse Pass. Subsequently, the Canadian National Railway (CNR) built a more northerly line, surmounting the Rockies near Jasper, via the less severe Yellowhead Pass. Today, Canada's scheduled ViaRail trains use the CNR tracks. Only the plush Rocky Mountaineer tourist train runs trips on the original CPR line. Its 2-day 'First Passage to the West' Banff–Vancouver journey is not cheap. But the scenery and history are priceless.

The Rocky Mountaineer is designed for sightseeing, with big-windowed, glass-roofed observation cars and a mile-by-mile route guide flagging up sights including eagles and bears. Starting from the mountain-cradled resort town of Banff, the train hugs the Bow River, curving via pine forest and snow peaks past Lake Louise Station (the turquoise lake sadly out of sight). Soon after, a monument marks the Continental Divide and the Alberta-British Columbia border, also the trip's highest point at 1,625m (5,332ft).

ENGINEERING EXCELLENCE

373. Georgetown Loop Railroad
Colorado, United States

Opened in 1884, this 4.5-mile (7km) corkscrewing, mountain-conquering railway was one of Colorado's first tourist attractions, opening the Rockies to visitors.

ABOVE: The Rocky Mountaineer follows the original rail route across the Canadian mountains.

Beyond, the landscape drops to Kicking Horse Canyon, the toughest engineering challenge. The descent was conquered via a section of very steep, very dangerous track known as the 'Big Hill'. In 1907, this was replaced by two spiral tunnels, which still corkscrew through the mountain. Emerging from these, the Rocky Mountaineer zigzags over the milky-blue river, eventually crossing the arched steel girders of Stoney Creek Bridge.

Next the train passes Craigellachie where there's a monument and museum. There were actually four 'last spikes'. The unused silver spike is in the Museum of Civilization in Ottawa. The original bent spike and a spare fourth one were taken by Donald Smith and fashioned into commemorative jewellery. The actual last spike driven in by Smith was also later removed. It's thought to still belong to the family of chief patent officer WJ Lynch, present at the ceremony in 1885.

After Craigellachie, the train passes the town of Sicamous, on Lake Shuswap. Soon, big mountains become sandy hills flanked by hoodoos (rock chimneys). It's all a lot more arid as the train arrives at the city of Kamloops, where passengers overnight in a hotel.

From Kamloops to Vancouver the lines of the CPR and CNR run in parallel, often either side of the river. This means both the Rocky Mountaineer and ViaRail's scheduled service share the same views of the dusty plains, Cascade Mountains and verdant Fraser Valley before reaching Vancouver – though the Rocky Mountaineer does it with more style.

PEAK TRAM

Hong Kong, China

Catch Asia's oldest funicular railway for views
of the region's most dazzling metropolis.

Need to know
- *Point in time: 1888 (Peak Tram opened)*
- *Length: 0.85 miles (1.4km)*
- *Minimum time: 5 minutes*
- *Key stops: Garden Road, Kennedy Road, MacDonnell Road, May Road, Barker Road, The Peak*
- *Countries crossed: Hong Kong (China)*

When the British first occupied Hong Kong Island in 1841, during the First Opium War with China, there wasn't much there. But within a few decades, as the British colony became established, the population exploded from around 7,000 people to more than 150,000. A few of those residents started to make their homes on Victoria Peak, the island's highest mountain. The trouble was that the only way to access its slopes was by foot or sedan chair.

In 1881, Scottish ex-railwayman Alexander Findlay Smith – who also happened to own a hotel on 'The Peak' – proposed the building of a tram system. Construction started in 1885, each heavy section of track being hauled up without mechanical assistance. When the line opened in

375. Valparaíso Funiculars
Chile

Hill-tumbling Valparaíso has twenty-six funiculars, the oldest dating to 1883. Many are defunct but these 'elevators' are part of the seaport's UNESCO World Heritage site.

376. Lookout Mountain Incline Railway
Tennessee, United States

One of the world's steepest passenger railways (opened 1895) crawls up to Lookout Mountain, site of an 1863 Civil War battle.

377. Drachenfels Railway
Rhine Valley, Germany

Access both a medieval ruined castle and a 19th-century Gothic one via this 1-mile (1.6km) rack railway up Drachenfels (Dragon Rock), opened in 1883.

378. Carmelit
Haifa, Israel

An underground funicular runs up and down Mount Carmel, home to the sacred shrine of the Bab, the holiest site for the Baha'i faith (founded 1863).

RIGHT: Traditional and modern meet in this fascinating Asian metropolis.

FAR RIGHT: Hong Kong's Peak Tram has been in operation since 1888.

1888, it was the first cable funicular in Asia. The open tramcars, each with space for thirty passengers, were powered by coal-fired steam boilers. On its journey from the lower station at Garden Road to the terminus at Victoria Gap pass, the tramway climbed 378m (1,240ft) in just under a mile.

There have been plenty of changes since then. The steam boilers were replaced by an electric motor in 1926. During the Second World War, the line was damaged and didn't reopen until Japanese occupation ended in 1945. In 1989 the line underwent a massive revamp, with new tracks laid and computerised operations installed.

Hong Kong has also changed immeasurably since 1888. Today the 4-million-plus passengers who ride the Peak Tram each year get magnificent views of not just Victoria Harbour, the Kowloon Peninsula and the leafy mountains but also of the thrusting, skyscraper jungle that Hong Kong has become.

SETTLE–CARLISLE RAILWAY

Northern England, United Kingdom

Travel through the picturesque Pennine Hills
via England's highest main-line station.

Need to know
- *Point in time: 1876 (Settle–Carlisle Railway opened)*
- *Length: 72 miles (116km)*
- *Minimum time: 1 hour 30 minutes*
- *Key stops: Settle, Ribblehead, Dent, Kirkby Stephen, Appleby, Carlisle*
- *Countries crossed: United Kingdom*

First, the Settle–Carlisle Railway in numbers: this 72-mile (116km) line through northern England has 380 bridges, fourteen tunnels and twenty-one viaducts. It has twenty stations (eleven are functional), twelve signal boxes and one aqueduct. And it took an army of 6,000 navvies to build.

It was audacious in the extreme to attempt to construct a railway through the glorious but challenging undulations of the North Pennines, Eden Valley and Yorkshire Dales. However, the Midland Railway company was determined to have its own route from England into Scotland, to compete with the West Coast and East Coast Main Lines.

Construction began in 1870. Labourers lived in shanty towns alongside the tracks and worked with nothing more sophisticated than shovels and dynamite. But somehow they created astonishing structures, not least the great Ribblehead Viaduct, a twenty-four-arched span rising 32m (104ft) above Blea Moor. It came at a cost, however: so many navvies lost their lives that Midland Railway had to pay to extend local graveyards. Memorials can be seen at the churches of St Mary's Outhgill and St Leonard's Chapel-le-Dale.

Ridden south to north, the railway starts in the market town of Settle. It runs through Stainforth Tunnel, then over Ribblehead Viaduct towards Grade II–listed Dent Station, the highest on the English main line, from where the panorama is breathtaking. From Dent the line climbs to its highest point, 356m (1,169ft) Ais Gill summit. Then it descends into the lush Eden Valley, running via viaducts, tunnels and the pretty market town of Appleby before finishing in the town of Carlisle, founded by the Romans. It's a regular main-line railway, though heritage steam trains often run the route.

MORE BRILLIANT BRIDGES

- - - - - - - - - - - - - - - - - -

380. Forth Rail Bridge
Scotland, United Kingdom

Take the train from Edinburgh to Aberdeen to cross this iconic 2,467m (8,094ft) cantilever span across the Firth of Forth; it was first opened in 1890.

ABOVE: The impressive Ribblehead Viaduct has twenty-four stone arches.

LEFT: Occasionally, steam train specials run along the Settle–Carlisle line.

381
CALEDONIAN SLEEPER

United Kingdom

Sleeper train services between
London and Scotland started
operating in the 1850s when the
East Coast and West Coast Main
Lines first forged railways up the
length of the United Kingdom.
Today, the Caledonian Sleeper
remains the most romantic way to
travel to the north. There's nothing
quite like falling asleep among the
bright lights of London and then
waking amid deer-roamed glens.
Sleeper trains run from London
Euston to Glasgow and Edinburgh
and then onwards to either Fort
William (beneath Ben Nevis),
Inverness (capital of the Highlands)
or east-coast Aberdeen. Even
better: new, cutting-edge sleeper
carriages are scheduled to launch
in 2018.

382
GREAT CENTRAL
RAILWAY

Leicestershire, United Kingdom

A day-trip in the English East
Midlands may not sound like the
most exotic holiday – but it was
one of the most significant.
On 5 July 1841, British travel
pioneer Thomas Cook took
500 people on a rail journey
from the city of Leicester to
a temperance meeting in the
town of Loughborough – his
first organised excursion and the
world's first-ever package tour.
Now the 12-mile (19km) journey
can be made via the Great Central
Railway, the United Kingdom's only
heritage main-line railway and the
only one on which full-size steam
engines still puff past each other.

383
PARK LINE

Montana, United States

In 1872, Yellowstone became the United States' first national park. At first, few people visited its hot springs and geysers – it was hard to reach. But railway developers spotted an opportunity. By 1882, the Northern Pacific Railroad had built a station at Livingston, Montana, creating a gateway to Yellowstone. By 1902, the 50-mile (80km) Park Line ran south from Livingston over Bozeman Pass to Gardiner, by Yellowstone's north entrance. Gradually, trains were usurped by automobiles; the last Park Line passenger service ran in 1960. But Livingston's historic depot, now a community centre, is still the hub of the town.

384
ENTIRE EUROPEAN RAIL NETWORK

Europe

The railway boom in Britain in the 1830s created the need for a guidebook to this newfangled network. In 1839, the cloth-bound *Bradshaw's Railway Time Tables, and Assistant to Railway Travelling* was published by English cartographer George Bradshaw. A review of a later edition declared that 'seldom has the gigantic intellect of man been employed upon a work of greater utility'. In 1847, the first *Bradshaw's Continental Railway Guide* was released, covering all of Europe. This gargantuan tome was produced yearly until the First World War, then again until 1939, when the Second World War made rail travel in Europe too dangerous.

INDIAN PACIFIC

Southern Australia

Make an epic journey between Perth and Sydney, following hardy outback pioneers across the desolate Nullarbor Plain.

Need to know
- *Point in time: 1841 (first European crossed the Nullarbor Plain)*
- *Length: 2,704 miles (4,352km)*
- *Minimum time: 65 hours*
- *Key stops: Perth, Kalgoorlie, Cook, Adelaide, Broken Hill, Sydney*
- *Countries crossed: Australia*

BELOW: Traverse the vast open outback on the historic route from Sydney to Perth.

English explorer Edward John Eyre described southern Australia's Nullarbor Plain as 'the sort of place one gets into in bad dreams'. Eyre should know. After a long, desiccating expedition with Wylie, his indigenous Australian companion, he became the first European to traverse this nightmare of nature in 1841. Thanks to the advent of rail, the journey across no longer needs to be so arduous, although the Nullarbor itself remains just as unforgiving.

'Nullarbor' means 'no tree'. Formerly the bed of a shallow sea, it's the world's largest single piece of limestone, scattered with saltbush, blue bush scrub, emus, kangaroos and wild camels, descendants of those brought by early outback pioneers. For thousands of years the Pila Nguru people made the Nullarbor their home. Now a few remote roadhouses and hardy farming communities dot the emptiness.

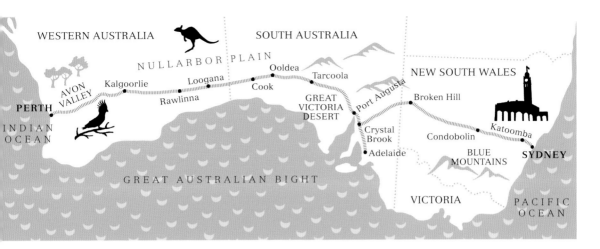

Most of those communities can be found along the Trans-Australia Railway, construction of which began in the early 20th century. By that time, railways had already been built from Western Australia's capital Perth to the goldfields of Kalgoorlie and from east-coast Sydney to the South Australian city of Port Augusta. In 1912, work began from both sides to connect the two. In 1917, the tracks met at the tiny siding of Ooldea in the midst of the Nullarbor Plain.

Although a railway now spanned Australia east to west, this wasn't the birth of a great transcontinental train ride. The newest Kalgoorlie–Port Augusta section was built to 1,435mm (4ft 8.5in) standard gauge. The railways at either end were 1,067mm (3ft 6in) narrow gauge. So passengers had to switch trains several times. It wasn't until 1970 that the whole route was standardised and the first continuous train traverse could be made. Ever since, the Indian Pacific service has connected Sydney with Perth, a journey of 2,698 miles (4,343km). The original 1970s stainless-steel carriages still run, pulled by diesel engines. The train has two classes, Gold sleeper and more deluxe Platinum sleeper. There are also restaurant cars serving local delicacies such as saltwater barramundi and grilled kangaroo.

The Indian Pacific runs once a week. Eastbound, it leaves Perth at 9 a.m. every Sunday. It glides into the Avon Valley, where cockatoos preen in the trees, before crossing Western Australia's endless wheatfields. First stop is the town of Kalgoorlie, which exploded onto the map in 1893 after three prospectors hit one of the world's richest gold seams here. There's an off-train excursion to the vast open-pit mine and the town's historic centre.

Beyond Kalgoorlie lies . . . nothing. Lots of it, as the Indian Pacific starts day 2 crossing the Nullarbor Plain,

AWESOME OUTBACK

- - - - - - - - - - - - - - - -

386. Spirit of the Outback
Queensland, Australia

Take a 24-hour train ride from Brisbane to the quintessential outback town of Longreach – home to Stockman's Hall of Fame, which celebrates Australia's 19th-century pioneers.

387. Westlander
Queensland, Australia

Follow in the footsteps of Australian outback explorers on a journey from Brisbane to the town of Charleville (established 1865) via vineyards and the Great Dividing Range.

388. Cockle Train
South Australia

Built in 1887 to link Goolwa, on the Murray River, with the ocean at Victor Harbor (near Adelaide), this 10-mile (16km) coast-hugging line is Australia's oldest steel-railed route.

as bleak as it is mesmerising. This traverse includes the world's longest stretch of dead-straight railway track, 297 miles (478km) between the sidings of Loogana and Ooldea. The train makes a brief stop on this section, at the almost-ghost town of Cook. Founded in 1917 to house railway workers, the town now has a single-figure population and an eerily abandoned main street, although a small shop still sells 'I crossed the Nullarbor' certificates.

Eventually the Indian Pacific exits the plain, gradually segueing into the sandy hills and scrub of the Great Victoria Desert. It passes Tarcoola – the junction for the northbound Ghan train – and turns south at Crystal Brook to detour to Adelaide. Day 3 dawns amid the green outskirts of this elegant city. Passengers have a few hours off-train to look around Adelaide's handsome streets before reboarding, backtracking north to Crystal Brook and then turning east.

The fertile farms of South Australia slowly turn to woody mallee scrub before the train crosses into New South Wales. It stops at Broken Hill, a remote outback mining town with unexpectedly impressive buildings and art galleries. Next, sand dunes, lakes and an extinct volcano roll by. Early on day 4, the Indian Pacific enters the eucalypt-hazed Blue Mountains before commencing its final, curving descent towards the coast, finishing at Sydney's Central Station.

BROCKEN RAILWAY

Harz Mountains, Germany

Ride a steam train up a mountain where witches
gather and where spies once lurked.

Need to know

- *Point in time: 1808
  (publication of Johann
  Wolfgang von
  Goethe's* Faust*)*
- *Length: 12 miles
  (19km)*
- *Minimum time:
  50 minutes*
- *Key stops: Drei Annen
  Hohne, Schierke,
  Brocken Summit*
- *Countries crossed:
  Germany*

BELOW: The meteorological
'Brocken spectre'
phenomenon adds more
mystery to the mountain.

So much strangeness swirls around the Brocken, the
highest mountain in the Harz Range. This 1,142m (3,743ft)
peak is said to be where Europe's witches convene on
Walpurgisnacht (30 April), a ghoulish gathering included in
Goethe's literary masterpiece *Faust*. The mountain is also
allegedly roamed by the giant 'Brocken spectre' – actually
a meteorological oddity of fog and shadows.

Three connected rail lines swirl the haunting Harz, too.
The Harz Narrow Gauge Railways network totals 87 miles
(140km), including the 12-mile (19km) Brockenbahn (Brocken
Railway). This branch runs from Drei Annen Hohne Station
into Harz National Park. It stops at the Alpine-style village of
Schierke, follows the Bode Valley, crosses the Eckerloch
Bridge and spirals right around the mountain to slowly reach
the top – an ascent of almost 600m (2,000ft) via regular
adhesion railway, hauled by vintage steam locomotives.

The line opened in 1899 and ran until 1945, when Second
World War damage and occupying Soviets restricted services
for several years. The mountain's location, on the former
border between East and West Germany, meant that the
Brockenbahn was severed by the Iron Curtain – passengers
with special passes could ride between Drei Annen Hohne
and Schierke but only goods transport could continue to the
summit. From 1961, the Brocken was commandeered by
Russian and East German spies carrying out surveillance
from this strategic vantage point. Since the line was restored
and reopened in 1992, everyone is allowed up, and one of the
Brocken's old Cold War listening posts is now a museum.

RIGHT: Germany's Harz
Mountains are laced with
lakes, legends and railways.

JOURNEYS WITH PHILEAS FOGG

396. London–Brindisi
United Kingdom–Italy

Jules Verne's fictional hero Phileas Fogg began his adventure with a train ride from London to the Italian port of Brindisi. Today, using the London–Paris Eurostar then trains via Munich and Bologna, it takes around 30 hours.

397. San Francisco–New York
United States

It took Phileas Fogg 7 days to take the train across the United States, a journey interrupted by bison and Sioux warriors. It can now be done in 3 nights.

LEFT: Kolkata has the oldest operating electric tram network in Asia.

398
DURBAN–
JOHANNESBURG

South Africa

Three heavyweights of history dot this 449-mile (722km) ride. From the coastal city of Durban the line heads to Pietermaritzburg. In 1893, Mohandas K. Gandhi (not yet the Indian independence legend honoured as Mahatma) was thrown off a train at the station here for deigning to ride in first class. Further north, the line passes the town of Estcourt where young war correspondent Winston Churchill was based during the Anglo-Boer War. In November 1899, Churchill was taken prisoner during a train ambush nearby. The line finishes at Johannesburg Park Station, near Constitution Hill and the Old Fort prison where Gandhi and, later, anti-apartheid icon Nelson Mandela were both incarcerated.

399
CRIMEA–
ST PETERSBURG

Russia

On 29 October 1888, Tsar Alexander III, his family and their extensive retinue were travelling from the Black Sea to St Petersburg when the imperial train derailed near Borki Station (now in Ukraine). Twenty-one of the passengers were killed and thirty-seven injured. Miraculously, though, not a single royal was hurt (although the tsar's dog Kamchatka was killed instantly). It's said that a heroic Alexander singlehandedly held up the dining car's collapsed roof, allowing his children to escape. The popular belief was that the survival of the royals was God's reward for the holiness of the Russian people.

400

WASHINGTON DC–ELBERON

Eastern United States

On 2 July 1881, United States President James Garfield was boarding a train at Washington DC's Baltimore and Potomac Railroad Station when disgruntled lawyer Charles Guiteau shot him in the back. Garfield survived for 11 weeks. Towards the end of his life, he was taken by train to Francklyn Cottage in Elberon, New Jersey, for fresher air. So that the dying president didn't need to change trains, a rail track was built right to the cottage's door. Washington's 'B&P' station was demolished in the early 20th century; the National Gallery of Art now occupies the site. Francklyn Cottage and its temporary railway have also gone, but a stone memorial commemorates the spot.

STRIKING STATIONS

401. Berlin–Potsdam
Germany

The first trains from Berlin to Potsdam, former residence of Prussian kings, ran in 1838. Later, Kaiser Wilhelm II had a private terminal (Sanssouci Station) built here.

402. Atocha Station
Madrid, Spain

Opened in 1851, rebuilt in 1892, retired in 1992, bombed in 2004 – Atocha remains Madrid's most handsome station, an airy, plant-filled space.

403. Chhatrapati Shivaji Terminus
Mumbai, India

Admire Mumbai's most majestic (and busy) terminus, a riot of Mughal and Gothic Revival architecture opened in 1888.

404. Corinth Station, Mississippi
United States

Corinth Station lay at the meeting of two key railways and, in 1862, was the site of an American Civil War siege. Both lines are now defunct but a museum marks this 'Crossroads of Confederacy'.

UNDERGROUND RAILROAD

Eastern United States

Ditch real trains to explore the human 'railway' that
helped transport escaped slaves to freedom.

Need to know

- *Point in time: 1849
  (Harriet Tubman
  escaped from slavery)*
- *Length: 1,000-plus
  miles (1,600km)*
- *Minimum time:
  Several weeks*
- *Key stops: Dorchester,
  Wilmington,
  Philadelphia, Auburn*
- *Countries crossed:
  United States*

The Underground Railroad was not actually a railway. But it's
an appropriate name for the network of secret routes used in
the 19th century by slaves fleeing America's southern states
for the northern states and Canada where slavery was
prohibited. Real railways took off from the 1830s, and the
human version, which peaked from around 1830 to 1865,
borrowed the terminology. The Underground Railroad had
many 'tracks' dotted with 'stations' (hiding places). The
'cargo' (escaped slaves) were guided by 'conductors' and
facilitated by 'agents'. Arriving at the 'terminal' meant
making it to the north – to freedom.

One of the most famous fugitives was Harriet Tubman.
She absconded from her plantation in Dorchester County,
Maryland, in 1849. Her exact route isn't known but she
likely headed northeast along the Choptank River, through
Delaware and into the free state of Pennsylvania. Like
other escapees, she travelled at night, guided by the
North Star. What made Tubman remarkable is that she
returned to Maryland many times, risking her own
freedom to help others.

It's possible to experience something of Tubman's journey
today. In Maryland, the Harriet Tubman Underground
Railway Byway links several related sites, including
Bucktown Village Store – where she received a blow that
left her injured for life – and the new Harriet Tubman Visitor
Center, built near the plantation where she laboured.
Wilmington, Delaware is home to the Quaker Meeting
House where Thomas Garrett, railroad 'agent', abolitionist
and Tubman's friend, worshipped. The Home for the Aged
in Auburn, New York, is where Tubman died in 1913.

Tubman was a civil rights heroine and a matchless
'conductor'. As she said: 'I never ran my train off the track
and I never lost a passenger.'

FOUR MORE FASCINATING JOURNEYS

----

406. Volk's Electric Railway
United Kingdom

Opened in 1883, this 1-mile (1.6km) line along Brighton seafront is the oldest operating electric railway in the world, still fresh from a 2017 renovation.

407. Ring Tram
Vienna, Austria

Make a 3-mile (5km) tram lap of the Austrian capital's Ringstrasse, the grand, palace-lined ring road built from the 1860s to the 1890s.

408. Paris–Lourdes
France

It's a 524-mile (843km) rail journey from Paris to miraculous Lourdes, where a young girl reputedly saw a vision of the Virgin in 1858.

409. Tbilisi–Gori
Georgia

Travel by train 47 miles (76km) from the Georgian capital to the town of Gori, where Soviet leader Joseph Stalin was born in 1878.

LEFT: The Underground Railroad's matchless 'conductor' Harriet Tubman is commemorated by a statue in Boston, Massachusetts.

CHAPTER SIX

20TH CENTURY AND BEYOND

Trace the evolution of the railway from steam to super-speed, via hippies, upheavals and two world wars.

MOSCOW METRO

Moscow, Russia

Soak up Stalin's socialist propaganda on the world's most magnificent subway network.

Need to know
- *Point in time: 1935 (Moscow Metro Line 1 opened)*
- *Length: 210 miles (339km)*
- *Minimum time: 50 minutes (Line 1)*
- *Key stops: Kropotkinskaya, Mayakovskaya, Ploshchad Revolyutsii, Dostoyevskaya, Komsomolskaya*
- *Countries crossed: Russia*

BELOW: Komsomolskaya station features depictions of heroic Russian generals.

Russian philosopher Nikolay Chernyshevsky once said that 'art is no use unless it serves politics'. This could well be the strapline for the Moscow Metro, where architectural splendour serves to deliver the Stalinist message.

The first plans for a Moscow Metro were drawn up in 1902 during the reign of Tsar Nicholas II. Moscow wanted its own underground to rival those in cities such as London and Paris. However, events kept getting in the way: the Russian Revolution of 1905, the First World War, the 1917 Bolshevik Revolution. Construction finally started under Soviet dictator Joseph Stalin in 1932.

Stalin had specific ideas. The metro would provide cheap transportation for everyone (a ride still costs less than US$1). And its stations would be 'palaces for the people' with elegant vaulting, stirring mosaics and chandeliers. The metro would also prove the supremacy of socialism, when much of the capitalist world was suffering the Great Depression.

MOSCOW

SOKOLNICHESKAYA
Line 1

ARBATSKO-
POKROVSKAYA
Line 3

• Dostoyevskaya

Komsomolskaya •

Mayakovskaya •

Ploshchad
Revolyutsii •

Red
Square

Kropotkinskaya •

Universitet • Sportivnaya

Thousands of Russian workers, Great Purge victims and labour camp inmates dug out the tunnels with pickaxes; scores of them died in the process. Engineers were brought in from London; however, when Stalin started fearing they had learned too much about Moscow's layout, he had them arrested on charges of espionage and deported.

Originally 7 miles (11km) long with thirteen stations, Line 1 (the Sokolnicheskaya Line) opened on 15 May 1935, to much fanfare. A quarter of a million passengers travelled the new subway that day, and choirs sang out the 'Songs of the Joyous Metro Conquerors'. The line was a triumph of technology, design and propaganda. One of Line 1's most impressive stations was Dvorets Sovetov (now Kropotkinskaya), a cathedral of marble columns and grey and pink granite. It was designed to be an underground hall for a new Palace of the Soviets, but the palace was never built.

Construction of the Metro continued apace, even during the Second World War. At that time, stations were used as air raid shelters and offices for government departments. Stalin even made speeches from the platform of Mayakovskaya (opened 1938), one of the network's most striking stations. Here, shimmering steel and pink-marble

MARVELLOUS METROS

- - - - - - - - - - - - - - - - - -

411. Pyongyang Metro
North Korea

As befitting the world's most secretive nation (established 1948), the Metro in the North Korean capital is one of the deepest in the world – so it can double as a nuclear bunker.

412. Paris Métro Line 2
Paris, France

This line has run the same route (Porte Dauphine–Nation) since 1903. It stops at Sacré-Cœur and Père Lachaise Cemetery, and still has some original art nouveau entrances.

413. Stockholm Metro
Sweden

Stockholm's Tunnelbanna was built in 1950 and is often called the 'world's longest art gallery' – many of its stations are adorned with paintings and art installations.

414. Post Office Railway
London, United Kingdom

Between 1927 and 2003, an automated underground delivered mail beneath London's streets. At its peak, the 6.5-mile (10km) network shuttled 40 million pieces of mail each day.

415. Holborn–Aldwych
London, United Kingdom

During the Second World War (1939–45), the British Museum stored many of its treasures in the tunnels of this branch line. Aldwych Station closed in 1994.

416. Shanghai Metro
China

Shanghai's Metro is the world's most extensive. By 2025, it's set to be even bigger – the aim is that nowhere in the city centre will be more than half a mile from an underground station.

RIGHT: Mayakovskaya station, opened in 1938, depicts a Soviet utopia.

columns rise curvaceously to ceiling mosaics depicting a Soviet utopia: athletic swimmers, daring parachutists, farm women standing nobly amid sheaves of wheat.

Later, at the dawn of the Cold War, a whole section of the Arbatsko–Pokrovskaya Line (Line 3) was built very deep underground, to be used as a refuge in case of nuclear attack. Station design was also more minimalist for a time, although a flamboyant neo-Stalinist aesthetic became popular again from the 1970s.

Now, with 203 stations, fourteen lines, 210 miles (339km) of track and a daily passenger load of 9 million people, the Moscow Metro is one of the world's biggest, busiest and most astonishing undergrounds. There's also said to be a whole 'Metro-2' network, a deeper, secret subway connecting government shelters and command centres. It's all hush-hush, although mysterious ventilation shafts, blocked stairways and a strange dead-end line (between Sportivnaya and Universitet stations) can be seen.

More than forty Moscow Metro stations are listed as cultural heritage sites, including aforementioned Kropotkinskaya and Mayakovskaya. Ploshchad Revolyutsii (the most convenient stop for Red Square) is adorned with 76 bronzes of soldiers, farmers and others who helped defend the Soviet nation, including a little bronze dog – rubbing his nose is said to bring good luck. Stark grey-white Dostoyevskaya (opened 2010) is named for author Fyodor Dostoyevsky and decorated with grisly scenes from *Crime and Punishment* and his other works. Baroque Komsomolskaya is the height of Stalinist splendour, with a vaulted yellow ceiling, stucco-work and gilded depictions of Russian generals doing heroic deeds.

417
LEYTONSTONE–FINCHLEY CENTRAL

London, United Kingdom

This route on the London Underground honours the man who made negotiating the Tube a whole lot easier. In 1931, while working as an underground engineering draftsman, Harry Beck devised a new Tube map in his spare time. When it first launched in 1933, it was an immediate hit, beautifully simplifying the complex network. The map is still used today and has become a design icon. A blue plaque adorns 14 Wesley Road, Leyton, where Harry Beck was born in 1902. From Leyton, you can take the Central Line then the Northern Line to Finchley Central, where another plaque marks the station Beck used on his daily commute.

LITTLE TRAIN OF THE UPPER SOMME

Northern France

Ride an old field railway across some of the
bloodiest battlefields of the First World War.

Need to know
- *Point in time: 1916
  (Battle of the Somme)*
- *Length: 4.5 miles (7km)*
- *Minimum time:
  30 minutes*
- *Key stops: Froissy,
  Cappy, Dompierre*
- *Countries crossed:
  France*

BELOW: The French
cemetery at Dompierre
is a moving memorial.

Riding this little heritage railway, looking out over peaceful
green fields and the meandering Somme River, it's impossible
to imagine the carnage that once took place here. From 1 July
to 18 November 1916, this inconspicuous patch of northern
France was the site of one of the First World War's bloodiest
battles. Entrenched British and French soldiers faced off
against the Germans for 141 days, during which more than
1 million men were killed and wounded. On the first day
alone, 19,240 British troops died.

The 600mm (2ft) gauge Froissy–Cappy–Dompierre
Railway is one of a network of field railways that was built
by the French from 1915, in the build-up to the battle. It was
used to supply the trenches with artillery and other goods

throughout the war. Afterwards, a factory at Dompierre used the section to Cappy, a station on the Somme Canal, to transport its sugar beet. Now the line is run as the Little Train of the Upper Somme, a seasonal tourist service pulled by steam and diesel engines.

Railway HQ is in the hamlet of Froissy. Here, a Narrow Gauge Railway Museum displays a large collection of locomotives and wagons, mostly dating from 1910 to 1930. This includes various military models, many of which were used during the First World War. From here, the 'Little Train' heads west along the canal towpath, through the marshes, fields and woodland of the Somme Valley to Cappy. It then enters a curved tunnel and begins its climb to the Santerre Plateau via an ingenious zig-zag constructed after the war. It finishes in Dompierre, where a cemetery remembers just a few of the casualties of that terrible clash.

LIKE THAT? TRY THIS

- - - - - - - - - - - - - - - - - - -

419. Paris–Compiègne
Northern France

Take a train to the town of Compiègne. The First World War armistice was signed in a railway carriage in the forest here in 1918; the local museum has a replica.

BELOW: The Little Train of the Upper Somme uses tracks built during the First World War.

NAZI 'GOLD TRAIN'

Western Poland

Search for the legendary Second World War treasure
train, allegedly hidden in the Polish mountains.

Need to know

- *Point in time: 1945
  (Nazi 'Gold Train'
  allegedly left Wroclaw)*
- *Length: 44 miles
  (70km)*
- *Minimum time: 1 hour
  15 minutes*
- *Key stops: Wroclaw,
  Smolec, Imbramowice,
  Swiebodzice,
  Walbrzych*
- *Countries crossed:
  Poland*

BELOW: Underground
tunnels around Walbrzych
could house the 'Gold Train'.

The 'Gold Train' is a thing of legend. It's said that in
1945, towards the end of the Second World War, the Nazis
loaded a train with a bevy of riches – maybe 300 tonnes of
gold, precious jewels and priceless works of art. This train
was then supposedly driven southwest from the city of
Breslau (now Wroclaw). And it was concealed in a warren
of tunnels hacked out beneath the Owl Mountains by
prisoners of war and concentration camp detainees. The
train hasn't been seen since.

In fact, there is no evidence such a train ever existed – but
that hasn't stopped people from looking. For instance, in
2016 the world's media suddenly became focused on a leafy
embankment at KM65 of the Wroclaw–Walbrzych railway
line. Two amateur treasure-hunters using ground-
penetrating radar claimed to have found the train, buried
right there. A high-profile dig revealed nothing but soil.

The loot-filled locomotive may remain elusive but plenty of passenger trains run between Wroclaw and Walbrzych. Before boarding, explore handsome Wroclaw, Poland's fourth-largest city, with its Germanic churches, baroque palaces and Flemish-style mansions. Then ride the railway 44 miles (70km) to Walbrzych, looking out for the 'treasure' site en route.

In Walbrzych you can visit 13th-century Ksiaz Castle, which was seized by the Nazis in 1944 and was allegedly being refurbed to house Adolf Hitler himself. Beneath the castle is a network of tunnels (some visitable). They are part of Project Riese, the gigantic subterranean safe haven planned by the Nazis, in which officials could retreat, weapons could be manufactured and – maybe – trains could be hidden.

SECOND WORLD WAR RAILWAYS

421. Berchtesgaden Land Train
Germany

This 22-mile (35km) line through the Bavarian Alps from Freilassing leads to Berchtesgaden, Hitler's retreat of choice. His Eagle's Nest villa was built here in 1938.

BELOW: Nazi tunnels, part of Hitler's Project Riese, lie under Ksiaz Castle.

REUNIFICATION EXPRESS

Vietnam

Take a ride on the railway that was severed by the Vietnam War but which now binds the country together again.

Need to know
- *Point in time: 1976 (North–South Railway reopened)*
- *Length: 1,072 miles (1,726km)*
- *Minimum time: 36 hours*
- *Key stops: Hanoi, Hué, Danang, Nha Trang, Thap Cham, Saigon (Ho Chi Minh City)*
- *Countries crossed: Vietnam*

The French started building railways in Vietnam in the 1880s. Keen to link their colonial interests in the region, they soon prioritised a route running the length of the territory, from Hanoi in the north to Saigon (now officially Ho Chi Minh City) in the south. It would be the 'backbone of Indochina'. Construction began in 1899 but it took until 1936 before the full, single-track 1,072-mile (1,726km) line – the Transindochinois – was complete. Initially, the journey took about 60 hours.

It wasn't to last. The North–South Railway, as it was also called, soon became a target for attack. Towards the end of the Second World War, when occupying Japanese troops

were utilising the Transindochinois, Viet Minh guerrillas and United States bombs sought to sabotage the line. Then, during the First Indochina War (1946–54), the independence-seeking Viet Minh continued to attack it in their battle against the French. In 1954, Vietnam was divided along the 17th parallel into communist-ruled North Vietnam and quasi-democratic South Vietnam. The railway, of course, was divided too, split at the Hien Luong Bridge. For the next two decades it was impossible to travel the length of the line and it became a key target during the Vietnam War (1954–75) – for both sides. Communist Viet Cong forces derailed services in the south; American bombardment disrupted transportation in the north.

However, on 31 December 1976 the Transindochinois began running again. Many of the 1,334 bridges and twenty-seven tunnels had been completely destroyed and had to be repaired, despite scant technology and limited materials. But miraculously, less than 2 years after the surrender of South Vietnam and the reunification of the country, a full Saigon–Hanoi rail journey was possible once more. The route, seen as a powerful symbol of solidarity and integration, earned itself an unofficial name: the 'Reunification Express'.

There is no service actually called the Reunification Express but several trains run the route, a slow reveal of rice paddies, water buffalo, pagodas poking through the trees, palm-fringed sands, tiny villages and locals in conical hats riding bicycles. The line provides a window onto a country recently ravaged by wars but risen from the ashes.

ALTERNATIVE VIETNAM
- - - - - - - - - - - - - - - - -

423. Da Lat–Thap Cham Railway
Vietnam

The tracks of this railway were dismantled to repair Vietnam's North–South main line. Now a tourist train runs along a restored 4.5-mile (7km) section from Da Lat's Art Deco station.

LEFT: Railway tracks squeeze through the streets of central Hanoi.

The railway's southern terminus is Saigon – the name most people use for the city despite its rebranding as Ho Chi Minh City in 1976. Saigon throngs with commerce, French colonial landmarks and reminders of past struggles. The War Remnants Museum is particularly poignant.

From Saigon the train heads north, leaving the suburbs to pass farmers' fields and forested, boulder-scattered peaks. For much of the way the railway sticks close to the South China Sea. It's most spectacular between the city of Danang and the former imperial capital of Hué. On this section, the railway wends along jungly cliffs, looks out over golden beaches and scales verdant mountains via Hai Van (Ocean Cloud) Pass.

It takes around 36 hours to complete the full Saigon–Hanoi ride but it's worth breaking the journey. The laidback resort town of Nha Trang is a welcoming beach stop. Danang, set amid the Marble Hills, is the railhead for Hoi An, a charming old port of canals, covered Japanese bridges and silk shops. Hué, on the banks of the Perfume River, is home to the impressive Imperial Citadel, which tells of a Vietnam long before the railways.

Capital Hanoi is a frenetic, energetic terminus. You can visit the ancient Temple of Literature and Ho Chi Minh's Mausoleum. You can also retreat to a tiny bar, right by the rail tracks, and raise a glass of rice wine to the Reunification Express as it comes screeching by.

BELOW: Dynamic Saigon marks the southern terminus of the Reunification Express.

424
OPERATION PIED PIPER

United Kingdom

Operation Pied Piper wasn't one train journey – it was hundreds. The United Kingdom's mass evacuation of people to the British countryside at the start of the Second World War saw more than 3 million souls – mostly children – relocated from at-risk cities to rural safety. It was an enormous logistical challenge. Special timetables were arranged, and evacuation trains ran out of London's main stations every 9 minutes for 9 hours. Children were labelled and loaded aboard for destinations unknown, far from home. Though well intentioned, the effects were often devastating. A 1941 report concluded that 'separation from their parents is a worse shock for children than a bombing'.

425
PERMITTENTTRAFIK

Sweden

Sweden remained neutral during the Second World War. But its railways did play a small, controversial, part. The Nazis invaded Denmark and Norway in 1940, and pressured Sweden to allow German soldiers to travel across its territory, so that they could go home on leave, the so-called *permittenttrafik*. From mid-1940 to August 1943 there were daily return trains between the southern Swedish city of Trelleborg and Kornsjö, south Norway, and weekly trains between Trelleborg and the far-north Norwegian port of Narvik. More than 1 million military personnel travelled between Norway and Germany across Swedish soil.

426
KRAKOW–OSWIECIM

Southern Poland

The 40-mile (64km) train ride from
the handsome city of Krakow to the
town of Oswiecim is a poignant
one. During the Second World
War, Oswiecim was known as
Auschwitz. The Nazis built
concentration camps here and,
between 1940 and January 1945,
around 1.3 million people – mostly
Jews – were interned. At least
1.1 million died. They were brought
to Auschwitz en masse aboard
'Holocaust Trains'. Some historians
have even postulated that Hitler's
'Final Solution' (the extermination
of all Jews) would have been
impossible without railways.
At the Auschwitz-Birkenau State
Museum, rail tracks leading into
the camp can still be seen.

427
U-BAHN

Berlin, Germany

When the Berlin Wall divided the
city, it divided its underground,
too. The infamous wall was
erected in 1961 to separate the
enclave of democratic West Berlin
from communist East Germany.
U-Bahn lines that previously
spanned the city turned around at
the border. Lines that ran mostly
under West Berlin but dipped
under East Berlin didn't stop there
– the empty platforms became
Geisterbahnhöfe (ghost stations).
Friedrichstrasse was the only East
Berlin stop still served by U-Bahn
trains from the west. It was a key
checkpoint for West Germans
visiting family in the East, and
their emotional farewells saw
Friedrichstrasse nicknamed
Tränenplast: 'Palace of Tears'.

BALKAN ODYSSEY

Hungary—Italy

Board a luxurious Golden Eagle train to explore the
ancient and modern history of the Balkan region.

Need to know
- *Point in time: 1912–
  1913, 1991–2001
  (Balkan wars)*
- *Length: Around
  2,000 miles (3,200km)*
- *Minimum time:
  11 days*
- *Key stops: Budapest,
  Brasov, Belgrade,
  Mostar, Sarajevo,
  Ljubljana, Venice*
- *Countries crossed:
  Hungary, Romania,
  Bulgaria, Serbia,
  Bosnia and
  Herzegovina,
  Slovenia, Italy*

The 20th century was a troubled one for Eastern Europe's
Balkan Peninsula. Its early years saw states here battle for
freedom from the Ottoman Empire. Then, in 1914, the
assassination of Austro-Hungarian Archduke Franz
Ferdinand in Sarajevo (now capital of Bosnia and
Herzegovina), proved to be the catalyst for the First World
War. More recently, the deadly Yugoslav Wars (1991–2001)
ravaged the region.

Thankfully, Balkan countries once off limits due to conflict
are now open for tourism. The 11-day Balkan Odyssey trip,
aboard a luxurious Golden Eagle train, is perhaps the
classiest way to visit them. Starting in Hungarian capital
Budapest and finishing in canal-veined Venice, the trip takes
in many of the Balkans' highlights aboard the wood-panelled,
five-star sumptuousness of one of the world's plushest trains.

LIKE THAT?
TRY THESE

- - - - - - - - - - - - - - - - - -

429. Vienna–Bad Ischl
Austria

Travel between the capital of the former Austro-Hungarian Empire and summer home of Emperor Franz Joseph I. Here, on 28 July 1914, he signed the declaration of war on Serbia that escalated into two conflicts that would change the world.

430. Šargan Eight Railway
Serbia

Ride a 5-mile (8km) remnant of the Belgrade–Sarajevo line (closed 1974). The section around Šargan-Vitasi describes a dramatic figure-of-eight amid the hills.

RIGHT: The Balkan Odyssey train journey calls at Mostar, where the rebuilt bridge is a potent symbol of unity.

For instance, the Golden Eagle calls at the ancient Bulgarian cities of Veliko Tarnovo and Plovdiv, both of which have splendid, hill-perched medieval old towns. And it visits Serbian capital Belgrade, located astride the Danube and Sava Rivers. Here you can visit the memorial to former Yugoslavian President Marshal Tito at the Museum of Yugoslav History.

In Bosnia and Herzegovina the train stops at Sarajevo, which from 5 April 1992 to 29 February 1996 endured the longest siege of a capital city in the history of modern warfare – some 1,425 days. Amid the minarets and old bazaar, battle-scarred buildings remain. The train also visits Mostar, once one of the Ottoman Empire's most important cities. The iconic 16th-century bridge here was destroyed in 1993 by Croat bombing but repaired and reopened in 2004 – a symbol of the region's new beginnings.

DEATH RAILWAY

Thailand and Myanmar

Trace the infamous Southeast Asian line that was
hacked through the jungle by prisoners of war.

Need to know
- *Point in time: 1943
(Thailand–Burma
'Death Railway'
completed)*
- *Length: 258 miles
(415km)*
- *Minimum time:
3 hours (Nong
Pladuk–Nam Tok)*
- *Key stops: Nong
Pladuk, Kanchanaburi,
Kwai Bridge, Nam Tok,
Konyu, Songkurai,
Thanbyuzayat*
- *Countries crossed:
Thailand, Myanmar*

The Thailand–Burma 'Death Railway' is one of the most
chilling stretches of track the world has ever known. It's
said that a life was lost for every sleeper laid.

In the 19th century the British surveyed a possible railway
linking Thailand and Myanmar via the Three Pagodas Pass,
but the terrain was deemed too difficult. However, decades
later, during the Second World War, the Japanese decided
to take on the challenge. Having invaded Myanmar in 1942,
they were keen to establish an overland supply route to their
new territory. Linking the existing railheads of Nong Pladuk
in Thailand and Thanbyuzayat in Myanmar – a distance of
258 miles (415km) – seemed like the best option.

Construction began from both ends in June 1942. The
Japanese initially reckoned that it would take 5 or 6 years

to complete the line. However, by inflicting a gruelling regime on a vast workforce of around 60,000 Allied prisoners of war and more than 200,000 Southeast Asian *romusha* (forced labourers), it was done in a mere 16 months. The two lines met at Konkuita, near present-day Sangkhlaburi, on 17 October 1943 – but at some human cost. It's estimated that around a third of those who worked on the construction of the railway died in the process. Working punishing 18-hour days on pitiful rations in steamy, malarial jungle, it's a wonder any of them survived at all.

Also a wonder was the line itself, an engineering masterstroke comprising 9 miles (14km) of bridges, hacked out of inhospitable wilderness. But the line was in use for less than 2 years. After the Japanese surrender on 15 August 1945, the railway came under the control of the British, who ripped up a section at Three Pagodas Pass. The rail link between the countries has been severed ever since. Now only a fragment of the route is traceable by train.

In Thailand, it's possible to ride the scenic 80-mile (130km) section between Nam Tok and Nong Pladuk, a short train ride from Bangkok. From Nong Pladuk, the Death Railway heads northwest to the regional hub town of Kanchanaburi. It's worth spending time here to visit the Allied war cemeteries and the Thailand–Burma Railway Centre, which helps put the line into context.

Shortly after Kanchanaburi, the train crosses the infamous 'Bridge on the River Kwai'. This steel bridge, immortalised (fictitiously) in David Lean's 1957 film, was battered by Allied bombs but soon repaired. Souvenir shops and cafes are now clustered nearby.

Next the line cuts through the Kwai Noi valley. The most dramatic section comes after Wang Sing station, with the train pressing through narrow cuttings somehow hewn out of the rock by starving men with little more than picks and shovels. Further on, the train inches slowly towards Tham Krasae station and on to the 300m (985ft) long Wang Po Viaduct. This breathtaking structure teeters around the edge of a curving cliff, the river churning below. Nearly every man who worked on this section of the railway died.

Beyond is Wang Po station, followed by a scenic unravelling of verdant river banks backed by distant mountains. End of the line is the small town of Nam Tok, from where it's easy to continue 6 miles (10km) by road to the Hellfire Pass Memorial Museum.

A short stretch of the line here has been cleared. This enables visitors to walk along the old tracks and through Konyu Cutting (nicknamed Hellfire Pass), one of the railway's toughest, and deadliest, sections.

BELOW: Trains still ply sections of the Death Railway, including Wang Po Viaduct.

436
BAIKAL–AMUR MAINLINE

Siberia, Russia

It took 70 years to complete the Baikal–Amur Mainline (BAM), at a cost of up to 400,000 lives. Construction began in the 1930s under the Soviet leader Joseph Stalin. Gulag prisoners and then Japanese and German prisoners of war did the arduous work on this line across Siberia. After Stalin's death, BAM construction halted but resumed in the 1970s – this time by paid labourers who built miles of tunnels and bridges across the permafrost. The 2,687-mile (4,324km) line, between the town of Tayshet and the eastern port of Sovetskaya Gavan via enormous Lake Baikal, finally opened in 2003.

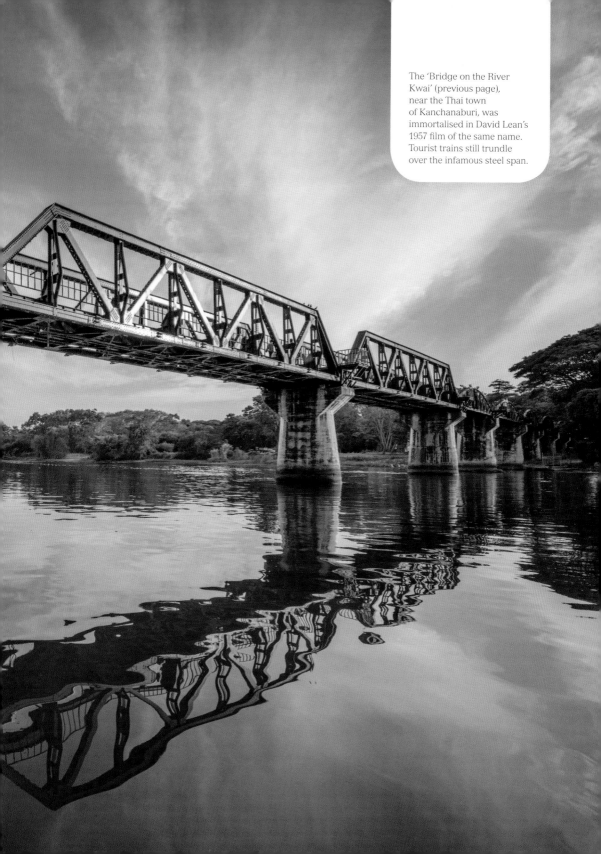

The 'Bridge on the River Kwai' (previous page), near the Thai town of Kanchanaburi, was immortalised in David Lean's 1957 film of the same name. Tourist trains still trundle over the infamous steel span.

QUEEN OF JAFFNA

Sri Lanka

Travel across the tropical island on a railway that's been reborn following the end of the Sri Lankan Civil War.

Need to know
- *Point in time: 2014 (Colombo–Jaffna Northern Line reopened)*
- *Length: 247 miles (398km)*
- *Minimum time: 6 hours 15 minutes*
- *Key stops: Colombo, Anuradhapura, Vavuniya, Kilinochchi, Jaffna*
- *Countries crossed: Sri Lanka*

Thousands of cheering souls welcomed the flower-garlanded Queen of Jaffna as she pulled into Jaffna Station on 13 October 2014. This was the first time in 24 years that a train had made the full 247-mile (398km) journey from the capital Colombo to the far-north city of Jaffna.

Built by the British and opened in 1905, the Colombo–Jaffna Northern Line was one of Sri Lanka's key rail routes, linking the island's north and south, and helping connect the Sinhalese majority and Tamil minority. During the bloody Sri Lankan Civil War (1983–2009), when the guerrilla organisation known as the Tamil Tigers fought to create an independent Tamil state in the north, services were disrupted. Government troops used the railway, making it a prime target for Tamil rebels. Services were suspended in 1990.

The conflict ended in May 2009, after more than 70,000 people had lost their lives. The resumption of Northern Line services in 2014 not only restored a vital transport connection but also acted as a symbol of unity for a healing country.

The Queen of Jaffna takes just over 6 hours to travel from the sprawl of Colombo to Jaffna, with plenty of tropical lushness en route: gardens filled with mango and papaya trees, coconut plantations, endless rice paddies, leafy outcrops topped with Buddhist temples. It also stops at Anuradhapura, Sri Lanka's ancient capital, which is now a UNESCO World Heritage–listed scatter of *dagobas* (stupas), towers and temples. Jaffna itself, geographically closer to India than Colombo, is distinctively Hindu and still bears reminders of both its Dutch and British colonial heritage, as well as its more recent war-torn past.

RIGHT: The resumption of the Queen of Jaffna service was a cause for celebration at Jaffna station.

438
PHNOM PENH–SIHANOUKVILLE

Cambodia

Cambodia has never been over-endowed with railways. A main line northwest, between capital Phnom Penh and Poipet (on the Thai border), was built in the 1930s and 1940s; a line south from Phnom Penh to the south coast port of Sihanoukville was constructed in the 1960s. But much damage was done during the Cambodian Civil War (1967–75) and by the turn of the 21st century the country's meagre railway network was in a terrible state. However, in 2016 things started looking up. Phnom Penh Station was redecorated and limited services resumed on the 158-mile (254km) southern line, providing a scenic way to access Sihanoukville's palm-lined beaches.

439
TITO'S BLUE TRAIN

Serbia and Montenegro

It took 23 years to blast the
296-mile (476km) Belgrade–Bar
Railway through the Balkan
Mountains. Finally opened in 1976,
the line negotiated 254 tunnels
and 435 bridges to get from the
Serbian capital Belgrade to the
resort of Bar, on Montenegro's
Adriatic coast. The completion
of the project was overseen by
Marshal Tito, President of
Yugoslavia from 1953 to 1980.
Tito also had his own lavishly
appointed locomotive, the
Blue Train, aboard which he
entertained many dignitaries, from
Ethiopian Emperor Haile Selassie
to Queen Elizabeth II. The railway
was bombed during the Yugoslav
War in the 1990s but has since
been repaired. Private charters
of Tito's loco also make the
magnificent journey.

440
ZURICH–ST PETERSBURG

Switzerland—Russia

The train journey taken by Russian
communist revolutionary Vladimir
Lenin in 1917 was one of the most
momentous in European history.
Lenin was in exile in Switzerland
during the First World War, but
when Russia's 1917 Revolution
erupted, he was keen to return.
The Germans, then fighting a
draining battle on the Eastern
Front, hoped that Lenin's return
would destabilise Russia and end
the war. So, on 9 April 1917, Lenin
left Zurich by train in a sealed
carriage and travelled across
Germany. He then sailed
to Sweden, continued by train to
the Finnish border, crossed Finland
and arrived in St Petersburg on
16 April. His fateful return was
pivotal in the establishment of
Soviet Russia.

441
CHILDREN'S RAILWAY

Budapest, Hungary

This line in the Hungarian capital isn't a railway *for* kids, it's a railway run *by* them. The narrow gauge Gyermekvasút (Children's Railway) opened in the 1940s, in the aftermath of the Second World War. Hungary was then a socialist state and the ruling party believed that giving its youth division a giant train set would help them learn teamwork skills. Not that this is a toy. The Gyermekvasút is a full-sized, fully functioning 7.5-mile (12km) line that runs through deer-grazed woodland between the stations of Szechenyi-hegy and Huvosvolgy. Children work as ticket-sellers and conductors; adults do the driving.

442
INLAND LINE

Sweden

Opened between 1908 and 1937, Sweden's Inland Line was both a vital communication link and an insurance policy. The country's first south-north main line ran close to the east coast, leaving vast swathes of lake- and forest-filled interior extremely isolated. Also, if Sweden was invaded from the east (a threat at the time), its coast railway would be vulnerable. An alternative was required. Today, the 800-mile (1,288km) Inlandsbanan, which connects the southern town of Kristinehamn to Gällivare in the Arctic Circle, is less a security solution, more a brilliant way of travelling through remotest Sweden, providing access to wonderful wilderness en route.

EUROSTAR

United Kingdom, France and Belgium

Pass through the pioneering Channel Tunnel to bridge the gap between the United Kingdom and continental Europe.

Need to know

- *Point in time: 1994 (Eurostar launched)*
- *Length: 307 miles (495km) (London–Paris)*
- *Minimum time: 2 hours 16 minutes (London–Paris)*
- *Key stops: London, Ebbsfleet, Lille, Paris, Marne-la-Vallée, Brussels, Lyon, Avignon, Marseille*
- *Countries crossed: England, France, Belgium*

TREMENDOUS TUNNELS

444. Hokkaido Shinkansen
Japan

This bullet train links Honshu and Hokkaido islands. It runs through the Seikan Tunnel, the world's second-deepest operational main-line rail tunnel, opened 1988.

445. Eurostar
United Kingdom–Netherlands

By the end of 2017, high-speed English Channel-crossing services will directly connect London and Amsterdam.

The idea of building a transportation tunnel under the English Channel to link the United Kingdom with France was first mooted more than 200 years ago. In 1802, French engineer Albert Mathieu-Favier came up with a plan for a paved, oil-lamp-lit passage to be used by stagecoaches.

By the 1830s, following the advent of steam trains, an undersea rail connection was being considered. And in 1867 Queen Victoria and French Emperor Napoléon III approved a design, although the Franco-Prussian War (1870–71) prevented it from getting off the ground. Preliminary tunnel excavations were made in the 1880s but were soon stopped, this time by British Prime Minister William Gladstone, on the grounds that such a link was a risk to national security.

During the 1950s, Anglo-French negotiations on the project began again. However, it wasn't until 1987 that the Fixed Link Treaty paved the way for the Channel Tunnel to become a reality. Construction began in 1988. Eleven boring machines, working from both French and English shores

simultaneously, drilled through the chalk mudstone, creating two rail tunnels and a service tunnel. The two sides first met in December 1990 and the tunnel officially opened in May 1994, with Queen Elizabeth II aboard the ceremonial train. The first Eurostar passenger services from London to continental Europe commenced on 14 November 1994.

The Channel Tunnel is quite some achievement. Measuring 31.4 miles (50.5km) long and up to 75m (250ft) deep, it has the longest undersea portion of any tunnel in the world. Up to 400 Eurostar trains pass through it each day, collectively carrying an average of 50,000 passengers. Using the tunnel you can travel between three of Europe's greatest capitals, London, Paris and Brussels, in just over 2 hours.

Thirty-five minutes of that journey is spent inside the tunnel itself. It's not so exciting to ride through. There's not much of a view as the train barrels through the black hole below the seabed. But the possibilities it opens up are endless. Having boarded the Eurostar at London's grand St Pancras International station, zipped over the fertile fields of Kent and plunged underground at Folkestone, you pop out in rural northern France, the whole of Europe spreading out ahead.

Since the tunnel's inauguration, Eurostar trains have run direct to two French cities: the Flemish-influenced university town of Lille (1 hour 22 minutes) and peerless Paris (2 hours 16 minutes), city of love, lights, art, *amour*. In addition, trains run direct to Marne-la-Vallée, for Disneyland Paris, and to *frites*-and-finance-fuelled Brussels (2 hours 1 minute), capital of Belgium and, in a de facto capacity, the European Union. However, the Eurostar network has expanded over the years and direct routes are now spidering further afield.

BRILLIANT BRIDGE

446. Seto–Ohashi
Japan

The Seto–Ohashi line links the prefectures of Okayama (Honshu) and Kagawa (Shikoku) via the 8-mile-long (13km) island-hopping Great Seto Bridge, built 1978–88.

LEFT: A statue of writer John Betjeman greets passengers arriving at Eurostar's London terminal.

RIGHT: Eurostar runs direct to the fairy-tale turrets of Disneyland Paris.

These days trains also run straight from London to the gastronomic French city of Lyon, in the Auvergne-Rhône-Alpes, taking 4 hours 41 minutes. In 5 hours 49 minutes you can reach the Provençal city of Avignon, seat of the popes in the 14th century and home to a magnificent papal palace. The recently regenerated (but still appealingly gritty) Mediterranean port of Marseille is just 6 hours 27 minutes away. In winter, seasonal services from London to Bourg-Saint-Maurice, Aime-la-Plagne and Moûtiers speed skiers straight to the snowy French Alps, too.

These are just Eurostar's direct services, of course. From the main hubs, Europe is your oyster. Indeed, disembarking at Paris Gare du Nord or Brussels-Midi stations and gazing up at the departures board is like browsing one of travel's most tantalising menus.

GOTTHARD BASE TUNNEL

Alps, Switzerland

Travel under the Alps through the longest,
deepest railway tunnel in the world.

Need to know
- *Point in time: 2016 (Gotthard Base Tunnel opened)*
- *Length: 35 miles (57km)*
- *Minimum time: 17 minutes (tunnel); 2 hours 40 minutes (Zurich–Milan)*
- *Key stops: Zurich, Erstfeld, Bodio, Milan*
- *Countries crossed: Switzerland, Italy*

The view inside the Gotthard Base Tunnel isn't up to much. But the bigger picture – a continent connected better than ever – is beautiful indeed.

The twin-bore Gotthard Base Tunnel, opened in June 2016, is the world's longest and deepest rail tunnel. Officially, it measures a record-breaking 35 miles (57km) long, although adding up both of the main tunnels, the subsidiary shafts and cross passages, there are 95 miles (152km) of tunnelling in total, buried up to 2,300m (7,545ft) below the surface of the massif above. The engineers had to burrow through seventy-three different types of rock; the boring machine itself was 410m (1,345ft) long.

The first Gotthard Tunnel, a 9-mile (14km) engineering marvel of its time, was dug between 1872 and 1882; 199 men died in the process. Running between the Swiss villages of Göschenen and Airolo, it was the first modern railway link between northern and southern Europe, and is still used today.

BELOW: Trains now speed through the Gotthard Base Tunnel, cutting journey times.

MOUNTAIN TRACKS

----

451. Corcovado Rack Railway
Rio de Janeiro, Brazil

A 2.5-mile (4km) rack railway climbs from Cosme Velho Station up Corcovado summit to the feet of Rio's beatific Christ the Redeemer statue, unveiled in 1931.

452. Bernina Express
Switzerland and Italy

Possibly the Alps' most awesome rail ride, the mountain-slicing, 90-mile (144km) Chur-Tirano service opened in 1910. It has 196 bridges and fifty-five tunnels.

453. Saint-Hilaire du Touvet Funicular
Rhône-Alpes, France

The mountain village of Saint-Hilaire was only accessible by foot until 1924, when this 1,480m (4,860ft) funicular opened to enable tuberculosis patients to visit sanatoriums.

454. Nilgiri Mountain Railway
Tamil Nadu, India

Steam locomotives operate on this 16-mile (26km) UNESCO World Heritage–listed line. It was built by the British and opened in 1908.

RIGHT: The Gotthard Base Tunnel burrows under the Alps near the village of Erstfeld.

Plans for a new deep tunnel (the Gotthard Base Tunnel) between the Swiss villages of Erstfeld and Bodio were conceived in 1947. Construction didn't begin until 1999 and took 17 years. Nine workmen lost their lives – a plaque commemorates them near the northern entrance. There is also a shrine to St Barbara, patron saint of miners.

The new high-speed tunnel will revolutionise European freight transport, with 260 freight trains set to traverse the Gotthard daily, hitting speeds of 100 miles per hour (160kph). It will also slash travel times for passengers, with sixty-five daily scheduled trains whizzing through at over 125 miles per hour (200kph). For instance, the journey time between the powerhouse cities of Zurich and Milan has been reduced by an hour to just 2 hours and 40 minutes.

455
LHASA–SHIGATSE RAILWAY

Tibet Autonomous Region, China

The 157-mile (253km) Lhasa–Shigatse Railway, opened in 2014, is one of the smoothest ways to get within almost-touching distance of Mount Everest. Built as an extension of the Qinghai–Tibet Railway, this line reaches heights in excess of 3,500m (11,500ft) as it connects Tibet's capital Lhasa with its second city, Shigatse, via the Brahmaputra Grand Canyon. Shigatse is the nearest railhead to Everest. However, it's still a long, bumpy haul by jeep to reach the mountain's North Base Camp near Rongbuk Monastery. This is the end of the road – but also the starting point for summit attempts via Everest's northeast ridge, first climbed in 1960.

456
RAMAL TALCA–CONSTITUCIÓN

Chile

The Talca–Constitución Railway was begun in 1889, completed in 1915 and declared a National Monument of Chile in 2007. The 55-mile (88km) route is the country's last remaining narrow gauge *ramal* (branch line), linking the city of Talca, south of Santiago, to the beachside city of Constitución, on the Pacific coast. The little single-track line runs along the banks of the Maule River, crossing it over the Gustavé Eiffel-designed Banco de Arena Bridge. It trundles via fields, lakes and hills, stopping halfway at the small town of González Bastía so that trains running in opposite directions can pass.

457
BRECON MOUNTAIN RAILWAY

Wales, United Kingdom

The Brecon Beacons, a marvellous expanse of heather-cloaked mountains, was designated a national park in 1957. The narrow gauge Brecon Mountain Railway, opened in stages from 1980, allows people to explore the park without using cars. The 5-mile (8km) line from the village of Pant to the remote station of Torpantau runs along a section of the Brecon and Merthyr Railway, opened in the 1860s but closed in 1964. Today, heritage steam locomotives leave new Pant Station, enter the national park and climb to the entrance of Torpantau Tunnel, giving passengers the chance to get off and explore the park on foot.

458
TALYLLYN RAILWAY

Wales, United Kingdom

Many railways worldwide owe a vote of thanks to the little Talyllyn Railway – the line that proved old tracks *could* be saved. Running for 7 miles (12km) along the Fathew Valley, between the seaside town of Tywyn and inland Nant Gwernol Station, Talyllyn was the world's first preserved railway. It originally opened in 1865 to cart slate but by the early 1950s looked destined for closure. That's when the Talyllyn Railway Preservation Society (the world's first such organisation) was founded. Through hard work and passion, the group restored the line and original rolling stock so that this rural byway can still be enjoyed today.

MARRAKESH EXPRESS

Morocco

Ride the fabled train through North Africa to the
city that enticed a thousand hippies.

Need to know

- *Point in time: 1969 (Crosby, Stills and Nash released single 'Marrakesh Express')*
- *Length: 354 miles (570km)*
- *Minimum time: 8 hours*
- *Key stops: Tangier, Rabat, Casablanca, Marrakesh*
- *Countries crossed: Morocco*

BELOW: The souks of Marrakesh were a popular destination for many a hippy.

It's the 1960s and a counter-cultural movement is brewing. Hippies, the flower-garlanded offspring of the 1950s Beat Generation, have arrived – first in San Francisco, then spreading across the United States, then the world. Embracing peace, love, long hair and psychedelic trousers, they're reacting against growing materialism, middle class repression and the Vietnam War (1955–75). They believe in non-violent protest, communal living, beards and the liberal use of recreational drugs.

Many of them also believed in travel. Keen to escape from the evils of the capitalist West, they set off in search of spiritual enlightenment elsewhere. An overland hippy trail emerged, heading east from Istanbul into Asia, where free spirits could live cheaply and imbibe the mysticism (and hashish) of the east. Another popular destination was Morocco. By the late 1960s, the North African country was becoming an essential stop-off for those seeking exotic unconventionality, including hippies, artists, authors and rock stars.

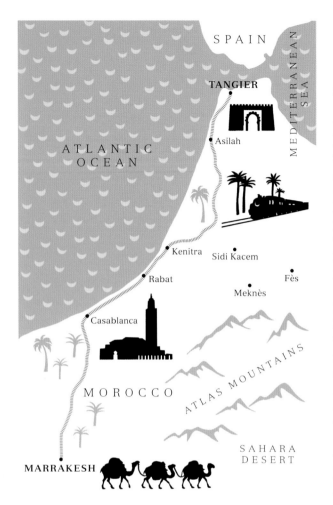

English musician Graham Nash made his own trip to Morocco in 1966, catching a train between the cities of Casablanca and Marrakesh. He quickly ditched his first-class carriage (full of 'rich American ladies') for the bustle of third class, 'where it was all happening' – chickens, goats, people in *djellaba* robes cooking on tiny stoves. The experience inspired Nash to write 'Marrakesh Express', released as a single by Crosby, Stills and Nash in 1969. This in turn inspired thousands more hippies to head to Morocco, and specifically to Marrakesh. The millennium-old imperial city seemed the embodiment of exoticism; it was also an important seat of Sufism, an ancient, esoteric branch of Islam that appealed to hippies.

Today, travellers of all sorts ride the so-called Marrakesh Express. Morocco's first railways were built at the beginning of the 20th century by the ruling French, initially to assist the movements of the French Foreign Legion. Although not an extensive network, it's possible to travel by train from the Mediterranean port of Tangier to Marrakesh, in the foothills of the Atlas Mountains.

Tangier, just across the sea from southern Spain, is the gateway to Africa. Over the centuries, Berbers, Phoenicians, Romans, Byzantines and Arabs have settled this strategic spot but by the middle of the 20th century Tangier was attracting beatniks, artists and alternative types. It was, after all, fairly easy to hide in Tangier's crumbling, labyrinthine medina (walled old town). The city, which went on to develop a dodgy reputation, has been cleaned up in recent years and is well worth exploring before boarding a train at Tangier Ville Station to head south.

The train takes around 8 hours to reach Marrakesh. There's no third-class option these days – just second or first, plus first-class couchette cabins on the overnight

LIKE THAT? TRY THIS

- - - - - - - - - - - - - - - - - - -

460. Festival Express
Canada

Hop from Toronto to Winnipeg to Calgary, channelling the spirits of Janis Joplin, the Grateful Dead and more. These stars made a rock band train tour in 1970.

service. The train still calls at the Atlantic port city of Casablanca, where it's worth getting off to explore the French colonial art deco architecture. These buildings were only a few decades old when Graham Nash boarded the train here, and are still looking good today.

Of course, the ultimate destination of this express is Marrakesh. The city may have lost its hippy edge; most of the souls escaping here now are mini-breakers booking into exquisite *riad* hotels. But Marrakesh still oozes exotica from every alleyway. Take a *petit taxi* from Marrakesh Station into the old town and wander to the huge main square, the Djemaa el-Fna. Here, pans sizzle with fragrant spices, storytellers weave tales, acrobats leap, snakes are charmed and the modern Western world can feel far, far away.

BELOW: The Tangier–Marrakesh train calls at the city of Casablanca.

461
FREEDOM TRAINS

United States

The 1947–49 Freedom Train
was the greatest ever travelling
exhibition. With the United States
entering an era of post-war
prosperity, the Freedom Train set
off to remind people what it meant
to be American. The seven-car
train, loaded with treasures
such as the Declaration of
Independence and the Gettysburg
Address, made a 37,160-mile
(59,800km) countrywide tour.
It's the only train to have operated
in all forty-eight contiguous states.
In 1975–76, a second Freedom
Train made a similar grand tour
for the United States Bicentennial.
This time the cargo included items
such as Martin Luther King's
robes and a rock from the moon.

462
TRANS-ASIA EXPRESS

Turkey and Iran

From the 1960s, countless hippies
seeking to escape the consumerist
West made an exodus eastwards.
They amassed in Istanbul, then
trucked or hitched across Turkey
to Iran, Afghanistan, India and
beyond. One way to follow in their
footsteps is the 3-day, 1,844-mile
(2,968km) Trans-Asia Express.
Linking Turkish capital Ankara to
Iranian capital Tehran, this service
cuts across the craggy Anatolian
plains to Tatvan Pier, where
passengers (and the baggage car)
board a ferry to cross Lake Van,
picking up another train from Van
Pier to reach Tehran. Sadly, the
Trans-Asia Express was suspended
in 2015 following security
incidents, but hopefully one day
the 'hippy train' will ride again.

463
THE GREAT
RAILWAY BAZAAR

Europe and Asia

Published in 1975, *The Great Railway Bazaar* is a travel-writing classic. In it, American author Paul Theroux recounts a 4-month rail journey he made from London across Europe, the Middle East, India and Southeast Asia. He boarded evocative trains such as the Orient Express, the Khyber Pass Local and the Trans-Siberian Railway. And he found that trains are the mirror of their people and places: 'The trains [in a country] contain the essential paraphernalia of the culture,' Theroux noted. 'The railway bazaar with its gadgets and passengers represented the society so completely that to board it was to be challenged by the national character.'

464
'BANDRIKA'–ENGLAND

Europe

Bandrika is 'one of Europe's few undiscovered corners' – largely because it doesn't exist. Bandrika is the location of Alfred Hitchcock's 1938 movie *The Lady Vanishes*. The protagonists board an England-bound train in this fictitious Balkan nation, and must solve the mystery of the disappeared Miss Froy as the claustrophobic carriages trundle across the countryside. The train itself is the starring character. Its whistles imitate terrified shrieks. Its movement echoes the thrill of the chase. And its confined spaces help build the sense of tension. Indeed, the entire film set was just 27m (90ft) long.

FRIEND EXPRESS

Pakistan and India

Cross the fraught India-Pakistan border via the excruciatingly slow 'Agreement' train.

Need to know
- *Point in time: 1947 (Partition of India)*
- *Length: 17 miles (28km)*
- *Minimum time: 4 hours+*
- *Key stops: Lahore, Wagah, Attari*
- *Countries crossed: Pakistan, India*

BELOW: Amritsar's Golden Temple is the most sacred Sikh site.

It may look like a timetabling typo, but no. The Samjhauta Express – or 'Friend Express' – usually takes more than 4 hours to complete its 17-mile (28km) journey between the Pakistani city of Lahore and the Indian town of Attari. It's not that the train travels excruciatingly slowly (although it isn't fast). Most of the time is spent dealing with red tape either side of the border.

Ever since the Partition of India in 1947, when the British Indian Empire was divided along the Radcliffe Line into India and Pakistan, relations between the two countries have been strained. The transborder Samjhauta (Agreement) Express started running in 1976. It's been briefly discontinued twice since and was targeted in a terrorist attack in 2007. Now the service operates twice a week, run alternately by India for six months, then by Pakistan for six months.

From Lahore, trains trundle 15 miles (24km) to the village of Wagah on the border. This is where India-Pakistan relations become a pantomime. Every evening, just before sunset, a flag-lowering ceremony is held as the road border is closed. Cue magnificently dressed soldiers goose-stepping and gun-rattling at each other across the divide.

Procedures are more dismal for train travellers, who are inevitably delayed beyond the scheduled stopping time as papers are checked. And then checked again at Attari, just 2 miles (3km) further along the line. Here, at the old 19th-century station, armed guards patrol the platforms, which are separated by wire fences. If your documents pass the immigration test, you're free to board onward trains. Onward services run to the sacred Sikh city of Amritsar and Indian capital New Delhi.

FRIENDSHIP RAILWAYS

466. Vivek Express
India

India gained independence in 1947. Its longest rail journey is the 2,655-mile (4,273km) ride from northerly Dibrugarh in Assam to Kanyakumari, mainland India's southern tip.

467. Thai–Lao Friendship Bridge
Thailand and Laos

The small section of railway from Nong Khai (Thailand) to Thanaleng (near Vientiane, Laos) opened in 2009 – Laos' first rail connection.

468. Maitree Express
India and Bangladesh

This Dhaka–Kolkata train, the only service between India and Bangladesh, was relaunched in 2008 after a 43-year hiatus following the 1965 Indo–Pakistani War.

LEFT: The Border Closing Ceremony at Wagah on the border between India and Pakistan is a bit of a pantomime.

FFESTINIOG AND WELSH HIGHLAND RAILWAYS

North Wales, United Kingdom

Ride two restored heritage lines in Snowdonia that
triumphantly prove just what rail enthusiasts can achieve.

Need to know
- *Point in time: 1982 / 2011 (Ffestiniog Railway / Welsh Highland Railway reopened)*
- *Length: 13.5 miles (22km) / 25 miles (40km)*
- *Minimum time: 1 hour 10 minutes / 2 hours 10 minutes*
- *Key stops: Caernarfon, Waunfawr, Rhyd Ddu, Beddgelert, Porthmadog, Minffordd, Penrhyn, Blaenau Ffestiniog*
- *Countries crossed: United Kingdom*

In some ways, the Ffestiniog and Welsh Highland lines
in North Wales are more rollercoaster rides than railway
journeys. The fortunes of these two mountain-slicing tracks
are as up and down as the terrain they cross; there are
highs, lows, twist, turns – but, ultimately, a thrilling ending.

Originally opened in 1836, the 13.5-mile (22km) Ffestiniog
Railway (FR) ran downhill from the slate quarries of Blaenau
Ffestiniog to the coastal town of Porthmadog. At first, the
loaded wagons – and horses in dandy carts – were carried
to the sea by gravity; the horses then hauled the empty carts
back uphill. In 1863 the FR became the world's first narrow
gauge railway to use steam locomotives. It also pioneered
the Fairlie double-bogie engine, which looked like two
engines back-to-back. These could provide more power
while still being able to swing around sharp bends. More
slate could be hauled, and tourist cars were added. But as the
20th century progressed, the slate trade declined and tourists
increasingly favoured the roads. In 1946, the FR closed.

CAERNARFON

Bontnewydd

Dinas Tryfan Waunfawr
Junction

Plas-y-Nant

Snowdon Ranger

SNOWDONIA
NATIONAL PARK

Llyn Cwellyn
reservoir

Rhyd Ddu MOUNT SNOWDON

Meillionen

Beddgelert ABERGLASLYN BLAENAU
PASS FFESTINIOG

Nantmor

Tanygrisiau

Welsh Highland
Railway

Tan-y-Bwlch Dduallt
Pont Croesor

Ffestiniog
Railway

Penrhyn

Porthmadog Minffordd

Glaslyn Estuary Boston Lodge Halt
Portmeirion

TRADING TRAINS

470. Jiayang Coal Railway
Sichuan, China

In high-speed China, opt for old-school steam on this 12-mile (20km) line. Opened in 1938 to serve the local coal mine, it's now a national cultural heritage site.

471. Hershey Electric Railway
Cuba

Cuba's only surviving electric railway, the 57-mile (92km) Havana–Matanzas line was built in 1917 by American chocolate company Hershey to carry sugar from its plantations.

472. Pingxi Line, Taipei
Taiwan

Opened in 1921 to transport coal, this 8-mile (13km) line is now a day-tripper's treat, running via mountains, waterfalls and right through the streets of traditional mining towns.

The West Highland Railway (WHR) fared worse. Comprising a handful of earlier lines and some new segments, it opened its full 25-mile (40km) Caernarfon–Porthmadog route in 1923. But it was mired in debt from the start, and never recovered. By 1937 it had ceased to operate; by the end of the Second World War it didn't even exist, its track having been pulled up for use elsewhere during the war. So, two lines gone – but not forgotten . . .

As early as 1951 a group of enthusiasts looked to rebuild the FR. They had successes, with small sections of track reopening from 1955. But there were huge setbacks, not least a new hydroelectric plant that flooded part of the former route. Undeterred, the Ffestiniog crew – largely volunteers – devised a 2.5-mile (4km) deviation around the new reservoir. This required hacking out the new Moelwyn Tunnel and constructing a spiral at Dduallt in order to reach Blaenau Ffestiniog. The railway fully reopened on 25 May 1982.

The WHR had a longer road to recovery. The original, stripped-back track bed remained largely intact. But there were many obstacles, from legal wranglings to an outbreak of foot and mouth disease. Again, the workforce comprised

LEFT: The Ffestiniog Railway originally carted slate from the quarries of Blaenau.

many volunteers, who toiled tirelessly to lay the track and restore the steam engines. The WHR reopened in stages from 1997, and finally relinked Caernarfon and Porthmadog in 2011. In 2014, Porthmadog Harbour station was expanded so that trains from both lines could use it simultaneously.

Both the FR and WHR are beauties. From Porthmadog, the eastbound FR crosses the Glaslyn Estuary. First stop is Boston Lodge Halt, where the heritage rolling stock is maintained – the FR still uses three of its original 150-year-old locomotives. The next stop is Minffordd, walking distance from the incredible Italianate resort of Portmeirion. The line then rises into a landscape of sheep meadows, woodland and waterfalls. It burrows through hills, grips mountainsides and describes tight curves, climbing 210m (700ft) to Blaenau Ffestiniog.

The WHR heads north from Porthmadog, through the Glaslyn Valley and into Snowdonia National Park. It negotiates the tunnels of the Aberglaslyn Pass and stops at the pretty village of Beddgelert before tackling the reverse curves up to Rhyd Ddu station – a hiking trail leads from here to the top of Mount Snowdon. Tracing Llyn Cwellyn reservoir, the train enters the Gwyrfai Valley, pausing at the engine sheds of Dinas before eventually trundling into Caernarfon station, stopping in the shadow of the town's massive medieval castle.

RIGHT: The Welsh Highland Line passes marvellous mountain scenery around Beddgelert.

CROWN EXPRESS

Bulgaria

King Boris III of Bulgaria, who
reigned from 1918 to 1943, was
an avid railway fan. He modernised
Bulgaria's railways, and often
drove his private *tsarski vlak* (royal
train). Known as the Corona
(Crown) Express, the train
comprised three luxurious
1930s–40s German-manufactured
carriages, decked out specifically
for Boris and his family. Boris
used it for state visits but now
tour companies sometimes
commandeer the fancy old saloon
cars for private trips. They're fixed
to heritage steam engines and
pulled along the Bulgarian rail
network's most scenic lines, such
as through the Rhodope Mountains
and along the Black Sea coast.

THE OCEAN

Eastern Canada

Follow in the rail tracks of the hundreds of thousands
of immigrants who populated Canada by train.

Need to know
- *Point in time: 1928–1971 (Pier 21 operated)*
- *Length: 836 miles (1,346km)*
- *Minimum time: 21 hours*
- *Key stops: Halifax, Amherst, Moncton, Mont-Joli, Rivière-du-Loup, Sainte-Foy, Montréal*
- *Countries crossed: Canada*

Between 1928 and 1971, almost 1 million people passed through Pier 21. This huge immigration facility in the harbour city of Halifax, Nova Scotia, was Canada's equivalent of New York's Ellis Island, processing boatloads of new settlers and refugees hoping to make a new life in the New World.

Inside Pier 21 there were customs offices, Red Cross volunteers and a canteen where arrivals could eat before their long onward journeys. Pier 21 was connected by ramp to Halifax's railway station. Here, most immigrants boarded special trains comprising basic colonist carriages in order to travel to their new homes across Canada. Those with more money could take the higher-class Ocean Limited instead.

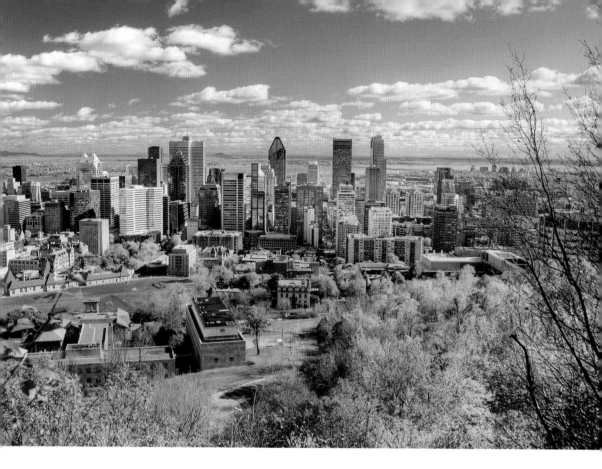

Now known simply as the Ocean, this train service links Halifax to Montréal on a scenic run through the Canadian Maritimes. In operation since 1904, it's North America's oldest continuously operated named passenger train.

The Ocean starts from the station near Pier 21 (now an excellent museum) and heads north, around Bedford Basin and past Nova Scotia's forests, lakes and farmland. It cuts through the Cobequid Mountains into New Brunswick, where it calls at Moncton. In 1872 this city was designated HQ of the Intercolonial Railway of Canada, the original company behind railways in the Maritimes.

The Ocean continues north into Québec, meeting the banks of the St Lawrence River, then veering southwest along its shore. Passengers can hop off at Sainte-Foy to access the old walled centre of Québec City or continue to the terminus at Montréal, a city of fine food and plentiful festivals. In Montréal, you could board another train and keep heading west, just like many of those early immigrants.

ABOVE: The Ocean ends up in the lively French-Canadian city of Montréal.

LEFT: The city of Halifax is where many immigrants boarded trains to start their new lives in Canada.

The Ocean train (previous page) runs through forest, farmland and mountains as it travels between Halifax and Montréal. The sugar maple and yellow birch-covered Cobequid Mountains in Nova Scotia are a highlight.

475
RAIL BALTICA

Latvia, Lithuania and Estonia

The three Baltic states gained independence from the Soviet Union in the early 1990s. Soon after, discussions began on a plan to better link the trio to the rest of Europe. 'Rail Baltica' is still in its nascent phase, with technical studies being carried out and land being acquired. But the vision is for a standard gauge railway connecting the capitals Tallinn (Estonia), Riga (Latvia) and Vilnius (Lithuania) with cities such as Warsaw and Berlin. Construction is hoped to start in 2020, with a route from Tallinn to the medieval Lithuanian city of Kaunas finished by 2025.

476
NSW TRAINLINK SYDNEY–CANBERRA–MELBOURNE

Southeastern Australia

Sydney and Melbourne – Australia's two biggest cities. Both beautiful, historic and thriving. Both dead set against the other being capital of Australia. This was the problem in 1901, when the six self-governing British colonies united to form the Federation of Australia. The compromise? Canberra: a purpose-built capital sited between Sydney and Melbourne. Construction began in the early 20th century; parliament moved there in 1927. You can visit all three cities with NSW TrainLink. There are two trains a day between Sydney's gorgeous harbour and arty Melbourne, taking around 12 hours. There are also several daily services making the 4-hour trip between Sydney and Canberra's well-planned streets.

477
BEIJING–PYONGYANG

China and North Korea

It's not easy to travel in the
Democratic People's Republic of
Korea (DPRK). Those who do visit
the secretive nation (established in
1948) must join organised, state-
sanctioned tours. But travelling
into or out of North Korea by train
gives a window into the wider
country. Services on the 848-mile
(1,364km) Beijing–Pyongyang line
run several times a week, crossing
the Sino-Korea Friendship Bridge
from Dandong (China) to Sinuiju
(North Korea). This offers glimpses
of the real North Korea: looming
mountains, ramshackle villages
and crumbling stations all bearing
pictures of the DPRK's 'Dear
Leader' and 'Great Leader'.

478
DMZ TRAIN

South Korea

The South Korean 'Peace Train'
links capital Seoul to Dorasan,
the station nearest the Korean
Demilitarised Zone (DMZ).
The Korean DMZ is the world's
most heavily militarised border,
a 2.5-mile (4km) wide buffer along
the 38th parallel that has divided
the peninsula into North Korea
and South Korea since 1953. It's
where the two sides meet to
negotiate, and it's where several
altercations have occurred. The
35-mile (56km) train trip from
Seoul runs through unspoilt
countryside and delivers
passengers to the DMZ's civilian-
restricted area, where it's possible
to visit Dora Observatory and gaze
over at what's happening on the
other side of the border.

CITY OF NEW ORLEANS

United States

Make a musical rail journey along the Mississippi,
through the heartland of jazz and blues.

Need to know

- *Point in time: 1922
  (Louis Armstrong
  travelled from New
  Orleans to Chicago)*
- *Length: 926 miles
  (1,490km)*
- *Minimum time:
  19 hours*
- *Key stops: New
  Orleans, Jackson,
  Greenwood, Memphis,
  Chicago*
- *Countries crossed:
  United States*

All trains have a certain musicality: a rhythmic clack, sway, whistle and rumble. But Amtrak's City of New Orleans service has more than most. This 926-mile (1,490km) rail ride runs through the heartland of American musical history.

Jazz developed around the 1890s, born from a mixed parentage of African drumming, European traditions, ragtime and marching bands. It thrived in New Orleans, a city with a diverse ethnic mix, a liberal outlook and an obsession with festivals and fun. From the turn of the 20th century, the city's theatres, honky-tonks, bars and brothels hummed with jazz rhythms, largely performed by black artists. While segregation laws limited job prospects for people of colour, many found work in the entertainment industry.

LIKE THAT?
TRY THIS

**480. San Diego and
Arizona Railway**
*California,
United States*

The first spike of this 'Impossible Railroad' was hammered in 1907. Currently closed, its Goat Canyon bridge (hike there for a view) is the world's largest wooden trestle.

RIGHT: The streetcars of New Orleans are the perfect way to access all that jazz.

One such African-American was Louis 'Satchmo' Armstrong. Born in New Orleans in 1901, he grew up to become one of the most influential artists in the history of jazz. In 1922, the young Armstrong – already a trumpet virtuoso – took the train from New Orleans to Chicago to join King Oliver's Creole Jazz Band. Chicago became the nexus of the jazz world in the 1920s, and from here Armstrong spread his unique style across the world.

Today you can learn much about New Orleans' musical heritage aboard the City of New Orleans train. This was the service on which Amtrak launched its Rails and Trails programme in 2000. In partnership with the United States' National Park Service, the programme is designed to encourage travellers to use trains to reach the country's heritage sights. Park rangers board at selected stations and explain the passing history to passengers. On the City of New Orleans, guides from the New Orleans Jazz National Historical Park jump on.

The park itself is headquartered at the Old US Mint, on the edge of New Orleans' French Quarter. The park also comprises other sites, including Louis Armstrong Park's Congo Square – in the 19th century, enslaved Africans would gather here to sing and dance.

The City of New Orleans isn't all about jazz. As the train heads north, through the moss-draped, frog-croaked swamps of the Mississippi Delta, it enters the home of the blues. This slower, more melancholic African-American folk music, with its origins in slave work songs and spirituals, evolved just before jazz. Similarly, it began in the American south and moved northwards to music-hub Chicago.

The train stops at the town of Hazlehurst, where blues legend Robert Johnson was born (1911), and the town of Greenwood, where he died (1938) having – if you believe the stories – made a pact with the devil. It also calls at Memphis, Tennessee, arguably the United States' most musical metropolis. Many superstars of Delta blues, jazz, rock and roll, R & B and gospel started here, cutting their first tracks

**481. Dayton–
Perrysburg**
Ohio, United States

On 12 October 1984
Ronald Reagan rode
Ferdinand Magellan
(the United States'
presidential train)
for 120 miles (197km),
making speeches en
route. The Magellan
is now displayed at
Miami's Gold Coast
Railroad Museum.

482. Coast Starlight
Western United States

The 1,377-mile (2,216km)
Los Angeles–Seattle
route passes Hearst
Castle (built 1919–47),
where media magnate
William Randolph
Hearst once entertained
Hollywood stars.

483. Harlem Line
*New York, United
States*

Take a train from
New York City to
Appalachian Trail
Station, a stop
with no facilities, in
the middle of nowhere,
used by hikers
accessing the lengthy
Appalachian Trail
(launched 1937).

RIGHT: Many big names of
music have recorded at Sun
Studio in Memphis.

at Sun Studio (still open today) or playing the bars of Beale
Street. A Hollywood-style Walk of Fame pays tribute to the
city's many stars. Graceland, Elvis Presley's home and final
resting place, is also in Memphis.

From here, the train runs along the Mississippi River and
through the cornfields of Illinois, terminating in Chicago.
From the 1920s, the 'Windy City' was alive with the sound
of music. The so-called 'Great Migration' saw millions of
African-Americans travel from America's rural south to the
industrial north, taking their music with them. In Chicago,
new styles of jazz, blues and other musical genres developed.
The lakeside city remains a live music hotspot, with old
venues such as Green Mill Cocktail Lounge (reputedly the
favourite of gangster Al Capone) still going strong.

NEW YORK HIGH LINE

New York, United States

Stroll along a disused elevated freight railway that's
now one of the Big Apple's biggest draws.

Need to know
- *Point in time: 1934 /
  2009 (train line / park
  opened)*
- *Length: 1.5 miles
  (2.5km)*
- *Minimum time: 1 hour*
- *Key stops: Gansevoort
  Street, 14th Street
  Passage, Chelsea
  Thicket, Falcone
  Flyover, 34th Street
  West Side Yard*
- *Countries crossed:
  United States*

BELOW: Views from the
High Line reveal regenerating
neighbourhoods below.

New York City's High Line is the high-water mark of
21st-century railway repurposing. Once a scrap of
overgrown, abandoned track, it's now a thriving park
and one of the metropolis's hippest attractions.

The High Line was originally built as an elevated freight
railway to remove trains from the avenues below. From the
1840s, street-level railroad tracks ran down Manhattan's
West Side but there were so many accidents that an
alternative was sought. Opened in 1934, the High Line
viaduct carried goods south from 34th Street to Spring
Street, cutting right through city blocks. However, demand
gradually fell and the line closed in 1980.

The viaduct looked set for demolition but a portion was
saved by a local railway enthusiast. Plans were drawn up
to turn it into a recreational park, and construction began
in 2006. The first section opened in 2009; by 2014, the full
1.5-mile (2.5km) stretch was open.

485. Confederation Trail
Prince Edward Island, Canada

When Prince Edward Island's rail network was closed in 1989, it was quickly converted into a 292-mile (470km) walking and cycling trail.

486. Bermuda Railway Trail
Bermuda

Most of the historic railway that served this North Atlantic island from 1931 to 1948 is now a scenic 18-mile (29km) walking and cycling route.

487. Bristol and Bath Railway Path
United Kingdom

The former Midland Railway was axed in the 1960s but this part of it is now a much-used, 13-mile (21km) cycle path. The Avon Valley Railway runs steam trains here, too.

RIGHT: The New York High Line is now a verdant park in the Big Apple.

Today the High Line is a funky strand of urban greenery, design and creativity floating above Manhattan's cab-honked streets. It's short but varied. Some parts feature former rail tracks and exposed girders. Some lead through dogwood thickets and areas of wild planting inspired by the species – sedges, asters, crab apples – that grew naturally when the railway was abandoned. There are public artworks, passageways through tower blocks and views to the Hudson River and Statue of Liberty.

The High Line has also regenerated the area, boosting property prices and spurring on development projects. For instance, the new Whitney Museum of American Art was opened at the park's southern terminus in 2015.

488
RIMUTAKA RAIL TRAIL

North Island, New Zealand

New Zealand's Wairarapa Line runs for 107 miles (172km) between capital Wellington and the city of Palmerston North, tackling the Rimutaka Ranges via a tunnel. However, when the line was first built (in stages from 1874 to 1896), the Rimutaka section featured a steep incline with an average grade of 1 in 15; special track-gripping Fell locomotives were required. The tunnel deviation was made in the 1950s and now a 14-mile (22km) stretch of the abandoned line via the Rimutaka Incline has been repurposed, allowing walkers and cyclists to explore old stations, bridges, curves, tunnels and beautiful New Zealand bush.

LIKE THAT? TRY THESE

489. Dequindre Cut Greenway, Detroit
United States

This 1.4-mile (2.2km) Greenway opened in May 2009. It is a pedestrian link in downtown Detroit along a former stretch of the Grand Trunk Western Railroad.

490. Bloomingdale Trail
Chicago, United States

The abandoned Bloomingdale Elevated Railroad has been transformed into a 3-mile (5km), art-lined linear park in northwest Chicago, opened in 2015.

TOKAIDO SHINKANSEN

Honshu, Japan

Buckle up to board the bullet train from Tokyo to Osaka,
the world's first high-speed line.

Need to know
- *Point in time: 1964 (world's first bullet train launched)*
- *Length: 320 miles (515km)*
- *Minimum time: 2 hours 22 minutes*
- *Key stops: Tokyo, Shinagawa, Yokohama, Nagoya, Kyoto, Osaka*
- *Countries crossed: Japan*

The Tokaido Shinkansen is named after a centuries-old road. The Tokaido was one of five paved highways that from the 17th century linked Japan's former capital, Kyoto, to its new one, Edo (Tokyo). It was lined with fifty-three post towns, providing food and shelter for travellers making long and arduous journeys along the road, mostly on foot. On today's Tokaido there's little need for much wayside refreshment. The bullet train service makes the 320-mile (515km) journey from Tokyo to the port city of Osaka, just beyond Kyoto, in under 2.5 hours.

Japan's Shinkansen (meaning 'new main line') was the world's first high-speed train network. The first route, the Tokaido, opened on 1 October 1964, nine days before Tokyo hosted the Olympic Games. The futuristic-looking, blue-white 0 Series train sets – nicknamed *dangoppana* ('dumpling nose') – were soon hitting top speeds of 130 miles per hour (210kph), slashing the journey time between the cities from around 7 hours to just over three. Now Japan has six Shinkansen lines, and trains travel at up to 199 miles per hour (320kph).

Before 1964, Japan's train system was rather behind the times. The country's mountainous terrain had meant that

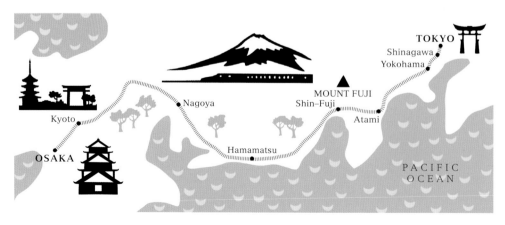

early lines, first laid at the end of the 19th century, were built to 1,067mm (3.5ft) narrow gauge and not suited to faster speeds. When the first train link between Tokyo and Osaka was completed in 1889, the journey took almost 19 hours.

In the 1930s plans were drawn up for a standard gauge *dangan ressha* (bullet train) system on the Tokaido route, but the Second World War halted progress. After the war there was a growing feeling that railways were old news and that the future would be all about automobiles and aeroplanes. But the idea of a fast train network persisted.

In 1957 the Tokyo-based Odakyu Electric Railway Company set a narrow gauge train world speed record of 90 miles per hour (145kph) with its 3000 series Super Express Romancecar. This success boosted confidence in the concept of high-speed rail. Two years later, construction of the first standard gauge Shinkansen began. On 20 April 1959,

BELOW: The ultimate view from a super-modern Shinkansen is of ancient Mount Fuji.

Japanese National Railways' President Shinji Sogo used a golden shovel to break ground on the line, at the mouth of the Shin-Tanna Tunnel near Atami. He declared: 'We'd like to build the most efficient railway ever, beyond what the rest of the world has been able to achieve.'

The Tokaido Shinkansen cost ¥380 billion (£2.2 billion) to construct – nearly twice its estimated budget – but it delivered on its promise. It's still a world-beater, by far the planet's most-used high-speed rail line. More than 340 trains carry 424,000 passengers on the route every day. It also has an enviable punctuality record – the average delay per train is less than 1 minute. The stats are only set to get more impressive. Japan has been developing the Linear Chuo Shinkansen, which uses superconductive maglev technology and can reach speeds of 310 miles per hour (500kph). Set to be completed by 2045, it will cut Tokyo–Osaka travel time to 67 minutes.

For now, though, three different services run the Tokaido Shinkansen line. Slower are the Kodama and Hikari services, which stop at more stations. Fastest is the Nozomi, which takes 2 hours 22 minutes and serves only the major cities en route: Tokyo; Shinagawa, site of the first post town on the former Tokaido road; Yokohama, Japan's second-largest city; Nagoya, home to a railway museum; temple-dotted Kyoto; and lively Osaka. All three trains offer the same view, though. On a clear day you can see majestic Mount Fuji, a sight little changed since those early Tokaido travellers were walking – not whizzing – by.

ABOVE: Slow down by hopping off the train in traditional, temple-dotted Kyoto.

LEFT: Thousands of people board Japan's high-tech bullet trains every day.

492
SHANGHAI MAGLEV TRAIN

Shanghai, China

Trains don't come faster or more futuristic that the Shanghai Maglev. Launched in 2004, this blisteringly quick shuttle has a top operational speed of 268 miles per hour (431kph), making it the world's fastest train in regular commercial service. It completes the 19-mile (30km) journey between Pudong Airport and Shanghai's Longyang Road Station in just 8 minutes. The train is one of the world's few operational maglevs, or magnetic levitation railways. These use magnets to create both lift and propulsion so that trains can float on a guideway, thus reducing friction and enabling extremely high speeds.

BEIJING–SHANGHAI HIGH-SPEED RAILWAY

Eastern China

Whizz between China's two biggest cities on the
country's flagship high-speed railway.

Need to know

- *Point in time: 2011
  (Beijing–Shanghai
  High-Speed Railway
  opened)*
- *Length: 819 miles
  (1,318km)*
- *Minimum time:
  4 hours 48 minutes*
- *Key stops: Beijing
  South, Nanjing South,
  Shanghai Hongqiao*
- *Countries crossed:
  China*

BELOW: Trains on this
high-speed line travel at up to
186 miles per hour (300kph).

By 2017, China's *gaotie* – high-speed rail (HSR) – network
stretched over 12,500 miles (20,000km). If all goes to plan,
in 2030 the total length of high-speed rail track will measure
28,000 miles (45,000km).

China's first HSR line opened in 2003 but it was 5 years
later that the superfast train-travel revolution really began.
When the line between Beijing and Tianjin opened in
August 2008 – in time for the Beijing Olympic Games –
it set the world record for the fastest conventional train
service. It was a big step towards transforming travel for
the planet's most populous country.

Then, in 2011, the Beijing–Shanghai High-Speed Railway
launched. It took 130,000 construction workers and
engineers just 38 months to build this 819-mile (1,318km)
route, the world's longest high-speed railway line
constructed in a single phase. Some 244 bridges were built,
including the Danyang–Kunshan Grand Bridge in the
Yangtze River Delta region. At 102 miles (165km), this

paddy-straddling span is the longest bridge in the world. The 71-mile (114km) Tianjin Grand Bridge, also on the line, is the world's second-longest bridge.

Travelling at 186 miles per hour (300kph), Chinese-designed CRH380A and German-designed CRH380B bullet trains have slashed the journey time between China's two biggest cities from around 10 hours to five. When China's then Premier Wen Jiabao officially opened the Beijing–Shanghai High-Speed line, he declared it to be a 'new chapter' in China's railway history, that would have a huge impact on the country's social and economic development. Longer and faster lines have opened since, but this remains the poster child of them all.

ABOVE: The rapidly modernising metropolis of Shanghai is China's biggest city.

OVRUCH–CHERNIHIV

Ukraine and Belarus

Take a train to Chernobyl to witness the eerie
aftermath of the world's worst nuclear disaster.

Need to know
- *Point in time: 1986 (Chernobyl disaster)*
- *Length: 109 miles (175km)*
- *Minimum time: 55 minutes (Chernihiv–Slavutych)*
- *Key stops: Chernihiv, Slavutych, Ilocha, Yaniv, Vilcha, Ovruch*
- *Countries crossed: Ukraine, Belarus*

UNFORTUNATE EVENTS

- - - - - - - - - - - - - - - - - - -

495. Belfast–Bangor Railway
Northern Ireland, United Kingdom

Ride this coastal train via Belfast's Titanic Quarter, where the ill-fated **RMS** *Titanic* was built in 1909–12. A museum now stands by the old dry dock.

496. Bridego Railway Bridge
Buckinghamshire, United Kingdom

This bridge at Ledburn was the site of the 1963 Great Train Robbery. A gang of fifteen felons held up the Glasgow–London Royal Mail train, stealing £2.6 million in cash.

On 26 April 1986, one of the four nuclear reactors at the Chernobyl nuclear power station in Ukraine exploded, releasing into the atmosphere at least 100 times more radiation than the atom bombs dropped on Nagasaki and Hiroshima. It remains the world's worst nuclear accident.

Incredibly, the Ovruch–Chernihiv Railway, which goes right past Chernobyl, continued to operate for several days. Trains full of passengers – oblivious to the scale of the disaster – were exposed to the dangerous fall-out. Today, unsurprisingly, services no longer run the full line, which is severed by the Chernobyl Exclusion Zone – the area of highest contamination.

Now trains run west from the city of Chernihiv as far as Slavutych (22 miles / 35km), a town of around 25,000 people, built to house those evacuated in 1986. From Slavutych, a short spur runs to the new terminus station at Semikhody, deep within Chernobyl's 10km Exclusion Zone. Most civilians ride no further than the Belarusian town of Ilocha. Only power-plant workers and travellers on authorised tours are allowed to go to Semikhody.

If you do have permits to enter the zone, it's possible to visit the old rail yard of Yaniv, main station for the abandoned ghost town of Pripyat. The locomotives and railway paraphernalia here were judged too toxic to be removed, so have been left to rot in situ, and hardy shrubs grow through rusting wagons. Tours also visit the railway bridge just outside Pripyat – now nicknamed the 'Bridge of Death'. This is where many locals gathered on the evening of 26 April 1986 to watch multicoloured flames leaping from the reactor's collapsed shell, unaware of the lethal radiation raining down on them.

RIGHT: The city of Pripyat was abandoned after the Chernobyl disaster.

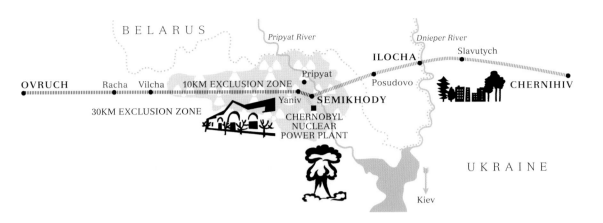

BELARUS

Pripyat River

Dnieper River

OVRUCH   Racha   Vilcha   10KM EXCLUSION ZONE   Pripyat   ILOCHA   Slavutych

Posudovo   CHERNIHIV

30KM EXCLUSION ZONE   Yaniv   SEMIKHODY

CHERNOBYL
NUCLEAR
POWER PLANT

UKRAINE

Kiev

MAEKLONG RAILWAY

Thailand

When the bell tinkles at Maeklong Railway Market, you know it's time to stop shopping and step aside. Space is tight in crowded Samut Songkhram and a market has populated a narrow rail corridor in the city's centre, with traders squeezing into the gap between the tracks and the shopfronts. The stalls spill onto the rails but several times a day, when the bell sounds, everything is moved aside as the trains of the Maeklong Railway (opened 1904) inch slowly by. Once the train has passed, awnings are unfolded, produce is laid out once more, and business resumes as usual.

MANDALAY–LASHIO

Myanmar

The rickety locos of the 175-mile (280km) Mandalay–Lashio line leave the city of Mandalay before dawn. They cross the plains in darkness and start climbing into the mountains at sunrise, heaving up to the old British-founded hill station of Pyin Oo Lwin. Then, after an unrolling of village-dotted countryside, the Gokteik Viaduct hones into view. This 689m (2,260ft) long railway trestle, supported by fifteen towers, was built by the Americans in 1901. The train inches over oh-so-slowly, offering vertiginous views to the jungle-fuzzed valley below. Once safely across, it continues to Hsipaw (home to a lively local market) before reaching Lashio, the end of the line.

499
SPIRIT OF QUEENSLAND

Eastern Australia

It took an awfully long time and an awful lot of negotiations to build the North Coast Railway Line along the eastern shore of Queensland. The first section opened in 1881 but there would be sixty more separate section openings – and several setbacks – before the full 1,044-mile (1,680km) line launched in 1924. Now the Brisbane–Cairns route is served by the Spirit of Queensland train, upgraded in 2013 to include seats that convert to flatbeds at night. Running five times a week, it's the most glorious way to glide along the east coast, with several stops giving access to the Great Barrier Reef en route.

500
BOSTON EXPRESS

New York, United States

Pulling out at 12.01 a.m. on 2 February 1913, a Boston Express was the first train to depart New York City's brand-new Grand Central Terminal. The first depot had opened on the same site in Lower Manhattan in 1871 but, as passenger numbers increased, a bigger station was required – a station befitting this increasingly important city. And that goal was undoubtedly achieved. Grand Central is the world's largest train station by number of tracks and platforms. It's also gorgeous, a Beaux-Arts beauty of sweeping staircases, gold chandeliers and – best of all – an astronomical mural on the main concourse's ceiling, featuring 2,500 stars.

INDEX

ACKNOWLEDGEMENTS

Sarah would like to thank her partner Paul Bloomfield, without whose general all-round greatness none of this would be possible (or as much fun). She'd also like to thank her Mum and Dad, who have always, always been there for her. On the publishing side, she is indebted to: Sonya Patel Ellis, for her incredible calmness, unwavering support and extremely hard work; Caroline Elliker, for her help and positivity; Lynn Hatzius, for her brilliant maps; Tony Seddon, for squeezing all these railways into one handsome book; and Emma Brown, for sourcing images.